The Definitive Guide to Terracotta

Cluster the JVM™ for Spring, Hibernate, and POJO Scalability

Terracotta, Inc.

Apress®

The Definitive Guide to Terracotta: Cluster the JVM™ for Spring, Hibernate, and POJO Scalability

Copyright © 2008 by Terracotta, Inc.

ISBN-13 (pbk): 978-1-59059-986-0

ISBN-10 (pbk): 1-59059-986-1

ISBN-13 (electronic): 978-1-4302-0640-8

Printed and bound in the United States of America 9 8 7 6 5 4 3 2 1

Trademarked names may appear in this book. Rather than use a trademark symbol with every occurrence of a trademarked name, we use the names only in an editorial fashion and to the benefit of the trademark owner, with no intention of infringement of the trademark.

Java™ and all Java-based marks are trademarks or registered trademarks of Sun Microsystems, Inc., in the US and other countries. Apress, Inc., is not affiliated with Sun Microsystems, Inc., and this book was written without endorsement from Sun Microsystems, Inc.

Lead Editor: Steve Anglin
Technical Reviewer: Jeff Genender
Development Editor: Matthew Moodie
Editorial Board: Clay Andres, Steve Anglin, Ewan Buckingham, Tony Campbell, Gary Cornell,
    Jonathan Gennick, Matthew Moodie, Joseph Ottinger, Jeffrey Pepper, Frank Pohlmann,
    Ben Renow-Clarke, Dominic Shakeshaft, Matt Wade, Tom Welsh
Senior Project Manager: Tracy Brown Collins
Copy Editor: Heather Lang
Associate Production Director: Kari Brooks-Copony
Production Editors: Jill Ellis, Laura Cheu
Compositor: Gina Rexrode
Proofreader: Linda Seifert
Indexer: Toma Mulligan
Artist: April Milne
Cover Designer: Kurt Krames
Manufacturing Director: Tom Debolski

Distributed to the book trade worldwide by Springer-Verlag New York, Inc., 233 Spring Street, 6th Floor, New York, NY 10013. Phone 1-800-SPRINGER, fax 201-348-4505, e-mail orders-ny@springer-sbm.com, or visit http://www.springeronline.com.

For information on translations, please contact Apress directly at 2855 Telegraph Avenue, Suite 600, Berkeley, CA 94705. Phone 510-549-5930, fax 510-549-5939, e-mail info@apress.com, or visit http://www.apress.com.

Apress and friends of ED books may be purchased in bulk for academic, corporate, or promotional use. eBook versions and licenses are also available for most titles. For more information, reference our Special Bulk Sales—eBook Licensing web page at http://www.apress.com/info/bulksales.

The source code for this book is available to readers at http://www.apress.com.

Contents at a Glance

Contents

About Terracotta, Inc.

Founded in 2003, **TERRACOTTA, INC.**, is a private firm headquartered in San Francisco, California. Terracotta delivers runtime plug-in capacity and availability for Java applications. Terracotta products simplify development, testing, deployment, and management of enterprise Java applications by adding clustering and distributed computing services to the JVM, allowing application development to focus on business features. Terracotta customers include leaders in a number of industries such as the packaged software development, financial services, telecommunications, travel, and online entertainment sectors.

About the Authors

ARI ZILKA is the CTO of Terracotta, Inc. Ari spends most of his time on the product roadmap and customer use cases, as well as speaking at conferences. Ari has worked as an architecture lead for several large-scale systems, most notably as the chief architect at Walmart.com.

GEERT BEVIN is a senior developer at Terracotta, Inc. Geert spends most of his time developing and optimizing the JVM internal hooks and libraries that make Terracotta transparent, as well as being an invited speaker at the largest developer conferences worldwide. Geert has worked as creator and contributor on several popular open source development projects such as RIFE, OpenLaszlo, and Gentoo Linux in addition to consulting with very large companies on implementing and improving their Java-based web applications. His work on providing continuations natively to Java contributed to him being elected as an official Sun Java Champion.

JONAS BONÉR is a senior developer at Terracotta, Inc. Jonas spends most of his time developing large-scale financial systems and integrating Terracotta with various products and tools, as well as lecturing and speaking at developer conferences worldwide. He has worked on the Terracotta core and the JRockit JVM at BEA and is an active contributor to the open source community; most notably, he created the AspectWerkz aspect-oriented programming framework and has been part of the Eclipse AspectJ team.

TAYLOR GAUTIER is a product manager at Terracotta, Inc. Taylor spends most of his time designing and using Terracotta's products. He is a converted, yet still devout, developer who has helped write parts of systems-level servers and technology at companies like Scale8 and Reactivity.

ORION LETIZI is a cofounding engineer at Terracotta, Inc. Orion spends most of his time designing and documenting clear use cases and guides for using Terracotta. He, of course, helped write the first two versions of the product but has since transitioned to helping others maximize their use of the technology. Orion has worked as a lead at several of the most popular e-commerce web sites and content portals on the Internet including Walmart.com.

ALEX MILLER is a technical lead at Terracotta, Inc. Alex leads and manages the transparency team at Terracotta. His focus is on transparently integrating cluster support into a user's application, the JDK, and third-party libraries. The transparency and server teams work together to optimize scaling and minimize the costs of clustered applications. Alex previously served as Chief Architect at MetaMatrix and worked on enterprise products at BEA. Alex speaks at conferences and blogs at http://tech.puredanger.com.

About the Technical Reviewer

JEFF GENENDER is the CTO of Savoir Technologies, Inc., a Java enterprise software consultancy. Jeff is an open source evangelist and Apache member who is an active committer on several Apache projects and a committer for Terracotta. He is the author of three books and serves as a member of the Java Community Process (JCP) expert group for JSR-316 (the Java Platform, Enterprise Edition 6 specification).

Jeff has successfully brought open source development efforts, initiatives, and success stories into a number of Global 2000 companies, saving these organizations millions in licensing costs.

Introduction

Imagine being able to call `wait()` on a Java object in one JVM, and imagine that later a thread in another JVM on another computer calls `notify()` on that same object and that `notify()` call penetrates the impermeable process boundary between the two JVMs to wake your thread from its slumber. Further imagine that all of the changes to that object made in the other JVM while you were waiting are now visible to your thread. Imagine now that the code you wrote to make this happen looked *no different* than code you would have written were this program to run only on a single JVM—no concessions to special frameworks, no callouts to special APIs, no stubs, no skeletons, no copies, no put-backs, and no magic beans.

What would it be like if you could automatically share Java heap between virtual machines so that threads running in different JVMs could interact with each other exactly as if they were running in the same JVM? Imagine what you could do with that kind of power—the power to express a computing problem in the simplest possible terms that stay true to the problem at hand yet be able to run that program on multiple computers at once while the program thinks it's running on one big computer. What would such a thing be? And wouldn't you really, really want it if you could have it?

Terracotta was born out of just such imaginings.

Terracotta is Java infrastructure software that allows you to scale your application to as many computers as needed, without expensive custom code or databases. Throughout this book, it is referred to as JVM-level clustering or network-attached memory. The question you now face is how to understand and leverage this technology best.

The goal of this book is to help you answer that question. While a total of almost fifty person-years of engineering have gone into the product, to date very little has been documented about Terracotta. After years of underground lab work and hundreds of production deployments under its belt, Terracotta's team of authors have come together to write this definitive guide to Terracotta. This book will help you learn the official definition and detailed architecture of the technology. It will also walk you through the most popular applications of JVM-level clustering. It will teach you how to tune and manage a production application running in a Terracotta environment.

Use this guide as a gateway. Terracotta is infrastructure just like a database, a file server, or even a networking switch. With it you can achieve many things and design many different use cases. Any technology that claims it is well suited to all use cases should be viewed with caution. We have put forth this work to help you both understand and trust Terracotta for certain use cases. While file servers and relational databases have been used with great success over the past 30 years, they have also been abused with varying levels of success (for example, we have seen a single relational database handle 1.5 billion inserts a day, filling it with data that was retained for only 30 days, all achieved by disabling rollback). We realize that databases succeed because a community of developers rallied around the concept and built a shared toolset and understanding of where databases fit and where they do not.

The Java community acts as a gateway to this understanding of database technology. Together, the community members help each other design systems that are generally accepted as successful. Terracotta has invented new nomenclature—calling itself network-attached memory. As a result, the community needs a foothold with which to establish a shared knowledge of this new thing, this network-attached memory. This book is your gateway into the universe of network-attached memory and the power it represents. Use it to help begin the conversation and thought process around what are good and bad use cases for a JVM-level clustering approach.

I think an example is in order. (By the way, we communicate mostly by example in this book. Hopefully, this style of teaching will be helpful to you.) Engineer A wants to use Terracotta to act as a point-to-point communication protocol on the Internet to stream movies to web browsers. Meanwhile, Engineer B wants to use Terracotta to maintain a centralized or shared view of her application configuration data without having to maintain each JVM's system properties or XML-based configuration separately. Engineer C wants to use Terracotta to replace his web application's current stateless architecture for a more natural stateful one. The product will integrate to each engineer's application with minimal initial effort, so how is engineer A, B, or C to know what to expect? For engineer A, Terracotta will seem unstable, slow, and generally cumbersome, while for engineers B and C, Terracotta will seem almost ideal.

If you can tell the differences among these application patterns, consider yourself among the few. If you are currently wrestling with an application running on Terracotta or are contemplating where to use it and where to not use it, this guide represents the foremost thinking on the subject.

Here, you will learn about several popular cases for using Terracotta. You will learn in detail how to configure the system in each case, and you will learn the details of what makes that case a potential success or sweet spot.

By the end of this book, you will see the patterns for yourself and be able to help your friends understand the differences too. It's an exciting time for those of us at Terracotta. The concepts we are discussing and suggesting to you will not prove new or radical. The concepts embodied within the product—centralized management, stateful development, stateless runtime, and more—have never been brought together or assembled into a package like this. This assembly of approaches and techniques is what makes Terracotta exciting. Communicating the new capabilities this technology provides to the application development team is challenging yet rewarding. We hope you find the book as engaging to read as we found it to write. With your help, this will be the first of several books on the topics of Terracotta, network-attached memory, and JVM-level clustering.

How This Book Is Structured

This book is structured as follows:

- *Chapter 1, Theory and Foundation*: We start with a look at what Terracotta is and the theory behind it.

- *Chapter 2, History of Terracotta*: This chapter provides a brief history of Terracotta to give the rest of the book some context.

- *Chapter 3, Jumping Into Terracotta*: In this chapter, we get into the practicalities of Terracotta, introducing the basic concepts of its configuration and showing a simple example of Terracotta clustering.

- *Chapter 4, POJO Clustering*: This practical chapter covers how to cluster an existing POJO application.

- *Chapter 5, Caching*: This chapter explains how to use Terracotta to alleviate some of the problems inherent in caching and how to bring the benefits of caching to distributed systems.

- *Chapter 6, Hibernate with Terracotta*: In this chapter, we show you how to scale Hibernate-enabled applications. We cover the concepts on which Hibernate is built so that you gain a full understanding of clustering with Hibernate.

- *Chapter 7, Extending HTTP Sessions with Terracotta*: You'll learn how to use Terracotta to cluster HTTP sessions in your web application in this chapter.

- *Chapter 8, Clustering Spring*: This chapter takes you through the process of turning a non-Spring clustered application into a Spring-enabled clustered application. It shows you how you can integrate Terracotta and Spring in a simple and effective fashion.

- *Chapter 9, Integration Modules*: We show you how to use Terracotta Integration Modules to cluster an external library or framework or modularize the configuration of your own application in this chapter.

- *Chapter 10, Thread Coordination*: In this chapter, we explain how to deal with threads and concurrency in Terracotta. We take a cookbook approach to give you a number of use case models that you can apply to your own applications.

- *Chapter 11, Grid Computing Using Terracotta*: This chapter showcases Terracotta's abilities to act as the platform for your own grid computing applications.

- *Chapter 12, Visualizing Applications*: The final chapter describes how to tune your Terracotta applications using Terracotta's visualization tools.

Prerequisites

To run the code in this book, you need to install the Java Software Development Kit 1.4 or greater.

Contacting the Authors

For more information about Terracotta, visit the web site at http://www.terracotta.org. There, you can find forums (http://forums.terracotta.org) and mailing lists dedicated to Terracotta, where members of the author team monitor and respond to queries from Terracotta users.

CHAPTER 1

■■■

Theory and Foundation
Forming a Common Understanding

Terracotta is Java infrastructure software that allows you to scale your application for use on as many computers as needed, without expensive custom code or databases. But Terracotta is more than this twenty-six-word definition. If you have picked up this book, you are looking for a deeper understanding of the technology and where to use it. To achieve that understanding, we must first break down the jargon surrounding scaling, clustering, and application architecture. In Chapter 1, we will spend some time defining terms and then explain the value Terracotta provides to applications. This will help us to build a shared understanding of the target audience of the technology.

Applications always have a developer and operator, although sometimes one individual may serve in both roles. The application developer works to deliver business logic that functions to specifications and is responsible for all the application code. The operator manages the production application and works with the developer to make sure the application is scalable enough to handle its potential production workload. The two must work together if the application is going to be successful, meaning that it is low cost to run and stable. Terracotta was designed with both the developer and operator in mind.

Terracotta was designed to free the application developer from the constraints of enterprise development frameworks, like Hibernate, Spring, and Enterprise JavaBeans (EJB). Whether or not applications use these frameworks, close reliance on the database leads to a lack of freedom of design. While Hibernate and Spring strive to help the developer by greatly simplifying application code, many applications fall short of the promise of freedom because they are never truly decoupled from the database. Terracotta uniquely provides a complete solution for decoupling from the database and scaling while simultaneously writing pure plain old Java objects (POJOs).

Terracotta was also designed to deliver the most stable operating platform for production Java applications, period. The system can be managed in a manner similar to databases—if you can operate a database, you can operate Terracotta. And data that Terracotta is managing on behalf of an application cannot be lost. Unlike the database however, Terracotta provides solutions for developing linearly scalable applications.

While most clustering vendors focus on application scalability, Terracotta manages to deliver scalability in conjunction with the highest levels of availability, and it does all this without a database. The system also provides unprecedented visibility across the application stack in a single vendor solution. Specifically, we can now monitor applications at the operating system level, the JVM level, and the application level through a single graphical dashboard or via Java Management Extensions (JMX). This means we can monitor not just application or application server performance but also hardware performance from a central location.

The developer and operator need a simple way to scale production applications. To date, that way has been the database, but it tends to work only because a database has a large array of management tools for production operation and because its development model (SQL queries, stored procedures, and object-relational mapping) is widely understood. The database is not really what developers would ask for had we the choice however, and Terracotta's founders have seen another option. In fact, Terracotta's dual focus on developmental and operational needs did not come about by chance.

Terracotta was born in the fires of a large-scale production Java application. While the business was growing by 100 percent year on year (which may not sound all that large until we explain that revenue was in billions of dollars), the platform team held itself to a standard of purchasing no new hardware after the first year of operation. The team came very close to meeting that goal for four years in a row. Terracotta takes lessons learned at that top-ten e-commerce website and significantly advances the state of the art of scalability by creating a general purpose extension to Java that any application can use to reap the benefits of simple development with simultaneously scalable and highly available production operation.

Clustering was once thought of as complex and highly unstable due to sensitivity to individual server failure, but with the advent of Terracotta, clustering is an idea whose time has finally come. Through the pages of this book, you will learn Terracotta's unique definition of clustering. The first four chapters focus on concepts and principles and the next few show how to apply Terracotta to common use cases such as clustered caching with Hibernate, clustering in Spring, HTTP session replication, and more.

Once these chapters have whet your appetite, this book will transition into covering both detailed techniques for building powerful abstractions using Terracotta and how to tune for any and all Terracotta usage. Now, let's dive into a more detailed definition of the technology.

Definition of the Terracotta Framework

As we've already stated, instead of filling your head with jargon by defining Terracotta using otherwise unclear terms, we will give a short definition and an explanation of the benefits of the approach. We'll break down each term in that definition into plain English, so that we have a strong basis from which to proceed to use cases.

Terracotta is a transparent clustering service for Java applications. Terracotta can also be referred to as JVM-level clustering. Terracotta's JVM-level clustering technology aids applications by providing a simple, scalable, highly available world in which to run.

To understand this definition, we need to define "transparent clustering service," as well as the operational benefits, including "simplicity," "scalability," and "high availability." We can then discuss the applications for this technology.

- *Transparency*: To users, transparency means that an application written to support Terracotta will still function as implemented with zero changes when Terracotta is not installed. This does not mean Terracotta works for everything or that Terracotta is invisible and does not require any changes to application code. Transparency for the Terracotta user denotes a freedom and purity of design that is valuable, because the application stays yours, the way you wanted to build it in the first place.

- *Clustering*: Clustering has had many definitions, and as a result, Terracotta struggled for some time with calling itself a clustering service. A clustering service is unique in that, while clustering refers to servers talking to each other over a network, a clustering service refers to technology that allows you to take an application written without any clustering logic or libraries and spread it across servers by clustering in the JVM, below the application. This moves clustering from an architecture concept to a service on which applications can rely when running in a production environment.

- *Simplicity*: Complexity and its antithesis simplicity refer to the changes that developers have to make along the road to building scalable applications. For example, to make an application scalable, objects may have to implement the `Serializable` interface from the Java language specifications in order to share those objects across servers.

- *Scalability*: Scalability can be confusing. This is a time when a background in statistics helps, because developers often confuse many of our performance-measuring terms, such as mean versus median and scalability versus performance. Scalability is important if you want to save money by starting small and growing only when demand requires. Scalability is the result of low latency and high throughput. An application can be very quick to respond but might only handle one request at a time (low latency and low throughput). Alternatively, an application can be very slow to respond but handle thousands of concurrent requests (high latency and high throughput), and the database is a great example of this latter type of application. Unlike the traditional relational database, Terracotta helps optimize both latency and throughput to create a truly scalable application.

- *Availability*: Availability means that every piece of shared data must get written to disk. If the datacenter in which the application cluster is running on top of Terracotta loses power, nothing will be lost when the power is restored. No individual process is critical, and the application can pick up where it left off.

With this common terminology, we will next look at analogies to Terracotta that already exist in the datacenter environment.

Network Attached Storage Similarities to Terracotta

Terracotta is a transparent clustering service, which can be used to deliver many different things such as session replication, distributed caching, and partitioning (otherwise known as grid computing). Transparency, as we have defined it, allows applications to depend on Terracotta without embedding Terracotta. There are several transparent services on which applications rely without embedding those services inside our application source code.

File storage is an example of a transparent service. Files can be stored locally on an individual server. File storage devices can change from tape to CD to hard disk without changing our application source code. What's more, file system performance can be tuned without changing our application. Files represent a popular mechanism for storing application data because they provide transparency of storage location, storage format, and performance optimization.

Terracotta brings the same capabilities to Java application memory. Thus, while networked file storage services are not a perfect parallel to Terracotta, file I/O is worth exploring a bit for these similarities. Their similarities should help you understand the value of transparent services before we jump into Terracotta and JVM-level clustering.

The file API can be summarized as having open(), seek(), read(), and write() methods. Underneath these methods, many different behaviors can be bolted on, each with specific strengths. A file can be stored on various types of file systems, allowing us to optimize performance for certain applications completely outside of source code.

Some file systems in use today include variants of the Journaled File System (JFS) architecture, the High Performance File System (HPFS), the Berkeley Fast File System (FFS), the MS-DOS File System, and Solaris's Zettabyte File System (ZFS). Each of these technologies has a specific performance character and sweet spot. For example, journaling is very good for production systems, because changes to the disk can be rolled back to repair file corruption that a bug in an application might have caused in the recent past. JFS is, therefore, well suited to highly available data. The Berkeley FFS is very good for large-scale random access usage underneath a multiuser server, where many tasks are writing to many files of different sizes for varying reasons at random times. Here, explicit fragmentation leads to predictable latency and throughput as a result of the random and even distribution of all data. Taking the opposite approach to Berkeley's file system, the DOS file system was tuned for sequential access underneath word processing applications in dedicated user scenarios. Microsoft's original file system approach worked well, because individual files were contiguous and in one place on the hard disk.

A Layer of Abstraction

It is quite interesting to see that these file systems each handle certain use cases very well and others not as well (we have all had to wait while the Microsoft Windows defragmenter rearranged our hard drives overnight for faster access). Nonetheless, when Microsoft changed its operating system architecture and adopted some of the HPFS or Berkeley techniques, many applications were none the wiser. No programs had to be rewritten if they used only the standard file APIs. Of course, any application that made assumptions about the performance characteristics and capabilities of the DOS file system had to change when the underlying file system changed.

Terracotta users find a similar abstraction with clustering that applications find with file systems. Terracotta users do not make assumptions about how objects move across the network, nor do the users write code explicitly to partition data among Java processes, as an example. Just like the operating system can switch file systems in production without changing an application's source code, Terracotta can run different optimizations (about which you will learn in subsequent chapters) without requiring the application to change.

Similarly, we can change the file system used by a production server to write to disk without going back to development and rewriting the application, and we can move the task of storing files outside any one server's scope. If a file is on a remote file server, the application does not care. Operations teams decide which file system to use. They may choose a file system technology because it makes the application run faster or choose a remote file server because it makes the application easier to manage or because the application can use the Network File System (NFS) protocol as a central broker for sharing information across processes.

Adding Networked File Storage

Exploring further, Network Appliance was founded in April 1992 to exploit the notion of network file storage for building large application clusters. At the time, Sun was dominating the Unix market as the premier platform on which to manually construct networked file servers using the NFS protocol that shipped inside most Unix variants. Novell was dominant in the PC market, providing similar networked file and logon services for MS-DOS and Windows users.

Network Appliance realized that setup, maintenance, and ongoing operation of networked storage was too expensive and decided to produce a hardware device that honored the NFS specification but required no setup other than plugging it in. The value of networked file storage is that the storage can be managed independently of the application server. The storage can be made highly available through well known backup and recovery techniques, such as backing up to expensive centralized tape robots or replicating data on a regular schedule to a disaster recovery site. The storage server can also be scaled to meet the I/O needs of the application without simultaneously buying bigger CPUs and more expensive application server hardware.

Parallels to Terracotta

Terracotta offers the operator benefits similar to networked file storage. Specifically, objects are stored remotely in Terracotta even though the objects are cached inside the JVM for fast application access. This means that the operator can focus on hardening the Terracotta server to deliver high availability, just as in the file system analogy. Terracotta's data can be replicated, backed up, and otherwise managed just like a file server. Thus, the application developer can use objects in Java just like simple file I/O, and Terracotta will move the objects from the process to a central location where those objects can be managed safely and cost-effectively.

The last parallel between files and Terracotta that we mentioned was that the two enable clustering through simple, straightforward sharing of data and locking events. Applications that write to files by locking the parts of the file they want to work on can safely be shared across users in real time. Without NFS or similar networked file sharing technology, this simple approach will not work. The developer would have to push data among application processes in the application layer using network sockets by hand far above the file system. As a result, operators would lose the ability to manage these clustered applications by managing only their storage.

Files are a good example of a transparent clustering service. Developers write inside a file as they desire, while operators store that file as they desire. In short, transparent services, such as NFS, help developers write applications as they would prefer, while allowing operators the freedom to build scalable, highly available production environments for managed data.

At this point, you might be asking yourself, "What's the difference between the NFS proto-col and the database?" With databases, developers use SQL, whereas with NFS, developers use the proprietary file layout. Also, with the database, the instance can run on any server we want without changing the application, and the database can be tuned without changing the appli-cation. The database certainly is a service. We are not asserting that NFS and files are better than SQL and a database. We are merely looking for good parallels to Terracotta. In its operat-ing character, a database is a good parallel. In its programming model, however, it is not.

A developer knows when writing to files is necessary and does so intentionally. In the modern application, much of the use of the database is through an object-relational mapping tool like Hibernate, and thus, a developer who would rather not write to a database is forced to do so.

Terracotta works more like file I/O than a database, because Terracotta presents itself in the manner the developer desires. Terracotta is consumed as memory inside the JVM. The notion of migrating memory from the local server to a service somewhere on the network, as can be done with files, is quite a leap of faith. Nonetheless, Terracotta is a new example of a transparent service.

At its core, Terracotta's goal is to allow several computers to communicate with each other as if they were one big computer through memory and pure memory constructs, such as threads and locks (mutex objects and the like). You might be tempted to think of Terracotta as functioning just like NFS, because Terracotta takes a local resource and moves it to the net-work. The similarities to NFS start an end there, however. Let us now explore the power in having a transparent memory location in more detail and learn how it is unique and impor-tant.

Transparency of Memory Location

Unlike when working with files, developers using Terracotta do not see an API. Recall that our definition includes the notion of JVM-level clustering. This means that to the application, Terra-cotta is the JVM, and to the JVM, Terracotta is the application. Figure 1-1 illustrates this concept.

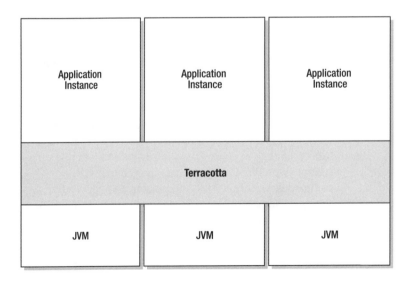

Figure 1-1. *Terracotta sits between the application and the JVM.*

Unlike file I/O, transparency of the memory location implies that Terracotta has to figure out what to share and move on its own. Think back to the file analogy and focus for a moment on the open() API call: open(<path_to_file>, mode). A developer decides where to write the file relative to the application's running directory. A developer who wants an application to write to a file usually makes the file name and directory in which it resides a start-up option for the user. Suppose our application wants to write to a data file named application.dat in the directory path /path/to/my/application/data. The application merely needs to invoke open("/path/to/my/application/data/application.dat"). An operator can then move our application's data using NFS. To use NFS, the production operations team needs to mount the remote file system underneath the directory the application writes to when that application calls open(). In our example, this would look something like the following:

```
mount //remoteserver/remotepath /path/to/my/application/data
```

Once the remote mount is established, our application will write its data to the remote server.

With Terracotta, however, everything works at a memory level. The interface, in this case, is the object orientation of the language itself. The parallel to mounting remote repositories applies, because objects have structure just like files and directories. Developers build object models, and the JVM maps those objects onto the heap at run time. Object models are the key to interfacing with Terracotta, because they contain all the information the JVM needs to map an object model to memory, and thus, all the information Terracotta needs at the same time.

To explore this idea further, consider that object models are made up of graphs of related objects. A user has a first name, last name, and ID. These are its fields. A home address and work address can be stored inline in a user object as fields, but they are usually broken out into their own address class. Users can also have friends. This simple object model is illustrated in Figure 1-2.

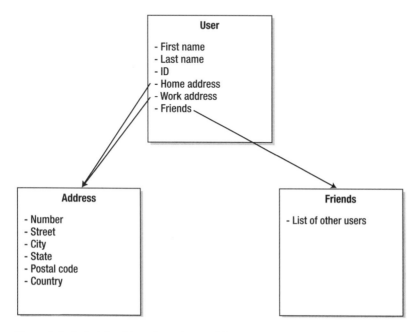

Figure 1-2. *A simple object domain model*

If a developer points to the User object, the expectation would be that the object references to Home address, Work address, and Friends would become shared automatically. In Terracotta, the developer need only specify the User object as being shared. Terracotta learns from the object definition itself what the fields of our shared object are (First name, Last name, etc.) as well as what the object relationships (Addresses and Friends) are. Consider this to be analogous to mounting a remote file system onto the local machine: the User object is mounted into memory from Terracotta, and after that, the memory operations can be cached locally but persisted remotely on the Terracotta service for sharing and later retrieval.

You will learn more about how this works in Chapter 3, but for now, know that Terracotta's ability to understand the intent of an application by analyzing the use of memory is what makes Terracotta transparent to our source code.

Putting Transparency and Clustering Together

Terracotta's transparent clustering service helps a developer share part of a Java process's memory across process boundaries and machines. This means that any object resident in memory in one Java process can be seen by another Java process, whether that process is on the same machine or somewhere else across the network. In the previous section, you learned that sharing part of a JVM means that we are mounting objects that appear local but are, in fact, stored in a central service. We should break this down in more detail.

First, let's build a simple class, ClusteredClass:

```java
class ClusteredClass {
  int id;
  String name;

  ClusteredClass( int id, String name ) {
    this.id = id;
    this.name = name;
  }

  final Integer getid( ) {
    return new Integer( id );
  }

  final String getname( ) {
    return name;
  }

  void setid( int id ) {
    this.id = id;
  }

  void setname( String s ) {
    this.name = s;
  }
```

```
  public String toString( ) {
    return ( "Customer id=[" + id + "] name=[" + name + "]\n" );
  }
}
```

Now, imagine that there are two servers, and we want those two servers to act together as one logical server. We have to be assured by the JVM that instances of ClusteredClass created in one server are available to the other under the same object ID. Why? Simply put, if an object created on one JVM were not the same object on all JVMs, the application would not reap any value from transparent clustering. Think back to the NFS analogy. If two application instances wanted to read from and write to the same file, they must mount the same remote file system and open the same file by name. In Java, an object ID is like a file name. Terracotta uses the object ID as the clusterwide path to a specific object in memory.

Without consistent object identifiers across JVMs, the application would find that any object created on one server would be different and have to be re-created or reconnected to object graphs when moving from one JVM to another. Somehow, all this fuss does not sound transparent. Let's, therefore, assume that objects created with a particular ID in one JVM will have the same ID in any and all other JVMs.

It would also be nice if the second server could see an instance of ClusteredClass constructed on the first server. However, there are several challenges inherent to our sharing goal. Objects created in one memory space will have different addresses in RAM, and thus different identifiers, than in another space. Not only do memory addresses not align across processes, but objects created in one memory space will eventually get modified, and those modifications have to make it from one server's memory to the other's. How can we make all this happen? It is, after all, quite a leap to assume that Terracotta can find all of our User objects (from the previous section) and share them on its own.

One way to think of this challenge is in terms of object scope. If an object o is not created or referenced at an appropriate level of scope, such that it can be accessed across threads or even by the same thread at some time later, the object is not shareable across servers. Method-local scope refers to an object whose life cycle is that of the method in which it is created; the object is created and destroyed within the method's scope. Method-local objects tend to be immediate garbage to the modern collector and are not, therefore, what we are after. This is important: *sharing every object between the two servers is not necessary.* Sharing objects in collections, singletons, statics, and global objects is more what we are after. Server two should only be able to see object o that server one created if server one creates the object in a scope that is accessible to more than one thread. So if we invoke a constructor in a method-local context, we should not worry about clustering, but in the global context we should:

```
void printAClusteredClassInstance( ) { // method-level scope
  ClusteredClass c1 = new ClusteredClass( 1, "ari" );
  c1.toString( );
}


ClusteredClass clone( ClusteredClass c ) { // calling-level scope
  ClusteredClass c2 = new ClusteredClass( c.getid(), c.getname( ) );
  return c2; // c2 escapes the method so it might be interesting…
}
```

```
static Map myMap = new HashMap();

void storeAClusteredClassInstance( ClusteredClass c3 ) { // Stored in a singleton...
  myMap.put( new Integer( c3.getid( ) ), c3 );
}
```

In the preceding examples, c1 is not worth clustering; c2 might be worth clustering, depending on what happens in the thread that calls clone(); and c3 should be clustered, because it joins myMap, which would likely be clustered. Thinking about it further, consider that if we are trying to get c1, c2, and c3 shared between servers one and two. c1 cannot, in fact, be shared because if server one creates it, there is no way for server two to reach c1. Similarly, there is no way for another thread in server one to reach c1 (unless we change the declaration of c1 to make it a static variable). c2 might be clustered if the thread calling clone() actually places c2 in a location in memory where multiple threads could reach it. c3 is definitely and easily reachable by server two, however, when server two executes myMap.get() with the appropriate key.

Now, we have to examine the constructor, because Terracotta usually has to do something with constructor calls to get a handle on objects when those objects are first created (the constructor is sort of like the call to the mount command in the NFS analogy). Terracotta can decide when to invoke the constructor sort of like an automatic file system mounter. Let's now walk through an example.

■**Note** automount first shipped with the Solaris Operating System. It detects the need for a remote file system and mounts that file system on demand.

In storeAClusteredClassInstance(), if we assume server one starts before server two, then we want only the first JVM to construct myMap, just like the code fragment would behave in one JVM. You are starting to see that Terracotta cannot only look for objects in memory but, in fact, has to address a few special instructions such as object construction, which translates into new memory allocation, as well as thread locking, which translates into mutex operations in the underlying operating system. In Chapters 3 and 4, we will explain how this works in more detail. For now, it is sufficient to know that there are only a handful of instructions that the JVM executes when manipulating memory, and Terracotta can observe all of them.

To round out our initial understanding of sharing objects across Java processes to achieve transparent clustering, threading and coordination must be considered. In the file analogy, an application process must lock the part of the file it wishes to write so that other processes do not corrupt it. For threads and locks, Terracotta can provide for cross-JVM locking just by using Java synchronization. You need to understand a bit about the Java memory model before you can fully understand this concept.

Threads are part of the clustering equation in that they manipulate objects and have to be synchronized when accessing those objects. Let's assume for a moment that Terracotta is deployed and working such that we have c3 on servers one and two and that c3 is exactly the same object in both JVMs. If one server wants to change myMap, it needs to lock myMap. Thus, locking and threading semantics must spread across processes, just like objects spread across Java processes.

Honoring the Java Memory Model

You know just about all you need to know to get started—except we still need to consider the memory model. We must synchronize our changes to myMap or c3 across Java processes just as we would across Java threads; at least, we do if we want changes to either object to be sent reliably between servers one and two. In a sense, the process boundaries have melted away. But when do the servers communicate? And what do they send? The memory model provides the answer.

The Java Memory Model is quite well documented elsewhere, but the key concept we should focus on is "happens before," as laid out in JSR 133. To the JVM, "happens before" is defined as the logical time before a thread enters a synchronized block. The JVM assures that the objects this thread will gain access to once inside the synchronized block will be up to date.

■**Note** The Terracotta authors relied on the graduate thesis of Bill Pugh at Carnegie Mellon University dated June, 2004 in designing the software, as did we when writing this book.

The model asserts that any changes that happened before a thread is granted entry into a synchronized block will be applied to main memory before the lock is granted. Terracotta uses the memory model to ensure proper cross-process behavior and semantics. For example, if object o has been changed by server one at some point in the recent past, server two will get those changes before entering into a synchronized block that is protecting access to o. Server one's changes in this case *happened before* server two began working with o, so server two sees server one's changes. Since locks are exclusive and pessimistic, meaning only one thread is allowed into a synchronized block at a time, the memory model proves sufficient for defining ordering in an environment where threads are spread across Java processes. We will go into more detail on this assertion in Chapter 4.

■**Note** To the highly informed reader, Martin Fowler's statement "remember the first law of distributed computing: don't distribute your objects" might seem to be questioned by Terracotta's transparency. In fact, it is. Fowler's claim is too simple and ignores the fact that distributing objects is indeed ambiguous. Fowler was focused on remote method invocation (RMI). RMI serializes an object, sends it to a remote JVM, deserializes that object, runs the specified method, serializes the object, and returns control back to the first JVM. Terracotta does, in fact, distribute object data and coordinating events, but Terracotta never moves the processing context from one JVM to another as RMI would. Just as we can remotely store the files underneath an application without breaking that application, we can remotely store application objects without breaking the application. Therefore, Terracotta is not bound by Fowler's law as stated, because Terracotta never uses RMI, serialization, or other frameworks—each of which is not transparent. In fact, such frameworks throw exceptions that only the developer can address in source code, such as RemoteMethodInvocationException.

Being a Service Has Advantages

It has already been established that the technology offers a Java developer transparent clustering. Let's now turn our attention to the "service" component of our definition of Terracotta. Terracotta is made up of only a few components. It feels and smells like the services that operators are used to, meaning that Terracotta is not only some sort of agent or library running inside existing Java processes but also itself is a Java process.

To restate, Terracotta is made up of libraries you install next to any JVM that is to join a cluster, and Terracotta is a separate Java process unto itself, as shown in Figure 1-3.

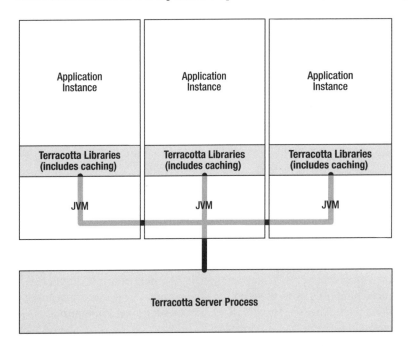

Figure 1-3. *Terracotta's two components include libraries and a server process that communicate over TCP/IP.*

The Java process running the Terracotta server runs *only* Terracotta. This Java process is the focal point of an operator's effort in managing a cluster of Java processes running on top of Terracotta. This means two things: scalability can be as easy as adding more JVMs, and high availability works similarly to that of the database or a file server. While applications use Terracotta to deliver availability and scalability, Terracotta itself delivers both scalability and availability when the operator managing the process can make the Terracotta service highly available. To simplify this concept, Terracotta makes an application highly available and Terracotta is, itself, made highly available much like a relational database.

Availability

In subsequent chapters, you will learn how Terracotta stores a copy of our shared object data outside our existing Java processes. This implies that if all our Java processes were to stop, we could, in fact, start the processes again and gain access to those objects as they existed in memory before Java was terminated. When running on top of Terracotta's transparent clustering service, an application does not stop running until the operator flushes the objects from Terracotta's memory and disk. This is how Terracotta delivers high availability as a runtime service.

The Terracotta process is designed to be reliable and restartable. If it were killed or stopped, Terracotta could restart where it left off, and the application processes would not see any errors or exceptions while Terracotta restarts. The ability to restart is helpful for small applications and in development environments. For production systems, a more nonstop approach is preferable. Terracotta server processes can be configured to identify each other on the network and to share the duties of object management for an application cluster. In essence, Terracotta doesn't just cluster your application but is also capable of being clustered for availability using built-in features in the software.

Scalability

In subsequent chapters, you will also learn how to use Terracotta to tune and scale applications that are spread across Java process boundaries. Tuning applications can be achieved on multiple levels, from limiting the scope of the clustering behavior purely in Terracotta configuration files to sometimes making changes to source code. Source code changes can result in the biggest bang for the buck in terms of getting more scalability from an application running on Terracotta. We will study in detail how to configure Terracotta, as well as how to write code that is best suited for the environment.

Once an application is perfectly configured, or is at least as good as it is going to get, there is still more that can be done. If scaling is defined as adding more JVMs, and throughput is defined as how many operations per second a single node can handle, Terracotta can help in delivering more throughput per node as much as it can help in delivering better scaling to apply against the business need.

To help a JVM perform, Terracotta provides built-in caching designed to allow applications to perform at nonclustered speeds even when clustered. To improve performance, an application needs to optimize its use of Terracotta's internal caches. Optimizing the use of cache is a function of optimizing workload routing. One example of workload routing is sticky load balancing for web applications. In sticky load balancing, the same user session gets routed to the same JVM for every request. If some sort of stickiness can be applied, Terracotta will keep objects in memory as long as it can. Load balancing is not always as simple as stickiness and session replication, though. In general, developers and operators have to work together to consistently route a workload to the same JVM over time.

■**Note** Several members of the Java community refer to Terracotta as a distributed cache. As you can see from the fact that Terracotta's caches are internal, and external load balancing is required to optimize cache efficiency, Terracotta is not a cache. It merely *uses* caching technology to ensure application performance and scalability.

By routing requests to the same JVM over time, we ensure that all the information a thread needs to process application requests is local to that JVM in memory. Without such assurance, our application will need Terracotta's server process to move the memory into context underneath us just in time. The application will have to wait for the network in order to complete an operation. This is commonly referred to as paging. Terracotta works at a byte level and not at a page level, but it has adopted the paging terminology from virtual memory inside operating systems because the notion is the same. In most operating systems, virtual memory allows an application to spill 4-kilobyte pages of memory to disk. The ability to page out unused memory frees the application to get more work done with less memory. When the application needs a page back from disk, that application begins to perform very slowly, however.

Here's another way to view the performance optimization Terracotta delivers through its use of caching inside the application's JVM: Terracotta will move as little data as possible given the changing workload it sees. This improves performance by allowing applications to move at the speed of memory instead of the speed of the network. Just like in the operating system and virtual memory, moving this caching feature into the transparent clustering service provides operators the configuration hooks to make runtime decisions about how large Terracotta's cache will be.

Terracotta can scale independently of the application above it. Much like a relational database, the Terracotta server's I/O and throughput are tuned using various IT strategies with which operators are familiar. These include disk striping and data partitioning. In a future release, Terracotta's designers also intend to provide the ability to cluster Terracotta servers for scale. Once the feature is implemented, Terracotta is able to stripe objects across Terracotta instances on its own.

Going back to our example code, Terracotta's core architecture can support storing myMap on one Terracotta server while storing c3 on a second Terracotta server. When the application runs myMap.get(id), Terracotta knows that the map is on one Terracotta instance, while c3 is on another, and routes I/O based on Terracotta object identifier and corresponding routing information. Terracotta honors object identity as well as the Java Memory Model so there are no copies of objects, only real objects, which allows the system to store parts of objects on one Terracotta instance and other parts on another. This architecture delivers the ability to scale linearly, because any number of Terracotta instances will split the responsibility of storing and manipulating objects evenly: two instances split the data in half, three instances in thirds, and so on.

Avoiding Bottlenecks

The hardest part of tuning an application is in storing data on disk for availability yet simultaneously avoiding I/O bottlenecks. Figure 1-4 illustrates why tuning is hard. Essentially, the database helps us deliver high availability but with high latency or low scalability compared to purely in-memory applications. Simultaneously, caching and purely in-memory applications provide low and sometimes zero availability, since nothing is written to disk.

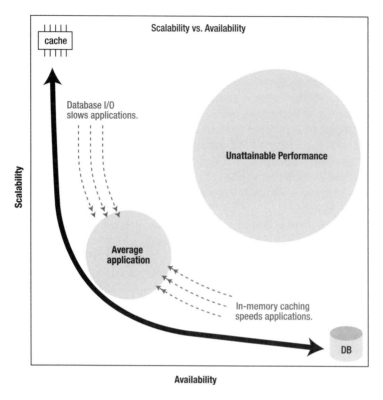

Figure 1-4. *Consider the scalability versus availability trade-off to help avoid bottlenecks and deliver reliability.*

The database can be mostly transparent through Hibernate and object-relational mapping, and it can support clustering if all application servers read and write to the same database tables. So why is the database not a transparent clustering service? The database should not be used for clustering, because it shifts the burden of scaling and clustering an application from application source code to production operations through complex and expensive database clustering technologies, such as Oracle Realtime Application Clusters (RAC). This is another way of saying what some of us might already know—the database is a bottleneck.

Unlike the database, Terracotta does not merely shift the object-sharing burden from the developer and source code to the operator. Terracotta's architecture and implementation contain several optimizations that provide an application with multiple lines of defense against disk I/O bottlenecks, the sum of these techniques make the solution over ten times faster than the database. Here are a few of these optimizations:

- Terracotta reads from in-memory caches when available.

- Terracotta reads only what it needs, and no more, from its server, and it can read in near-constant time from disk.

- Terracotta writes only what changes, and it writes the changes in batches.

- Terracotta writes in an append-only fashion. Objects are never sorted, indexed, or relocated/defragmented on the disk.

Let's analyze each of the four optimizations further, starting with reading from cache. First and foremost, the application has an in-memory cache of the data (see Figure 1-3) so that when reading, there is no disk I/O. This cache is on the application's side of the network with respect to the Terracotta server, so unlike a database's internal cache, Terracotta can respond to some requests at in-memory speed. Caching inside the application in a transparent fashion is only possible because Terracotta is transparent. This also serves to significantly lessen the workload on the Terracotta server process.

Second, Terracotta reads only what it needs. Terracotta stores an object's fields separate from each other on disk but near each other on the same disk block. Each field can be retrieved separately. Since the data is formatted on disk much like a HashMap would be in memory, Terracotta can take the identifier for a field to be retrieved as a key, hash that identifier into a file location, move to the appropriate block within the file, and load the field without loading any other disk blocks.

There is a further optimization here in that an object's fields are created at the same point in time that the constructor is called inside the application. Thus, the object's fields are all stored near each other on disk. Since Terracotta reads entire disk blocks at once, it usually reads, in a single disk operation, many objects and fields that were created together. Those objects and fields are often needed together, since they represent parts of the same object or closely related objects.

Third, the server writes what changes, and it writes in batches. As we pointed out, the Terracotta server writes to disk much like a hash map (HashMap) would write to memory. Each field can change without updating any other data. When several objects change, their changes are written together to the same block on disk so that they honor the block-level read optimization we discussed previously.

Fourth, the server writes in append-only fashion. This means that we needn't burden ourselves with changes in field data, and we needn't read blocks from disk in order to write blocks back to disk. Normally, changing data on disk requires reading the block where the data is located into memory, mutating the file buffers, and flushing the buffer back to disk. Terracotta avoids this extra read I/O. What's more, if the server running the Terracotta process has enough memory, the file data can all be cached in memory inside the operating system's file buffers. If this caching can occur, all read traffic is served from memory buffers (an additional line of defense), and the disk subsystem is only writing to the end of our data file. This implies that a Terracotta server can be tuned to utilize the entire disk subsystem's throughput, since it never has to seek to random locations on disk.

■**Note** If a Terracotta server needs to support more write traffic than a single disk can sustain, the operator can stripe Terracotta across multiple disks so that write traffic spreads across those disks. For example, if a single hard disk spinning at 10,000 rpm can sustain 100 megabytes per second of read or write traffic, striping four disks together under Terracotta would deliver a total capacity of 400 megabytes per second of highly available object I/O to Java processes running on top of Terracotta. 400 megabytes per second translates to over 4 gigabits of network throughput.

These scaling and disk I/O recipes, while quite standard fare for database administrators, were brought to the attention of Terracotta's designers at the large e-commerce web site and are now baked into Terracotta

So, while the database can append new records onto the end of a table like Terracotta does, indexes must be adjusted and maintained as data changes. Databases must be prepared for random I/O into sorted indexes, and this costs significant latency while the disk seeks the point on the disk where an index must change. Terracotta, however, does not burden itself with where on the disk an object is stored relative to other objects. It merely needs to be able to retrieve individual objects by their IDs. Terracotta's singular use of the disk, as compared with the multiple uses a database has for the disk, means Terracotta can optimize itself, whereas a database requires administrator intervention to tell the system which of many optimizations to leverage for specific data.

Use Cases

Terracotta makes several servers work together like one logical server. It can be applied in many ways and to many use cases, but it works in conjunction with the JVM to eliminate scalability/availability trade offs that we otherwise deal with application after application.

The basic use cases of Terracotta fall under the following umbrella categories:

- Distributed cache

- Database offload

- Session replication

- Workload partitioning

Distributed Caching

When used to distribute application cache data, Terracotta shares Java collections across Java processes. Under such architectures, typical cases require maps, lists, arrays, and vectors—in both java.util and java.util.concurrent—to be shared across processes. There are several Terracotta capabilities that will make this use case easier. The first is that object identity will work. This means that hashCode() and == will work as expected, for example, in maps and lists with respect to storing the same key more than once. This also means that the following code example will return TRUE:

```
Object foo1, foo2;
foo1 = cache.get( key );
foo2 = cache.get( key );
return( foo1 == foo2 );
```

Another benefit of transparent clustering services for distributed cache applications is that the cache does not impinge on the domain model. The classic example here is that of multiple indexes to a dataset. For example, a web site in the travel industry needs to be able to display hotels by location, price, room amenities, and availability. The natural place to store the hotel data is in a database where all these details amount to SQL queries against a data table and indexes are specified at run time. However, most travel web sites are not issuing queries against the database every time a user comes to the site and attempts to locate a hotel; rather, they use a cache. And, it would be nice to be able to do in the cache what we can do in the database, namely store the hotel once and only once but have alternate indexes with price ranges, location names, and other data as different keys.

I can store the Westin St. Francis Hotel in downtown San Francisco under the keys "San Francisco," "US POSTAL CODE 94102," and "Hotels between $300 and $1,000 per night". But the hotel is the same hotel no matter how it gets returned. This is all fine and good until we want to update the hotel's price to $259 on special; now, the hotel falls out of the price range under which it was originally stored in cache, because it is now less than $300. If we model this in the database, there's no problem. If we model it in memory, spread across machines—problem. Chapter 5 will detail the distributed cache use case and how to work with changing data over time.

Database Offload

The database is the bane of Java developers' existence and, simultaneously, our best friend. The key reasons for using a database are that the data gets written to disk and can be queried and updated in a well-known format and that the database can be tuned without significant impact to the business logic. The reasons not to use the database are that the object-relational translation complicates code, transactional architectures are hard to scale, and the database is a bottleneck.

Applications can use Terracotta to eliminate the database bottleneck. In such scenarios, leave objects in memory, and cluster them via Terracotta. Since Terracotta is infrastructure separate from any application process, objects in memory do not necessarily get lost (recall that Terracotta stores objects on disk, so objects will not get lost). Therefore, when using Terracotta, the database's role is well contained; it is used primarily for query and reporting of business data. It is used less as a central store for objects on disk and as a transactional control point where synchronization suffices.

Session Replication

Session replication has long been a feature of the application server or container. Apache Tomcat, BEA WebLogic, JBoss Application Server, IBM Websphere (CE), Jetty from Webtide, and Sun GlassFish each has a session replication solution bundled within the container. But transparent infrastructure for sharing objects across processes can provide unique value when compared to these frameworks.

Terracotta's transparency implies something new and different from all prior session replication approaches. Specifically, session replication usually pushes a few programming rules back up through the container to the application developer. Web application developers know that all session attributes must implement `java.io.Serializable`. Developers also know that those attributes must be small. And domain objects should not be referenced by the session attributes, or you risk serializing too much or serializing dangerous data. Last, any attribute that is accessed via `getAttribute()` must later be put back into session by calling `setAttribute()`.

These rules and more regarding the use of session replication are, in fact, direct results of containers' having used session serialization and replication when sharing objects in session. If we follow the session, what we would find is that the session is retrieved from an internal `HashMap` when the container receives a web request. That session is marked as clean when the container hands the session object to the servlet code. The session will get serialized and sent across the wire to other instances of the application only if we call `setAttribute()` when changing objects inside the session.

Transparent object sharing across Java processes is different. Transparent object sharing implies that if we, the application developers, can share the session `HashMap` and all the sessions and attributes inside that map, then we needn't signal to the container what we change and when. We no longer need to call `setAttribute()` when we change attributes. Nor do we have to make sure objects implement the serializable interface, nor worry about their size. In some cases, references to domain objects and singletons will even prove acceptable.

Workload Partitioning

Workload partitioning is currently referred to under more popular names like MapReduce, data grid, and compute grid. The idea here is to divide and conquer. With Terracotta, divide-and-conquer architecture is achieved either by using Java data structures for messaging along with thread coordination or by using JMS or socket communications instead of threading for coordination and using shared data structures for a different purpose.

Without going into too much detail now, Figure 1-5 illustrates the power of partitioning. Essentially, an application can spread computational workload such as querying, updating of large amounts of data, or similar use cases without the need for message queuing, a database, or other infrastructure services. A Java application and some multithreaded logic will suffice.

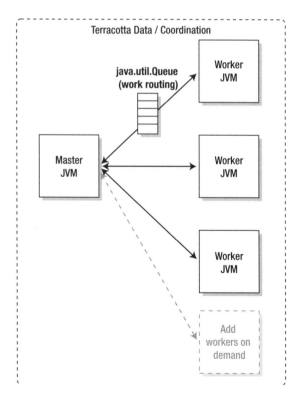

Figure 1-5. *Distributing workload to many computers using only memory, threads, and Terracotta (see Chapters 10 and 11 for details)*

Summary

Terracotta is a transparent clustering service with an object-oriented development model. "Transparent" refers to the pure Java language and JVM memory interface with no explicit programming model requirements, such as a requirement to use Spring or Hibernate. "Clustering" refers to the ability to allow multiple machines and Java processes to work together on the same data and to signal each other using pure objects and threading logic. And "service" refers to the infrastructure nature of this technology. A look at distributed caching APIs helps tighten this definition.

Distributed caches are not transparent clustering services. These libraries are designed to push bytes among networked servers when the cache is updated through get() and put() calls, and it's important to note the following details about them:

- *Transparency*: Distributed caches cannot be transparent. They require the developer to call get(), which copies data from the cache into objects when the API is called. Distributed caches also require the developer to call put() after objects are changed; this copies data back to the cache. get() and put() imply that the application code and the object model cannot support certain things. Methods in our source code cannot hold on to references to objects across calls to get(), because we will not get the up-to-date data from the cache from the last time a thread called put(). And object models cannot include rich domains where objects, like our User and his Address and Friends from earlier in this chapter, could actually be Java references. If our domain model is made up of regular references, the entire object graph will get serialized on put(), which means we will end up with different objects on get() than we initially created.

- *Clustering*: Distributed caches deliver Java developers a form of clustering. They do not provide clustering as a service, as we defined "service" earlier, because they are not transparent. An application cannot be written for a single machine and then operate across a group of machines in production. Furthermore, since most clustered caching libraries must be present at runtime for even threads on one machine to share objects, they cannot be removed from the application without rewriting that application to some degree.

- *Simplicity*: The relative complexity of distributed caches is quite high, not just because they force changes to the application source but also because they require changes to the production operating procedure. This is due to the fact that, in order to scale, distributed caches ask that we keep all objects in memory spread across many JVMs. For example, if we want to manage a 100-gigabyte dataset, and our JVM is 32-bit, we will need a minimum of 50 JVMs at 2 gigabytes of heap per JVM to store the entire data set. If we want that data to be highly available, we need to store each object in two JVMs, meaning we need a minimum of 100 JVMs. 100 JVMs are required just to manage 100 gigabytes of data, and this example ignores the application's actual purpose and business workload, which will surely drive even more servers.

- *Scalability*: Distributed caches have historically scaled better than applications clustered using only a database by putting objects at risk (recall Figure 1-4, where we trade off scalability and availability) and keeping our object data only in memory. Having JVMs hold our objects only in memory means that we cannot eliminate the database, because a loss of power would otherwise imply a loss of data. Thus we end up in a hybrid world with clustering plus databases and their associated scalability issues, which is back where we started

By our definition, distributed caches are not transparent clustering services. Consider now that distributed caches are rich networking libraries where developers do not see network stacks and APIs, such as sockets. Because these caches hide the network transport, compared to TCP or UDP, distributed caches are a higher form of networking. The higher form is valuable, but it is neither transparent nor a clustering service.

The definition of Terracotta as a transparent clustering service presented in this chapter is something new and worth exploring in further detail: in Chapter 2, you will learn about the history of the concept, and in Chapter 3, we will dive into our first example—HelloClusteredWorld.

CHAPTER 2

■ ■ ■

History of Terracotta

The galactic forces of Linux, Java, and the Internet have fundamentally changed application architecture, and the Java community is still trying to catch up with the impacts of the changes. Typical business applications in the past were rarely spread across servers; this has changed. Databases used to see much more than the networked SQL workload; they contained a significant portion of our business logic in the form of stored procedures or similar embedded execution technology. Today, they see mostly object-relational mapping (ORM) queries. Linux and the Internet have taken us down a different path than Oracle may have preferred.

With the Internet came the introduction of the n-tier architecture (see Figure 2-1). In their simplest form, enterprise applications can be viewed as either two-tier or three-tier. The third tier arose from the notion of the web server, which was first used to serve static HTML out of HTTP servers produced by vendors such as Apache. Eventually, this became a formal architecture paradigm involving presentation to users across the Internet behind a browser interface—we call the third tier the presentation tier for this reason.

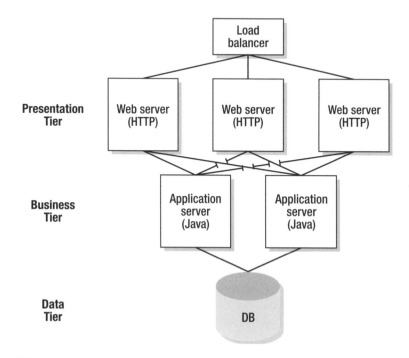

Figure 2-1. *The n-tier architecture*

The presentation tier quite rapidly changed from presenting static HTML to serving as part of the application tier in delivering a dynamic application development platform. For many reasons, the most important of which was the ubiquity of the web browser, three-tier architecture began to spill from Internet to enterprise applications.

For enterprises, the application tier caused a new problem. Operationally, there were now many requests coming in to the application tier from over the network (Internet, intranet, and extranet inclusive), yet the application tier was not scaling well. The database was a serious bottleneck. Also, application server stability and availability was at issue.

The database and application tiers are capable of finite capacity for any given design, whereas inbound traffic to an application can be unbounded. Individual users and use cases could exhaust application nodes or databases at any time. The data and application tiers proved to be expensive to deploy and manage, because scalability was hard to predict and ensure.

Architecture was shifting to a loosely coupled model wherein different components of the application could be abstracted behind interfaces and other components could ignore the implementation details. And loose coupling was accelerating the move toward n-tier architecture in that one service could be hosted on a completely different server from another without complicating the programming model.

In Chapter 1, we discussed the notion of files and file I/O as separate and apart from the notion of the file server on which the file lies. The value is in the operational ability to scale a service without changing the application. The trade-off for this flexibility is that many performance bottlenecks do not show at smaller scales and on nonproduction configurations and therefore are uncovered only in production, thus making capacity planning quite challenging.

In addition to the capacity-planning challenge inherent to loosely coupled application architecture, controlling the ongoing cost of development is often first priority, and many chose Java because of its flexibility and simultaneous simplicity. Java virtual machines (JVMs) in the early days could not capitalize on the entire CPU without very careful tuning. It was common to run two JVMs per CPU and two CPUs per node or four JVMs per node. The dominant application server vendors themselves chose Java as well. Java-based application servers were and remain very sensitive to workload. With all the JVMs came a hunger for memory, and the cheapest way to get lots of memory was to deploy small machines with 500MB to 2GB of RAM instead of buying expensive parallel processing machines with lots of RAM and CPU. The preferred deployment model was what many referred to as scaling out an application across many small machines, as opposed to scaling up an application inside one large multiprocessor server.

So while the Internet drove us to scale out, scaling out itself was simultaneously forced on us, since we now had multiple JVMs on the brain. Multiple JVMs on multiple nodes was not a difficult leap forward for IT departments. Perl scripts and the like helped to manage the sprawl, and managing the sprawl was the most important capability that kept operations teams from rejecting the scale-out model.

The last galactic force cemented the model of many JVMs on many servers. That force is Linux. Without Linux and the associated open source approach, license fees and support fees for expensive operating systems would have forced us to find ways to scale our applications on fewer servers; the backs of our IT budgets would have otherwise been broken as we bought more and more nodes across the enterprise.

So it came to pass that most architects chose to scale out, as opposed to scale up. At the time, neither scaling out nor scaling up mattered to database vendors like Oracle, because the database was handling the workload of all but the largest Internet web sites. Very few saw the impending rise of the database bottleneck. Instead, developers were busy choosing the easiest path for building applications. In the Java 2 Standard Edition (J2SE) world, Tomcat and Struts prevailed with stateless data access objects stored in the database. In the Java 2 Enterprise Edition (J2EE) world, EJB prevailed, and the container helped the developer store objects in the database. The database façade was destined to crack under the load of the new three-tier architecture. If the database was an immovable object, scale was the opposing unstoppable force. A tug-of-war began to play out regarding how to scale.

Let's now discuss this tug-of-war between complex expensive clustering and simple database-backed applications in more detail. This will help you come to the realization that an application that is trying to scale can use the same techniques as a multiprocessor motherboard architecture. Analysis of Terracotta's origin and founding principles will help you understand this analogy between the application and a modern motherboard. By the end of Chapter 2, you will know how a motherboard-style approach makes scaling out transparent and how transparency has helped elsewhere in application design.

Approaches to Scaling

At the start of the average development project, we must determine the business require-ments. Architects, developers, and people who manage production applications (Terracotta sometimes refers to this last group as application operators) can choose to start at the top and work down or to work from the bottom up. An example of top-down architecture would be deciding that the end user needs a graphical interface and wants to use a web browser, so we will need an HTTP server, a web development framework, a container in which to run it all, and a system in which to store business data. The inverse approach would be bottom-up where we start with the preferred data storage engine—database, file server, or what have you—and then look for the best, most scalable way to store data, working our way back to development frameworks that support our data store and eventually dictating how the end user can reach all this software. As a contrasting example to the top-down approach that resulted in a web application, starting from the bottom could result in a spreadsheet that users upload to a server for later processing.

Whether we're talking top-down or bottom-up, only those of us who have built large-scale applications before will include scalability frameworks and patterns early in our designs. The fundamental challenge in scalability is that applications are scaled across server processes, while business data is simultaneously accessed through each process. Concurrent access to data is either managed in a stateful or stateless manner. Neither stateless nor stateful architec-ture avoids the scalability bottleneck. Let's validate that assertion now.

Scale the Database

One approach to building an application that can spread across Java processes is to ensure that no process has information that other processes have at the same time. In the web appli-cation space, we call such architecture stateless, but the generic concept is more powerful than storing data in a database. The generic concept simply implies that no data can be stored in a single process's memory and that, ideally, no data should be stored in memory, period.

We can build a stateless application by writing all data to a database (or to flat files on a shared file server). We might even use durable message queuing to write out objects as messages that we can later retrieve. Regardless of the storage mechanism, stateless applications do not become a scalability challenge until those applications are spread across processes (Java or otherwise). This is due to the fact that, with a single application instance, we can perfectly cache the data coming from the database, thus reducing our dependency on that database.

A perfect cache is one where the cache never misses where we would expect it to hit. If a certain application workload pulls records from the database into memory as objects and those objects are cached, a developer would expect the database to see no queries regarding these objects until the cache is flushed. A scaled out application cannot exhibit perfect caching behavior, because each Java process needs to cache data separately and redundantly. Records pulled into memory in one JVM are not available to other JVMs.

When the application is scaled across processes, we need to distribute the cache in order to get the same benefit of caching on an application that is not clustered. Figure 2-2 illustrates the inefficiency associated with failing to distribute application caches.

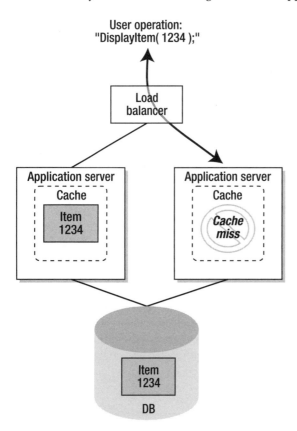

Figure 2-2. *Nondistributed caches leading to unnecessary cache misses*

If an application is designed to trust its own cache as consistent with the database at all times, when spreading the application across processes, the cache must be either disabled, as in the case of Hibernate second level caching, or distributed. Without a distributed cache, an individual process could return stale data to the end user if that node does not know that the data changed on another application instance. Imagine that one application server in Figure 2-2 changed item 1234 and did not tell the other that it had done so. Then both application servers would have a different version of item 1234 in cache, and only one would be in sync with the database.

Figure 2-2 illustrates that applications that don't store some state in the application tier are prone to bottlenecks, because they issue redundant SQL queries at the database. The redundant SQL queries sent to a database from various application nodes eventually crush it. The example also shows that, without distributing the cache, the application can become inconsistent. So, while developers get persistence and consistency from databases and stateless architecture, the application cannot scale without more work from the developer on stateful caching and replication of that cache.

The seemingly most expedient choice for an operator to scale a mature stateless application without demanding that the developer change the application is to scale the storage—database or otherwise. There are several problems with the notion of clustered databases. While database tuning is a topic for another book, suffice it to say that database latency is managed through indexing, building query plans, caching disk blocks, and otherwise optimizing queries. Meanwhile, database scalability is predicated on the concept of striping. Disk striping helps a single database server handle more application workload by summing the capacity of several hard drives together underneath a data table.

This idea can be extended to striping across database instances. If we take a customer table and split the table across two database instances on separate servers, we get twice the database capacity. However, we must now externally remember to check both instances for the data. The problem with partitioning the database is that the stripes across disks are purely up to database administrators and storage administrators, whereas striping data across database servers usually requires application-level support. Figure 2-3 shows a database partitioned across disks versus across servers and the resulting application changes required to support partitioned database instances.

If the database attempts to do this split on its own as a black box, then we do not get quite double the capacity because the instances have to route queries to each other on a miss. Thus, scaling the database is a misnomer, because the operator eventually has to ask the developer to make changes. Stateless architecture is not the silver bullet it appears to be on first blush. Either state or partitioning leaks back into the application through caching as a result of scaling out. Many Java developers have experienced this problem and choose to use in-memory replication.

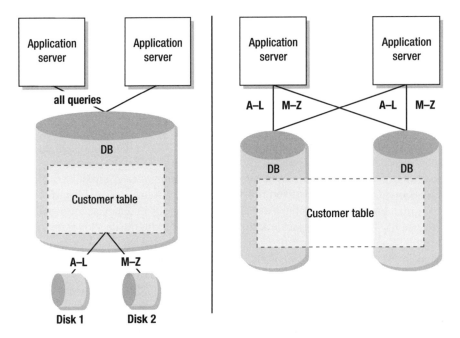

Figure 2-3. *Striping disks under databases (left) versus striping databases under applications (right)*

In-Memory Replication

The alternate approach is—again in the web application world—sometimes referred to as stateful. This model refers to keeping session data in memory. Application data kept in memory is made more highly available by replicating data to other application instances in case of failure.

The goals of stateful application programming are to eliminate the dependency on the database and improve application latency and scalability. In the Web world, where session cookies exist, applications can leverage the notion of sticky load balancing where the same user's session is routed to the same application instance over and over again. This solves one key problem with stateful programming: how should an application keep all its instances synchronized in real time? If the workload will always be routed to the same instance, then we can keep data in memory in only one or two nodes, and this will be fine. If work is sent around the application instances randomly, all instances need to know everything that has happened before in a particular context.

■**Note** The use of "happened before" is meant to remind you of Chapter 1, where we talked about multithreaded programming and the Java Memory Model's notion of "happens before." You will see in Chapters 3 and 4 that Terracotta delivers multinode scale out using only multithreaded programming. We will also discuss how to abstract multiple threads from most of our code so as to avoid the complexity of threading and concurrency in applications when appropriate.

In-memory replication can crush an application instance in two ways. First, the pressure to keep the application's entire working data in memory can push on the JVM's garbage collector to the point of exhaustion. Second, the pressure to replicate every change made on this instance to all others can be too great at as few as two nodes, depending on workload. Rarely can simple replication schemes scale past three or four nodes. It seems that in-memory replication and stateful programming models scale more poorly than stateless ones. There are good qualities to stateful architecture, however.

One can partition an in-memory architecture in any case where a database could have been partitioned. This means that if customer tables can be split in half, half of the in-memory customer data can be stored on one server and half on another. Once data is in memory, latency to access that data drops to nearly zero. Low latency is stateful architecture's best quality.

The only unaddressable risk in stateful architecture is that of availability. If the power to one process is lost, we may not lose anything with the help of replication, but if the power to all application processes is lost, we will most certainly lose everything in memory.

In exchange for the availability risk, we would hope that we gain a simplicity benefit. If we are working with objects in memory, can we not avoid the classic impedance mismatch between the application and the database? Sadly, the answer is no. Whether developing using EJB (remote or messaging beans), Java Messaging Service (JMS), HTTP session replication, remote method invocation (RMI), or another approach, the same data flow occurs:

1. An object is created in one server.

2. The object is serialized and pushed to all other servers.

3. The object is later changed in that server.

4. The object now must get updated in all other servers (meaning, go to step 2).

Since the object in memory is, in fact, going to get serialized to be sent on the wire, two servers would have different copies of an object. Serialization allows multiple threads to edit objects at the same time without corrupting the objects. The preceding data flow can be augmented as follows to prove the point:

5. The object is needed in one thread.

6. The object is deserialized from the cache or another JVM.

7. The object is changed in this server.

8. The object now must get updated in all other servers. If another server has edited this object at the same time, throw an exception, and discard the changes in either this server or the other.

This data flow implies that every thread that interacts with our objects must deal with a copy of the object. In other words, not only does the thread creating objects in step 2 have to serialize an object to send it to other JVMs but the thread consuming the object in step 5 must deserialize it to gain access to the object. Why? The answer goes back to concurrency. In a stateless model, it is clear that an object in memory is only a temporal representation of the database row, meaning that the database is the true system of record. However, in memory, it is not clear who maintains the system of record. In fact, all the JVMs together are the system of record. Transactional capabilities of the database are approximated when using in-memory replication by asking the application to work with object copies.

More to the point, the act of serializing object graphs to send them to the network and deserializing those byte arrays received from the network forces an application developer to live with a copy-on-read semantic. We will spend more time on object identity in Chapters 3 and 4. For now, let us assert that stateful programming is not simpler than stateless. And stateless programming is not more scalable than stateful, which is due to the fact that striping can work for both stateful and stateless paradigms.

All Paths Lead to Partitioning

So far in Chapter 2, all analysis has focused on replication versus partitioning. Partitioning, sometimes referred to as sharding or dividing and conquering, is an architecture that splits data across a cluster of servers. Partitioning can alleviate many typical bottlenecks in network and database traffic by dividing the data and corresponding work on that data along consistent lines. For example, a typical database application needs to support create, read, update, and delete operations. If create operations were to split data across two database instances, and read, update, and delete operations were to split data the same way, then two similarly sized database servers would provide twice the capacity of one. Figure 2-4 illustrates the concept of partitioning data between two servers by partitioning the business data into even and odd keys.

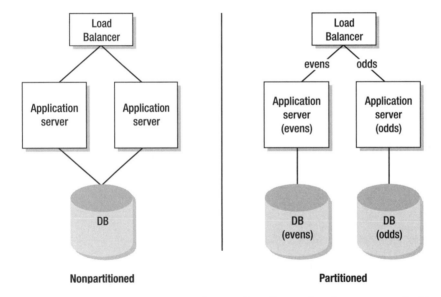

Figure 2-4. *Partitioning a CRUD application by splitting data into evens and odds*

■**Note** The nonpartitioned and the partitioned load balancers are different in Figure 2-4. The nonpartitioned version is simple and sends any traffic to either application server. The partitioned load balancer should be aware of the partitioning logic and route work to various application servers based on data partitioning rules.

Partitioning might seem the only path toward scalability for many application teams, because as applications grow, data replication or management turns into the number one bottleneck. As we already discussed, an application goes faster by either caching and keeping more data in memory or striping the data across multiple physical locations.

More accurately, availability is best achieved in a stateless architecture, whereas scaling out forces us to push data into memory and replicate it. In fact, most real applications are stateless and stateful simultaneously, and this is what Terracotta realized. Developers and operators need a way to fundamentally get past the trade-offs of availability and scalability (see Figure 1-4) without heading down the path of partitioning the application prematurely.

Terracotta's Origin in a Web Monster

In building an e-commerce site that has grown to be among the top ten in the world—a monster—some architectural decisions proved critical, while others were not as important as initially assumed. The application was to be load balanced and stateful with all business data and associated workflow managed via transactions in the database. Database transactions seem, in retrospect, an obvious mistake, mostly because transactions in a three-tier system imply spreading workflow between the database and the Java tier. The Java tier generates the update task and asks the database to make changes that can be rejected for various reasons. Now, this seems like having two conductors of an orchestra.

Discussing Terracotta's origins might seem like a tangent to the discussion of scaling the application tier. It is not: the architecture should have been predicated on workflow in the Java tier. But there was a problem with workflow in the Java tier in the year 2000. That problem was one of volatility of memory (or heap). If conversational state, otherwise known as workflow state, were to be maintained in memory, then conversations could be lost. At the time, there was no linearly scalable way to deliver high availability for in-memory replicated state. So the business data was stored in the database and cached in the application tier, thrusting the site into a stateful/stateless hybrid where database data was cached and replicated in memory to avoid database bottlenecks. Think of the architecture as "read from memory," because most database data was cached, and "write to disk," because all I/O was made in a durable fashion by flushing those updates to the database directly.

One alternative at the time was distributed transactions. The underpinnings of sharing state and coordinating updates across Java processes in a coherent fashion did not exist in the JVM or as a scalable Java service, and building a distributed in-memory system with transactional guarantees seemed hard. Another alternative was an eventually correct architecture. While other sites such as Amazon.com took an eventually correct approach where each application instance could complete transactions to local disk and eventually flush to the database, Terracotta's founders chose not to. The business was not prepared to discuss the ramifications of an eventually correct architecture, where users might be told that a previously confirmed purchase order could not be completed because of miscalculations in inventory long after checkout completed.

■**Note** By "eventually correct," we refer to the CAP theorem, which refers to the trade-off between consistency, availability, and partitioning. An eventually correct architecture is one that prioritizes partitioning over consistency. For example, an e-commerce purchase transaction can be conducted on two separate nodes and reconciled later by realizing that the same customer is buying the same products at the same time and thus one order should be canceled before debiting the customer's financial accounts.

The Application Is a Giant Computer

Within weeks of initial launch, the production application was failing to handle the user volumes, and the database was the culprit. We immediately learned our first lesson: the n-tier application should be viewed as if it were a giant multiprocessor computer. The modern Intel architecture calls for several levels of caching between the processor, which is running very fast, and the I/O subsystems, which cannot keep up with that processor. Multiprocessor computers have registers on the chip, an L1 cache on the chip as well, and an L2 cache that is external to the chip but can either be dedicated per chip or shared across processors.

The processor reads through these various caching layers of main memory. Data from main memory gets cached in the L2 and again in the L1. If a thread moves across processors, data in the thread's stack must move from one chip's cache to the other's as part of the process of context switching. The hardware deals with the coherence of each of these levels of cache somewhat transparently.

The L2 cache is much larger than the L1 cache but significantly slower as it is not on-chip. This implies a significant cost to go to L2, but modern servers have large L2 caches because the cost of going to L2 is still much lower than going to main memory. Sharing L2 can drastically reduce or even eliminate the cost of a context switch.

In the analogy between motherboards and applications, we can think of the L1 as caching inside the JVM, because the application pays almost no price for going to its own heap. In n-tier applications, the application server spends several hundred milliseconds on average per query waiting for the database. In the chip analogy, the CPU spends several thousand cycles waiting for main memory or disk. The database is expensive, like main memory on the motherboard.

Once we realized this, the presence of a cache in each Java process felt like an L1 cache on the processor. It became reasonable and acceptable, if not obvious, to introduce an L2 cache that could work as the superset cache of all L1 caches. This L2 service helped application instances avoid waiting for the database as well as lessening the cost of context switching tasks across those application server instances. If the L2 were to succeed for this web monster, it had only one requirement—calling the L2 had to be lower cost than calling the underlying database, ideally an order of magnitude faster.

Once delivered, this approach of L1 combined with an L2 caching service eliminated a few big scalability bottlenecks. First, just like on the motherboard, there no longer was pressure to fit all thread data into the L1 cache inside the application server. The entire dataset could, instead, be cached in L2 regardless of how much or little memory the application servers had as long as the shared L2 could spill to disk. This allowed application servers to stay very small. Second, the L1 could free memory when under high load simply by dropping parts or all of its cache data. The L1 could arbitrarily and unilaterally evict items from cache without causing downstream pressure on the database, since the L2 would protect the application from the database and vice versa. This allowed the application servers to maintain predictable throughput and simultaneously kept the database working at sustainable lower query volumes, well below the actual query traffic the site was generating.

A third benefit of running an L2 cache outside the application servers and sharing that L2 across application server instances was that the L2 provided availability to the data in cache even when the database was down. The L1 could use traditional caching techniques, such as least-recently-used/least-frequently-used, to flush the cache. Even if the database were busy or otherwise unavailable, the L2 was there to handle the requests. Getting the L2 to outperform the underlying database, therefore, provided not just scalability but high availability.

Because of the L2 concept, the web site could spread across machines to get easy scalability and availability. With the L2 service, the database's role in helping to scale the system was greatly diminished. And with the L1 cache inside the application server instances, linear scale was achievable.

Note With two machines, a well-designed application should be able to do twice as much work as one. In fact, spreading application instances across separate hardware, otherwise known as scaling out, should be superior to multiprocessing (scaled up) architectures, because everything is doubled; nothing is shared. We get twice the memory, disk, network, bus, and processor. Three servers, four servers, and so on will give us linear scale as long as the application can take advantage of all this hardware.

Terracotta's architecture, like that of its web monster parent, has both L1 and L2 components. The motherboard analogy maps to Terracotta, because Terracotta has libraries that install into the application's JVM and insert L1 object caches transparently, while Terracotta's server runs in its own process usually on a dedicated server, just like the L2.

Terracotta Makes L2 General Purpose

Running applications across servers seemed to be a good idea, especially considering the L2 solution. But Terracotta's web application experience proved that the costs were shifting from expensive database hardware to complicated application development. To inject L1 caches into arbitrary Java applications, Terracotta had to make a general purpose server (L2 server) that was smarter about what it was storing and when it was being invoked.

Original L2 Was Intrusive

The L2 cache, while critical, was not the entire solution. Terracotta leverages the power of the L2 concept, but also provides a solution to the complexities surrounding distribution of objects—replication and serialization. The L2 solution for the web monster was a simple networked cache service that took keys and associated values, pushed the pair across the network, and stored them on the L2 server instance. No objects ended up in the L2 that the developer had not put there on purpose.

Maintenance of the monster web site suffered because of constant regressions in correctness and performance. Sometimes, a developer would forget to serialize and replicate changes to L2-based objects, causing the application to break when the load balancer sent the user to other application servers because data was only in one JVM and coherence would be lost (as shown in Figure 2-5).

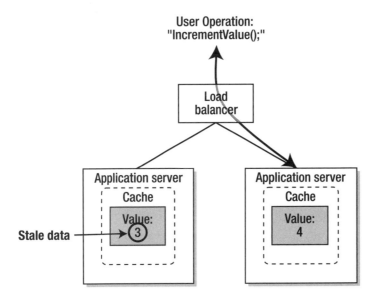

Figure 2-5. *Developer error where IncrementValue() operation does not update clustered cache*

Application performance would also suffer when the developer replicated changes too often or neglected in-memory caching and stored data straight to the database. The cost of scaling out was very high.

In founding the company, Terracotta's leaders sought to deliver the value of both stateless and stateful paradigms. Namely, the goal was to deliver a stateless runtime for operators with an L2 that persisted to disk and to simultaneously deliver a stateful programming model for developers where the L2 was transparent to the application and challenges with coherence and replication would not exist.

The reality of having hundreds of developers working in one code base led to misuse or nonuse of by-hand replication tools. No by-hand tool solves every problem and is only applicable if the use case for which it was designed happens to align with the developer's needs. These challenges are part and parcel of the issue with application programming interfaces (APIs). APIs do what the developer who is integrating them into the application asks. Any integration or application code changes required by an L2-type solution would risk negating the benefits of that L2-type product. Terracotta chose to create a better model for clustering—a transparent L2 server.

We Needed More Transparency

The goal was to build an application server that scaled out across Java processes and ran underneath a sticky load balancer, all without developers perceiving the existence of multiple processes (L1 and L2). The reality fell short of the goal, however, in that developers were well aware of the design of the cluster. The web site's creators built a very efficient session replication technology and several custom caches. All objects had to implement the Java serializable interface, and developers were constantly tuning session sizes so that the system could replicate sessions with minimal impact to end-user traffic. These caching and replication services suffered from the same marshal-across-the-network pratfalls that any other approach would.

The initial impact of developing a clustered web application seemed acceptable. However, many projects would stall not because they were hard to design but because they were hard to scale. Many application features could take down the core web infrastructure if poorly designed. And, most importantly, the application continually slowed down and presented itself as an ever-increasing challenge to maintain. What's more, the average project would go through phases such as Key Business Project Phase One, Phase Two, and so on, and phases usually encompassed refactoring existing code for performance, as opposed to introducing new features. Over time, the business noticed that the burden of maintaining a scalable application was slowing down new development.

Transparency Equals General Purpose

Decisions that seemed so critical to productivity, such as Struts versus Java Server Faces (JSF) or Tomcat versus another container, proved less important than the core scalability and availability model.

If an application is stateless and uses an object-relational mapper to store objects in a database, the team will likely work to lower database latency only to find that throughput is too low. The team may end up tuning the SQL that Hibernate generates. The database administrator might make changes to the database schema, while the Java developer changes the object model to compensate. The storage administrator may adjust storage array by striping tables across disks.

Ultimately, however, caching will appear. The Terracotta team's experience shows that this is inevitable. Caching is essentially the process of shifting an application from a stateless model to a stateful or hybrid model. As discussed earlier in this chapter, if the application is stateful and we want to scale the application across Java processes, a coherent protocol for editing objects across Java processes gets built as the application scales. In all cases, the domain model is affected, and business feature development slows as developers spend time tuning.

So the founders sought a transparent solution, one that works inside the JVM without serialization, thus avoiding the pratfalls of replication. The components of scalable application architecture are now in place. We need an L2 service for deflecting workload off the database and coordinating application activities, and we need a transparent interface that makes the notion of L2, L1, and application object all the same, just as in the motherboard analogy.

Transparent Scalability with Availability

Scalability and availability are opposing forces. Anything we write to disk slows us down, and anything we leave in memory is at risk of process or even power failure. Scalability comes from performance, and performance comes from alleviating bottlenecks. Memory is the least slow point of I/O on the motherboard. The disk is, of course, one of the slowest. Worse yet, the network is closer in performance to the disk than to memory.

What makes transparently spreading out an application difficult is that the application has to talk to the network, and the network is far slower than the CPU. Sun Microsystems attempted to build a clustered JVM, as did IBM, in 2000. The efforts quickly revealed that the network was painfully slow compared to the CPU and that most applications would have to be rewritten to take advantage of being spread across slow networks. So, it was decided that the CPU is too fast, clustering is too slow, and the developer would simply be handed tools to serialize and ship objects across the network when needed (RMI, JMS, and even JDBC can be used to share objects across Java processes).

This is what makes things hard today. Clustering in the name of scalability and availability requires the developer to copy objects around the Java processes in the cluster, and it requires the application to be aware that it is being deployed to many servers. In the past, developers wrote applications, tuned algorithms, and introduced I/O optimizations such as caching so that a process could fit in a small part of a large machine. As workload ramped, the process could be optimized, but at some point, the server had to be replaced. At the end of the day, very few tried to spread out an application on the network. It was too hard. And nothing has changed about pushing objects around processes—it is still hard.

One thing has changed with Terracotta, however: we no longer pass objects around to a group of application servers in a cluster. With the L2 that runs out of process introduced by Terracotta, a Terracotta application only passes objects to Terracotta. The Terracotta server (L2) can make an informed decision about which Java processes need what changes. And since the solution was designed to be transparent, Terracotta sees fine-grained changes as they occur, down to the byte level. This means that only a transparent solution with a central clustering server can write to disk, thus providing us availability without the need for Oracle. Why is that? The less we write to disk, the faster we go, remember? Terracotta writes only what changes to disk. And, it can write those changes at the same time it is helping our application processes share state.

Let's review. Recall the `ClusteredClass` from Chapter 1. If we change the `name` field or the `id` field, Terracotta can push only the changed information. If the `id` is an `int` (or `Integer`, it really does not matter), Terracotta needs to ship 4 bytes across the wire to the L2 process, and it needs to write the 4 bytes to disk. An instance of the class would otherwise be more like 30 bytes, so right there, we have a significant savings in I/O without writing custom code to make this possible.

The Terracotta server is also a separate process, currently referred to as an L2 for our application (we will stop using this nomenclature in Chapter 3). In Chapter 4 as well as in Chapter 13, you will learn more about how the Terracotta server can safely decouple its internal disk storage from application memory changes without risking data loss. The fact that the server is tuned to do disk I/O without making the application wait means that, for once, we can have our scalability and availability too.

Transparent Clustering Service Revisited

In Chapter 1, we defined Terracotta as a transparent clustering service that helps applications spread to as many machines as necessary for scale. While applications used to be stuck navigating a dark narrow tunnel of endless tuning through caching, replication, and partitioning, a light now appears at the end of the tunnel. Where we used to scale by doing lots of by-hand coding and marshalling objects across process boundaries, we now do nothing. The labor and complexity of scaling out change for the better when we find a way to move interprocess and interserver communication out of our own application code and down below somewhere in the runtime environment (as shown in Figure 2-6).

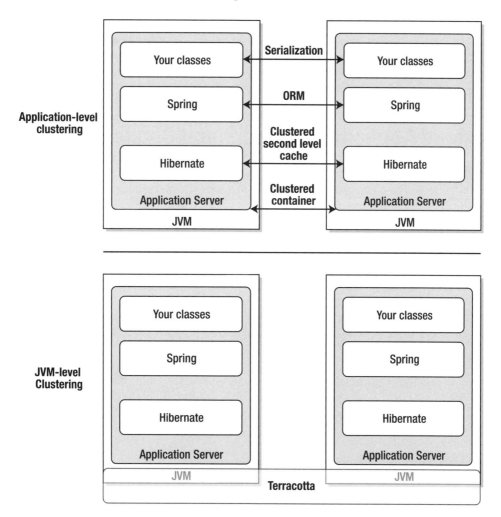

Figure 2-6. *Application clustering requires many different approaches; Terracotta does not.*

In Chapter 1, we concluded that Terracotta could be thought of as a transparent clustering service. Now, we have confirmed that the need for such a service exists.

Transparency Delivers Higher Scalability

We rely on transparency to help scale applications every day. The garbage collector is a transparent memory management service. For the most part, it works. It also does a better job than the developer not because its writers are smarter than the average developer (well, maybe they are smarter than most of us) but because the runtime environment has perfect information about usage patterns. It can make changes that the developer deems too complicated. User objects might be collected using one algorithm at noon and another at midnight, depending on how application workloads change.

Terracotta found that transparency and being a runtime service not only solves the complexity challenge developers otherwise face but also provides for scalability and performance beyond what the developer can build. One example of a runtime performance enhancement is greedy locking. Terracotta can decide at run time whether a lock should be pessimistic, centralized and exclusive, or decentralized and optimistic. A developer must make assumptions about exclusive access that protect for the worst case scenario only, and thus the JVM provides mostly pessimistic, exclusive locking semantics without Terracotta.

Clustered Application Servers and Clustered Caches

Terracotta is not just for caching data stored in the database. The data that has been entrusted to Terracotta is always stored on disk, thus Terracotta can be used without a database in certain use cases, most of which will be covered in Chapters 5 through 12 of this book.

If Terracotta did not exist, we have covered how applications could otherwise scale using a database. We also discussed in-memory replication and replicating state by hand across Java processes. There are alternatives to replicating objects by hand, or so it would seem.

In practice, there are no alternatives. OK, that was way too strong a statement, but it gets the point across that our analysis of stateless and stateful approaches does not change for application server vendors or clustering vendors as long as they use the same tools that application developers above the server or caching library use to replicate and cache state by hand (see Figure 2-6).

Today, clustered application servers, clustered caches, and other clustering libraries are measured on how they replicate data. Some use n-way replication, while others use a buddy system. Some replicate data when objects change, while others require the developer to directly inform the library of changes. And, of course, there are EJB, JPA, and Hibernate where replication is not needed, because the application state is stored in the database in a stateless manner.

We should not judge a framework on whether it is stateless or stateful or whether it is buddy-replication or n-way. We should, instead, judge a framework on whether or not it is a transparent service or a development tool.

A transparent service is one that is installed after the application has been written and deployed and whose behavior is controlled by configuration. One example is the garbage collector. The application makes assumptions about the presence of a garbage collector inside the JVM and thus never attempts to call delete() at some point after calling new(), as we would in C++. Counter examples to transparent services are Hibernate and Spring. While both are mostly transparent, their behavior is controlled as much by source code integration as by configuration. If a Spring or Hibernate application were loaded without the Spring or Hibernate libraries present, that application would cease to function.

Clustered caches and clustered application servers fail to realize that Hibernate and Spring both represent a development model and methodology. Clustered application servers are not supposed to represent a rigid development model. Spring, for example, provides a development model that is not rigid or fixed. But clustering frameworks ruin elegance and simplicity for the rest of the application. They are supposed to take any application that can be run inside the container and cluster the application. Clustered application servers and clustered caches fail at this goal and thus are a notoriously poor solution for scaling applications.

Summary

Since Terracotta provides transparent scalability and availability to Java applications, it allows those applications to spread out and run on as many machines as is necessary. Transparency allows the system to decide what to push among the JVMs and to the L2 server (otherwise known as a Terracotta server), and this provides very high scalability. Transparency has an additional benefit in that it does not enforce a programming model such as clustered caching, or EJB, or even Hibernate or Spring. Terracotta can take an existing application and scale it to many machines, whereas other approaches dictate a model that, if followed, can enable scaling out.

Let's now switch gears and work with actual Java program source code and Terracotta configuration to learn more about how this works. Chapter 3 introduces Terracotta configuration concepts.

■ ■ ■

Jumping Into Terracotta

Terracotta delivers a transparent scale-out model to Java programming. The lightweight nature of the development model is inherent in the fact that the software plugs in to an off-the-shelf JVM and allows developers to write applications without explicit in-memory replication or mapping data to an underlying data store. Those applications then spread across machines at run time. The point of such an approach is not just for scale but for high availability. Based on knowledge gained from some of the largest scale applications in the world, Terracotta helps you achieve scalability and availability with less effort. Let's now take a look at a system that illustrates ease, scale, and availability in a short, "hello world" style program.

Hello Clustered World

We call this application "Hello Clustered World." The relevant source code follows:

```
public class HelloClusteredWorld {
  private static final String message = "Hello Clustered World!";
  private static final int length = message.length();

  private static char[] buffer = new char [length ];
  private static int loopCounter;

  public static void main( String args[] ) throws Exception {
    while( true ) {
      synchronized( buffer ) {
        int messageIndex = loopCounter++ % length;
        if(messageIndex == 0) java.util.Arrays.fill(buffer, '\u0000');

        buffer[messageIndex] = message.charAt(messageIndex);
        System.out.println( buffer );
        Thread.sleep( 100 );
      }
    }
  }
}
```

HelloClusteredWorld will do something very simple. If we focus on the main() method, we notice right away that there is an infinite loop. In that loop, we are taking a static string named message containing the sentence "Hello Clustered World!" and copying the message into a buffer, one character at a time. The first time through the loop, the array named buffer will contain the character "H". The second time through the array will contain "H" and "e". The third time through it will contain "H" and "e" and "l". And so on. There is one small detail we have not covered. We test the loopCounter each time through the loop, and if the message has been fully copied into buffer, we empty the buffer. A quick run of this program at the command line produces what we expect:

```
% java HelloClusteredWorld
H
He
Hel
Hell
Hello
Hello
Hello C
Hello Cl
Hello Clu
Hello Clus
Hello Clust
Hello Cluste
Hello Cluster
Hello Clustere
Hello Clustered
Hello Clustered
Hello Clustered W
Hello Clustered Wo
Hello Clustered Wor
Hello Clustered Worl
Hello Clustered World
Hello Clustered World!
H
He
Hel
Hell
Hello
...
```

Now, let's cluster this application. What behavior should we expect? "Clustering" can be a confusing word. In the first two chapters, we have mentioned that Terracotta helps applications spread across Java processes. If this application were to spread out across processes, we would expect nothing actually. There is no multithreading in the application, and there is no state that is worth sharing.

Clustering HelloClusteredWorld

In a web application, one might define clustering as session replication. In an enterprise application, entity beans could be replicated or otherwise shared. Under both enterprise and web application contexts, we have the notions of object scope and life cycle, which means the container can do some clustering on behalf of the application. In HelloClusteredWorld, we have just a Java main() method.

The very notion of clustering is not clear in the context of a Java main(). At least, it appears unclear. In piecing together what it might mean to cluster this program, we should acknowledge that the only thing this main() method could do if it were simultaneously running on two or more Java processes would be to run the while loop, producing identical output to two different consoles simultaneously. After all, providing output is the only thing the application does.

Perhaps it makes sense to have multiple processes inside the while loop collaborating on copying the message into the buffer. If multiple Java processes are running inside the while loop at the same time, sharing the variables inside the HelloClusteredWorld class would allow the processes to somehow work together on this problem.

Working together in this case could imply that two processes each take half the copying workload. For example, if process one puts "H" into the buffer, process two would then put "e". Process one would not have to put "e" in the buffer and should put "l" into the buffer next; otherwise, something other than "Hello Clustered World!" would print to the screen.

■**Note** The synchronization logic in the main() method seems out of place when not writing the application with the intent of spreading main() across several processes. In the context of spreading out this main() method, however, we chose to prepare for concurrent object access by guarding any object updates with synchronization. In later chapters, we will discuss how to use Terracotta without explicit synchronization; there are several options.

If two virtual machines are running together, the desired behavior is to have the first JVM initialize the buffer and the loopCounter variables and set the buffer to "H". That JVM should then release the lock before sleeping for 100 milliseconds and trying to add another character to the buffer. Assuming a second JVM is started and the two are coordinating their efforts through Terracotta, while the first JVM is asleep, the second should acquire the lock on the buffer, add another character, and increment the loop counter before going to sleep. Thus, two JVMs working together will fill the buffer together in half the elapsed time, because each will put exactly one half of the total characters into the buffer.

The way all this works in Terracotta is to point at the class in which objects reside. Terracotta will take care of constructing shared objects and synchronizing the various JVMs where objects reside. The question now is which objects to share and how to share them?

In the case of HelloClusteredWorld, the ability to share buffer across Java process boundaries enables the two while loops running in each of the JVMs to work together on one instance of buffer. The loopCounter variable is the loop's index into the message, driving which character to copy into the buffer. Without sharing the loopCounter instance across JVMs, the two JVMs would not copy the appropriate characters. A few counter examples will help make this clear.

If the application did not share the buffer object across Java processes, the application would have to change. As written, the application copies only one character into the buffer. Assume the application were not sharing objects and the loopCounter was instead changed to increment by two instead of by one so that each of the two JVMs working together would not copy data redundantly to the buffer. Further, assume that in one JVM, the loopCounter starts at zero, while the other starts at one.

Two processes each doing only half the work in this manner would have corrupted the buffer after just two iterations of the while loop. Table 3-1 contains a listing of the state of the object named buffer in both JVMs at the end of each iteration through the while loop in main().

Table 3-1. *State of Memory at Key while Loop Iterations*

Iteration	JVM One Buffer State	JVM Two Buffer State
Initial state	null	null
1	"H"	"<empty character>e"
2	"H<empty char>l"	"<empty char>e<empty char>l"
3	"H<empty char>l<empty char>o"	"<empty char>e<empty char>l<empty char><space>"

Table 3-1 illustrates the problem with unshared buffer objects. We would have to edit the application to copy not just one character but all the characters from the message up to the loopCounter point. So it makes sense to share the buffer object.

Using loopCounter as an index into the message without sharing it would not work without making some changes to the application. We already discussed how it is possible to hard-code our application to increment the loopCounter by two instead of one, starting with an initial value of zero and one for each respective JVM. But what if we want three JVMs to work together on building buffers? We would have to edit the application so that each JVM incremented the loopCounter by three. It makes sense to share loopCounter as well as buffer.

By considering which objects need to be shared, we can conclude that the field names we want to cluster are HelloClusteredWorld.buffer and HelloClusteredWorld.loopCounter. With Terracotta, we can achieve this without altering the program. We write a Terracotta configuration file (more on that later) and tell it to share the buffer and the loopCounter, and we are almost done. A snippet of the configuration file follows:

```
<field-name>HelloClusteredWorld.buffer</field-name>
<field-name>HelloClusteredWorld.loopCounter</field-name>
```

■**Note** In this section, only snippets and code fragments are shown. The next section will you walk through repeating HelloClusteredWorld for yourself.

There is one more step: tell Terracotta to prepare the HelloClusteredWorld class for clustering, including honoring any threading logic present in our application. The most basic form of configuration is to tell Terracotta to prepare any and all classes for clustering using broad-reaching regular expressions, like this:

```
<instrumented-classes>
  <include>
      <class-expression>*..*</class-expression>
  </include>
</instrumented-classes>

<locks>
  <autolock>
    <method-expression>* *..*.*(..)</method-expression>
  </autolock>
</locks>
```

For now, we will not worry about how to configure threads and locking, since the focus is on how transparently sharing objects helps to cluster applications. Now, it is time to run the application as a clustered version of `HelloClusteredWorld`.

To run this application in a clustered fashion using Terracotta, the command line will have to change from `java` to `dso-java.sh`. The shell script is located in the directory named `bin` in the directory where you unpacked the Terracotta download (we will address the structure of the Terracotta kit in detail before the end of this chapter). The shell script adds the Terracotta libraries to the classpath for Terracotta's class loader to find. It also installs Terracotta's class loader as part of the boot class loader hierarchy and places itself in the boot classpath. Being part of the boot class loader hierarchy allows the JVM to connect to the Terracotta cluster at process start-up. As a boot class loader, Terracotta also has the privilege of helping to load almost all classes into the JVM. The command-line arguments to Java that you otherwise run will be passed undisturbed to the underlying JVM.

■ **Note** To learn more about boot class loaders, the boot classpath, and how Terracotta connects its libraries and agent into the JVM at run time, visit `http://java.sun.com/j2se/1.5.0/docs/tooldocs/findingclasses.html`.

When we run the application using `dso-java.sh`, we will find no change in output (these results are not shown here). The change comes when there are two instances of the application. The output of the second JVM when two processes are running follows:

```
% dso-java.sh HelloClusteredWorld
```

```
Hel
Hello
Hello C
Hello Clu
Hello Clust
```

Note that the very first line of output from the application is "Hel" as opposed to "H," as the result would have been without Terracotta. What has happened to our application? The two JVMs are moving through the infinite `while` loop together, which is quite interesting. Figure 3-1 shows a UML sequence diagram of this loop: each JVM has one thread whose starting point is signified by the thicker arrow. The JVMs then take turns synchronizing on the lock, adding a character, and sleeping. This continues in the infinite loop.

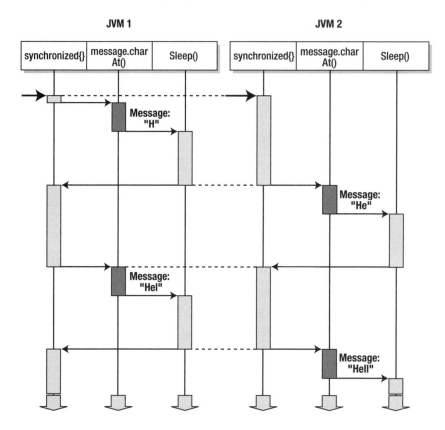

Figure 3-1. *UML sequence diagram of HelloClusteredWorld running in two JVMs in parallel*

Why HelloClusteredWorld Works

Hello Clustered World works with Terracotta, because Terracotta functions below the application to cluster at the level of the JVM itself. Terracotta inserts itself between the application logic and its memory, looking for calls to the heap. Those calls could be reads from memory or writes to memory.

A memory read or write results from Java instructions running in the JVM. For a moment, break down an object in your head into the class definition and the instance data. This is, in fact, what Terracotta does. The class definition contains the methods that implement the business rules and object model. The instance data contains only data in memory. So an instance of a class writes to memory via the assignment operator (=). And an instance of a class reads memory via the accessor operator (.).

```
class MyObject {
  int i = 0;

  // ...
  int playWithMemory( int input ) {
    int j;
    this.i = input;
    j = this.i;
    return j;
  }
}
```

At run time, the few lines of arguably silly code in the method named playWithMemory()
would turn into instructions to the JVM. The first line turns into a stack variable allocation of 4
bytes where the variable j will be stored. The next line writes to heap memory. The address in
memory at which to write is the address where this is stored. The size of the type of field i dic-
tates an offset into this, where the application intends to write. In this case, i is an int, so the
offset would be four. The argument to the playWithMemory() method will get copied into our
instance, this, thus causing a 4-byte write to heap.

The next line of code turns into a read from heap memory. Again, the read operation
occurs at a 4-byte offset into our instance where i is stored. The value of i gets copied into the
stack variable named j. Heap access is actually occurring transparently, line by line inside the
JVM as our application logic runs. Some logic will cause reads from heap memory, while others cause writes. Of course, the JVM can perform many operations other than reading and
writing to memory, but Terracotta is concerned mostly with these two byte code operations.
We will refer to these memory instructions by their proper names later, but for now, let's focus
on the concepts only; the names of these instructions would be confusing when looking at
alternatives to Terracotta in the next section. Also, there are many more instructions inside the
JVM to which Terracotta attaches, including constructor special instructions, and threading
instructions such as locking and unlocking objects, but the core concept is represented suffi-
ciently by these two.

The core concept behind Terracotta is that of bytecode manipulation. When
playWithMemory() is invoked and a heap memory read occurs with Terracotta enabled, the
read will do more than just read from memory. Things will be clearest using pseudo code. We
can see in pseudo code that the application logic does not change while Terracotta hooks into
the object:

```
class MyObjectWithTerracottaPseudoCodeForm {
  int i = 0;

  // ...
  int playWithMemory( int input ) {
    int j;
    // Terracotta inserts itself here because a memory operation is occuring
    if( Terracotta.isOutOfDate( this.i ) ) {
      Terracotta.updateFromNetwork( this.i );
    }
    this.i = input;
    // send deltas to the network since a shared object just changed
```

```
    Terracotta.sendDeltasToTheNetwork( this.i );
    // Terracotta inserts itself here as well
    if( Terracotta.isOutOfDate( this.i ) ) {
      Terracotta.updateFromnetwork( this.i );
    }
    j = this.i;
    // no delta is sent because the logic read memory as opposed to writing it.
    return j;
  }
}
```

In practice, the preceding pseudo code does not perform well when every operation on heap memory causes a network call to Terracotta, checking for updates when reading and sending back updates when writing. The real system is far more intelligent and is capable of sending many updates in a single batch to the network.

What is still not clear is how Terracotta knows to hook itself into the application at these particular places. The answer is bytecode. Bytecode turns arbitrary application logic into a very well formed syntax, regardless of coding style, frameworks, or development practices. That syntax can be thought of as HEAPREAD() and HEAPWRITE().

Terracotta does not insert itself into our Java source files; it inserts itself into our classes as they load. Those classes come from class files, which the compiler wrote to disk (in most cases). Terracotta does not understand Java syntax, because it does not have to. It only looks for HEAPREAD() and HEAPWRITE() logic operations and wraps them, as in the previous pseudo code example.

The Terracotta configuration file allows a developer to control where Terracotta inserts itself, on a class-by-class basis. For example, MyObject can be examined and made clustered by Terracotta, while MyOtherObject can be ignored.

Arguably, there are a couple of unanswered questions at this point:

- What is Terracotta's ability to figure out relationships among objects across JVMs?

- Does Terracotta have the ability to batch?

These topics are more advanced and will be covered in Chapter 4. For now, the concept of bytecode augmentation is the key. When reading memory, Terracotta inserts itself just before the read occurs in the original application logic. Before memory is trusted, Terracotta ensures all changes from other Java processes have been applied. Terracotta also inserts itself just after writes occur in the original application logic. After memory is changed, Terracotta ensures all changes are made available to any other Java process that may need them. In short, before and after existing application logic runs, Terracotta can insert itself into the logic updating local memory or informing the cluster of changes to local memory.

■Tip If you are comfortable with what you have seen thus far, try guessing what will happen if you kill the JVM running HelloClusteredWorld and start it up again. What will print next? Will "H" print out? No. Can you explain why not? We'll talk more about persistence and availability in Chapter 4.

Alternatives to Terracotta

Other approaches that you might use to build HelloClusteredWorld would actually require integration some sort of API. Think of these alternatives to Terracotta as get() and put() interfaces. If the application calls put(key, value), it can later call get(key) to obtain a copy of the value. The changed application would resemble the following pseudo code (differences are in bold):

```
public class HelloClusteredWorldWithAnAPI {
  private static final String message = "Hello Clustered World!";
  private static final int length = message.length();

  private static final char[] buffer = new char [length];
  int loopCounter;

  public static void main( String args[] ) throws Exception{
    while( true ) {
      // thread-level coordination no longer valuable
      // synchronized( buffer ) {

      // get the up-to-date version from the cluster
      // note: expect deserialization
      buffer = cluster.get( "HelloClusteredWorldBufferID" );

      // can't trust loopCounter because it is not a clustered object
      // int messageIndex = loopCounter++ % length;
      // drive the index from the current length instead
      int messageIndex = buffer.length;

      if(messageIndex == 0) java.util.Arrays.fill(buffer, '\u0000');

      buffer[messageIndex] = message.charAt(messageIndex);
      System.out.println( buffer );

      // expect buffer to get serialized
      Cluster.put( "HelloClusteredWorldBufferID", buffer );

      Thread.sleep( 100 );
      catch( InterruptedException e ) { e.printStackTrace( ); }
    }
  }
}
```

These are key changes to the application: synchronization is no longer important; the loopCounter is now derived from the current buffer length; and we serialize the buffer to the network and deserialize it from the network, copying the entire buffer each time. Without worrying about whether the get() and put() form of HelloClusteredWorld is better or worse than the Terracotta version, the information to take away is that JDBC, JMS, RMI, or other clustering and sharing approaches could be substituted in place of get() and put(). Table 3-2 maps the specific APIs to the logic concepts of get() and put() for each framework.

Table 3-2. *JDBC, JMS, and RMI Equivalents to the map.get() and map.put() Interfaces*

Framework	get() Equivalent	put() Equivalent
JDBC	[prepared]statement.execute() SELECT	[prepared]statement.execute() UPDATE INSERT UPSERT
JMS	MessageConsumer.receive()	QueueSender.send()
RMI	Portable.ObjectImpl._request()	Portable.ObjectImpl._invoke()

Where the preceding pseudo code calls Cluster.get( ), we could easily replace the logic with a relational database with the appropriate schema plus a JDBC query looking up a row in a one-row table. We might call that one-row table HelloClusteredWorld_TABLE. The table stores the buffer on our application's behalf so that any JVM can query the table for the buffer's current state and can update the table when changing the buffer. The database version of HelloClusteredWorld might contain some code like this:

```
try {
  String buffer;
  stmt = con.createStatement();
  rs = stmt.executeQuery( "SELECT * FROM HelloClusteredWorld_TABLE" );
  buffer = rs.getString( 1 );
  stmt.close();
  con.close();
} catch( SQLException ex ) {
  System.err.println( "SQLException: " + ex.getMessage() );
}
```

In the preceding example, we are simply calling get() and put() in the context of a database and JDBC connection. Terracotta does not need the developer to insert get() and put() calls, because Terracotta inserts itself into the application byte code looking for the application logic to read or write from the objects named buffer and loopCounter. The act of reading the loopCounter in memory with Terracotta inserted, in effect, asks Terracotta if loopCounter is up to date with respect to changes from other JVMs. If it is not up to date, Terracotta guarantees that loopCounter will be updated before returning control flow back to the application logic.

A Tour Through Terracotta

Now that you've seen HelloClusteredWorld at a high level, let's go step by step through the process of installing Terracotta, setting up a working version of HelloClusteredWorld, configuring it, and running it in a Terracotta cluster.

Downloading and Installing Terracotta

The first step is to download the software kit from `http://www.terracotta.org/`. Follow the Download link, and choose the download kit for your platform. The Terracotta kit comes in two flavors: one that comes with a Microsoft Windows installer and another that works on all platforms but does not come with an installer. For the purposes of this chapter, we will focus on the Windows kit, but other than the installer, there is little difference between the structure and behavior of the two downloads.

Once you have downloaded Terracotta, install it. On Windows, run the installer program. On other operating systems, use the tar program to unpack the archive. The Windows installer will place Terracotta in `C:\Program Files\Terracotta` by default. It will also add convenience items to your Start menu for running the administration console, the Terracotta Welcome screen, and the like.

Once the Windows installer has finished, it will automatically launch the Terracotta Welcome screen. On other operating systems, the Welcome screen may be launched manually by running the `welcome.sh` script in the top-level Terracotta installation directory. The Welcome screen is a good jumping-off place for exploring the Terracotta sample applications as well as starting the Terracotta administrator console, installing the Terracotta Eclipse plug-in, and working through some Terracotta tutorials. We will come back to the administrator console and the Eclipse plug-in later when we run through the Hello Clustered World example step by step.

Terracotta Installation Layout

Now that you've installed Terracotta and seen the Welcome screen, let's take a look at the contents of the Terracotta installation. It is important to note that the Terracotta kit contains everything needed for both the Terracotta client functions (the libraries that run inside your JVM) and the Terracotta server functions. In a typical Terracotta deployment, each application server machine running a Terracotta-enabled JVM would have an installation of the Terracotta kit on it. Likewise, the machine that runs the Terracotta server will also have the Terracotta kit installed. However, the application machines will use only the client parts of the Terracotta kit, and the Terracotta server machine will use only the server parts.

You'll find the following directories in the Terracotta kit:

`bin`: This contains all of the scripts needed to run the various Terracotta functions. Each script will be covered in more detail later.

`config-examples`: This contains example configuration files for various types of Terracotta deployments. You can use those scripts either as templates to start from or just as informative examples.

`docs`: This contains the small amount of documentation that comes with the Terracotta kit. Most of the Terracotta product documentation is kept online at `http://www.terracotta.org/`.

`lib`: This contains all of the JAR libraries on which Terracotta depends.

`modules`: This contains any prepackaged Terracotta Integration Modules (TIMs) that come with the Terracotta kit. Terracotta Integration Modules are JAR files that bundle Terracotta configuration together with any necessary supporting code and other resources into a single unit that may be included in your Terracotta configuration. You can think of them as plug-ins that provide Terracotta support for third-party applications. You can also build your own Terracotta Integration Modules to prepackage your own Terracotta-enabled libraries. More information about Terracotta Integration Modules and existing Terracotta integrations with third-party technologies can be found online at `http://www.terracotta.org/confluence/display/integrations/About`.

`samples`: This contains a wealth of sample projects that demonstrate various usages of Terracotta, including source code, Terracotta configuration, and start-up scripts.

`schema`: This contains the XML schema for the Terracotta configuration file.

`tools`: This contains tools for exploring Terracotta and to help configure Terracotta for HTTP session clustering.

`vendors`: This contains resources for third-party applications that are used in the Terracotta installation.

Terracotta Scripts

The important Terracotta scripts are in the `bin` directory. For each function, there is a Windows batch script and a corresponding Unix-style shell script. We will arrive at a more detailed description of the important scripts through our exploration of the Welcome screen later.

For a more detailed and up-to-date description of the Terracotta scripts and tools, see the online documentation at `http://www.terracotta.org/confluence/display/docs1/Terracotta+Tools+Overview`.

To get you started though, these are the main Terracotta scripts, in alphabetical order:

`admin.[bat|sh]`: This starts the Terracotta administration console. The administration console is a Java program that connects to the Terracotta server via JMX and receives telemetry data from a running Terracotta cluster.

`archive-tool.[bat|sh]`: This is used to package up all of the relevant data and configuration files of a Terracotta deployment for diagnostic purposes.

`boot-jar-path.[bat|sh]`: This is a helper script that sets the environment variable for the boot JAR location, creating the boot JAR if necessary. This is not intended for stand-alone use. It is used by the other scripts to help set up the Terracotta environment.

`dso-env.[bat|sh]`: The `dso-env.[bat|sh]` script prints out the JVM arguments required to launch a Terracotta-enabled JVM relative to the working directory from which the script is invoked. You can use this script to determine the appropriate JVM arguments to pass to your application's start-up scripts. For example, if you are running a Terracotta-enabled application within Tomcat, you might paste the output of the `dso-env` script into the `catalina.sh` script as follows; as a side effect, this script will create the boot JAR if it doesn't already exist:

```
export \
  JAVA_OPTS="-Xbootclasspath/p:/usr/local/terracotta/lib/dso-boot/my-boot-jar.jar \
  -Dtc.install-root=/usr/local/terracotta -Dtc.config=localhost:9510"
```

`dso-java.[bat|sh]`: This is a convenience script that you may use to start your application instead of using the `java` command. It will invoke the `java` command in your distribution with the Terracotta environment set up as much as possible.

`make-boot-jar.[bat|sh]`: This will create the Terracotta boot JAR. You can optionally pass in a configuration file that describes what additional classes to place in the boot JAR and a nondefault `boot-jar` file name and location.

`run-dgc.[bat|sh]`: By default, the distributed garbage collector will run in the Terracotta server at set intervals. This script will cause a Terracotta garbage collector cycle to start immediately.

`scan-boot-jar.[bat|sh]`: This is a helper script used by other tools to determine the validity of the Terracotta boot JAR. It will verify the contents of the boot JAR file against an L1 configuration. It will list all of the classes declared in the `<additional-boot-jar-classes/>` section of the Terracotta configuration file that are not included in the boot JAR, as well as classes in the boot JAR that are not listed in the `<additional-boot-jar-classes/>` section. It returns the exit code 1 if the boot JAR file is incomplete; otherwise, the exit code is 0.

`start-tc-server.[bat|sh]`: This will start the Terracotta server.

`stop-tc-server.[bat|sh]`: This will stop the Terracotta server.

`version.[bat|sh]`: This will print out the current Terracotta version.

Step-by-Step Hello Clustered World in Unix

At the beginning of this chapter, we introduced the standard "hello, world" program. For the sake of clarity, we left out specific instructions on how to run it. Let's return now to Hello Clustered World and walk through it step by step, exploring the details of how to get it running. The first pass through, we will use just a text editor and command-line tools. Then, we will explore how to get it running in the Eclipse IDE with the Terracotta Eclipse plug-in.

Creating a Project Skeleton

The first step is to create a project directory skeleton that looks like this:

```
hello_clustered_world/build
hello_clustered_world/src
hello_clustered_world/src/HelloClusteredWorld.java
hello_clustered_world/tc-config.xml
```

Make a top-level project directory called hello_clustered_world. Under that, create a directory called build that we'll use to put the compiled classes. Also under the top-level directory, create a directory called src that we'll use to put our Java source files. We will create the tc-config.xml file in a moment.

Creating HelloClusteredWorld.java

Once the project skeleton is created, using your favorite text editor, create a file under the src directory called HelloClusteredWorld.java. Type the following code into it:

```java
public class HelloClusteredWorld {
  private static final String message = "Hello Clustered World!";
  private static final int length = message.length();

  private static char[] buffer = new char [length ];
  private static int loopCounter;

  public static void main( String args[] ) throws Exception {
    while( true ) {
      synchronized( buffer ) {
        int messageIndex = loopCounter++ % length;
        if(messageIndex == 0) java.util.Arrays.fill(buffer, '\u0000');

        buffer[messageIndex] = message.charAt(messageIndex);
        System.out.println( buffer );
        Thread.sleep( 100 );
      }
    }
  }
}
```

Once you've saved the file, compile the program with the following command (make sure your working directory is the top-level project directory):

```
%> javac -d build/ src/HelloClusteredWorld.java
```

You should now have a file called HelloClusteredWorld.class in the build directory. Now, we can run it as a normal Java process as follows (again, make sure that your working directory is the top-level project directory):

```
%> java -cp build HelloClusteredWorld
H
He
Hel
Hell
Hello
Hello
Hello C
Hello Cl
```

```
Hello Clu
Hello Clus
Hello Clust
Hello Cluste
Hello Cluster
Hello Clustere
Hello Clustered
Hello Clustered
Hello Clustered W
Hello Clustered Wo
Hello Clustered Wor
Hello Clustered Worl
Hello Clustered World
Hello Clustered World!
H
He
Hel
Hell
Hello
```

Creating the Terracotta Configuration

The next step is to create a Terracotta configuration file. In a text editor, create a file called tc-config.xml in the top-level project directory. A good starting point is the POJO example configuration file in the Terracotta kit: config-examples/tc-config-pojo.xml. Copy the text of that configuration file into the tc-config.xml file currently open in your text editor. We will need to make a few alterations to this template configuration to work with HelloClusteredWorld.

■Note You can get a complete reference guide to the Terracotta configuration online at http:// www.terracotta.org/confluence/display/docs1/Configuration+Guide+and+Reference.

Making the Terracotta Server Run in Persistent Mode

The configuration file is split up into two main sections, one for the server(s) and one for the clients—from the perspective of Terracotta, the JVMs running your application are clients; although, from the perspective of the application developer, those JVMs are known as application servers. The first alteration will be to the server section of the configuration file.

The /tc:tc-config/servers section can contain multiple server entries, one of them being the primary active server. If there is more than one server entry, the clients will try to connect to them in order until the active server is reached. Should the active server become unavailable, the clients will try each of the other servers described here until they connect to the new active server. In this example, however, we will use only a single server.

The existing server configuration stanza, /tc:tc-config/servers/server, already contains some configuration information, namely the data and logs elements. The /tc:tc-config/servers/server/data element determines where the Terracotta server will write the Terracotta cluster data (clustered object data, connected client data, etc.). The /tc:tc-config/servers/server/logs element determines what directory the Terracotta server ought to write its logs to.

By default, the Terracotta server is not configured to persist the state of the cluster to permanent storage. This means that if the Terracotta server is restarted, it starts from scratch with no clustered application state. This is the equivalent of restarting a single JVM: all of the memory from the previous instantiation is wiped clean.

For this example, however, we want to see the Terracotta durable heap in action, so we want to configure the Terracotta server to run in persistent mode so that it may be safely stopped and restarted without resetting the clustered heap state. To do that, we must set the value of /tc:tc-config/servers/server/dso/persistence/mode to permanent-store by adding the following XML snippet to the existing /tc:tc-config/servers/server stanza:

```
<dso>
  <persistence>
    <mode>permanent-store</mode>
    </persistence>
  </dso>
```

Configuring the Terracotta Client

Now that we have the server configured, let's move on to the Terracotta client configuration. The client configuration consists of the client and the application sections. The client section describes general behaviors of the Terracotta client libraries.

The template configuration already has a clients stanza which, like the server stanza, describes where to write the Terracotta client logs. Unlike the Terracotta server stanza, though, the clients stanza does not contain configuration for specific Terracotta clients. The cluster configuration remains agnostic about how many Terracotta clients may join the cluster throughout the life of the cluster. We will leave the existing clients configuration stanza untouched.

The application section describes application-specific configuration. In the application section, we will be setting the clustered root fields, declaring which classes are eligible for Terracotta instrumentation, and declaring which methods should be augmented with Terracotta clustered locking and object change management.

Configuring Roots

In our previous discussion of HelloClusteredWorld, we determined that certain fields must be declared as clustered roots, which are the tops of clustered object graphs. Every object reachable by reference from a root field (that is not also declared transient) itself becomes a clustered object. Once instantiated the first time in the cluster, a root field becomes immutable, regardless of the modifiers applied to it in the source code.

HelloClusteredWorld has two fields that we want to declare as roots, buffer and loopCounter. To make those fields roots, we must add the following XML snippet to the /tc:tc-config/applications/dso/ section:

```
<roots>
  <root>
    <field-name>HelloClusteredWorld.buffer</field-name>
  </root>
  <root>
    <field-name>HelloClusteredWorld.loopCounter</field-name>
  </root>
</roots>
```

Configuring Instrumentation

Terracotta's transparency system augments Java byte code as it gets loaded into the JVM in order to observe changes to objects and coordinate cross-JVM locking and object updates. Our current configuration is set to instrument every class that gets loaded by the JVM. For our purposes in this example, this will work just fine. However, in real-life use, it is much more likely that you will want to restrict the set of classes that Terracotta instruments to just those that are necessary to eliminate the overhead of Terracotta instrumentation from the parts of your application (and third-party libraries that you are using) that do not interact with clustered objects.

To narrow down the instrumentation of HelloClusteredWorld to just what is necessary, let's modify the current instrumented-classes section to look like this:

```
<instrumented-classes>
  <include>
    <class-expression>HelloClusteredWorld</class-expression>
  </include>
</instrumented-classes>
```

This tells Terracotta to only instrument the HelloClusteredWorld class. Terracotta also instruments a number of other classes by default, all of which are found in the boot JAR.

Configuring Locks

Like the instrumentation section, our template configuration sets up locking for every method in every instrumented class. Again, this will work for our small example but is not generally practical for real-world use. To narrow down the methods that are sensitive to Terracotta locking, let's modify the locks section to look like this:

```
<locks>
  <autolock>
    <lock-level>write</lock-level>
    <method-expression>void HelloClusteredWorld.main(..)</method-expression>
  </autolock>
</locks>
```

This will tell Terracotta to put clustered locking only into the main method of HelloClusteredWorld. The two dots in the parameters section of this expression mean that it should match methods called main in HelloClusteredWorld with zero or more arguments of any type. This is a shortcut, since we know there is only one main method in HelloClusteredWorld.

Reviewing the Configuration

Our modifications to the template configuration are complete. Our tc-config.xml file should now look like this:

```xml
<?xml version="1.0" encoding="UTF-8"?>
<!--

  All content copyright (c) 2003-2007 Terracotta, Inc.,
  except as may otherwise be noted in a separate copyright notice.
  All rights reserved.

-->
<!--
This is a Terracotta configuration file that has been pre-configured
for use with DSO.  All classes are included for instrumentation,
and all instrumented methods are write locked.

For more information, please see the product documentation.
-->
<tc:tc-config xmlns:tc="http://www.terracotta.org/config"
  xmlns:xsi="http://www.w3.org/2001/XMLSchema-instance"
  xsi:schemaLocation="http://www.terracotta.org/schema/terracotta-4.xsd">
  <servers>

    <!-- Tell DSO where the Terracotta server can be found. -->
    <server host="localhost">
      <data>%(user.home)/terracotta/server-data</data>
      <logs>%(user.home)/terracotta/server-logs</logs>
      <dso>
        <persistence>
          <mode>permanent-store</mode>
        </persistence>
      </dso>
    </server>
  </servers>

  <!-- Tell DSO where to put the generated client logs -->
  <clients>
    <logs>%(user.home)/terracotta/client-logs</logs>
  </clients>

  <application>
    <dso>
      <roots>
        <root>
          <field-name>HelloClusteredWorld.buffer</field-name>
        </root>
```

```
    <root>
      <field-name>HelloClusteredWorld.loopCounter</field-name>
    </root>
  </roots>

  <!-- Start by including all classes for instrumentation.
       It's more efficient to instrument only those classes that
       hold shared roots or are part of a shared root's graph.
    -->
  <instrumented-classes>
    <include>
      <class-expression>HelloClusteredWorld</class-expression>
    </include>
  </instrumented-classes>

  <!-- Apply write level autolocks for all instrumented methods.
       It's more efficient to create finer-grain locks as dictated
       by your application needs.
    -->
  <locks>
    <autolock>
      <lock-level>write</lock-level>
      <method-expression>void HelloClusteredWorld.main(..)</method-expression>
    </autolock>
  </locks>
    </dso>
  </application>

</tc:tc-config>
```

Starting the Terracotta Server

The first step to running your application in a Terracotta cluster should be to start the Terracotta server using the `tc-start-server.[bat|sh]` script from the command line. Pass the location of our new `tc-config.xml` file to the `start-tc-server` script using the `-f` option.

Depending on where you installed Terracotta, you should see output that looks something like this (again, assuming you are executing the `start-tc-server` script from the top-level project directory):

```
%> /usr/local/terracotta/bin/start-tc-server.sh -f tc-config.xml
```

```
2008-03-09 15:01:29,005 INFO - Terracotta 2.5.2, as of 20080218-120204 (Revision 703
1 by cruise@rh4mo0 from 2.5)
2008-03-09 15:01:29,635 INFO - Configuration loaded from the file at
 '/Users/orion/hello_clustered_world/tc-config.xml'.
2008-03-09 15:01:29,791 INFO - Log file: '/Users/orion/terracotta/server-logs/terrac
otta-server.log'.
```

```
2008-03-09 15:01:30,374 INFO - JMX Server started. Available at URL[service:jmx:jmxm
p://0.0.0.0:9520]
2008-03-09 15:01:31,154 INFO - Terracotta Server has started up as ACTIVE node on 0.
0.0.0:9510 successfully, and is now ready for work.
```

Starting Two Clustered Instances of HelloClusteredWorld

Once the Terracotta server has started, start HelloClusteredWorld with Terracotta enabled. This is as simple as adding a few JVM arguments to the java command line, but an even easier way is with the helper script dso-java.[sh|bat], which adds those arguments for you automatically (it will also create the boot JAR if it hasn't already been created):

```
%> /usr/local/terracotta/bin/dso-java.sh -cp build HelloClusteredWorld
```

Now that Terracotta is enabled, you should see output that looks something like this:

```
2008-03-09 20:45:27,901 INFO - Terracotta 2.5.2, as of 20080218-120204 (Revision 703
1 by cruise@rh4moo from 2.5)
2008-03-09 20:45:28,434 INFO - Configuration loaded from the file at '/Users/orion/h
ello_clustered_world/tc-config.xml'.
2008-03-09 20:45:30,719 INFO - Terracotta 2.5.2, as of 20080218-120204 (Revision 703
1 by cruise@rh4moo from 2.5)
2008-03-09 20:45:31,328 INFO - Configuration loaded from the file at '/Users/orion/h
ello_clustered_world/tc-config.xml'.
2008-03-09 20:45:31,520 INFO - Log file: '/Users/orion/terracotta/client-logs/terrac
otta-client.log'.
```

This is output from the Terracotta client libraries that have been transparently inserted into your code path. After that, you should see the familiar output of HelloClusteredWorld.

Now, start another instance of HelloClusteredWorld in another terminal. The output should be very similar, but, as you saw in our initial discussion of HelloClusteredWorld at the beginning of this chapter, once the second instance joins the cluster, each instance will start printing with the messageIndex moved forward two characters instead of one. Again, as we discussed earlier, this is because the loopCounter variable is being incremented each time by the other instance between loop iterations—because the loopCounter is shared between them, the count advances twice per loop rather than just once.

Viewing Runtime Data in the Terracotta Administration Console

Now that we have a cluster running, let's use the Terracotta Administrator Console to get picture of the runtime data moving around our cluster. You can launch the Terracotta Administrator Console from the command line like this:

```
%> /usr/local/terracotta/bin/admin.sh
```

This will launch a Java Swing application that looks something like Figure 3-2.

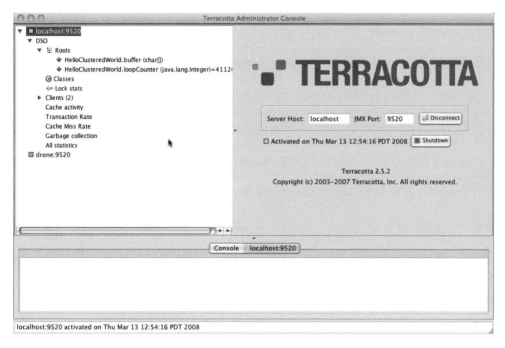

Figure 3-2. *Terracotta Administrator Console's initial display*

If you select or expand the Roots control, you will see a snapshot of the runtime state of the clustered object graphs. It should look something like Figure 3-3.

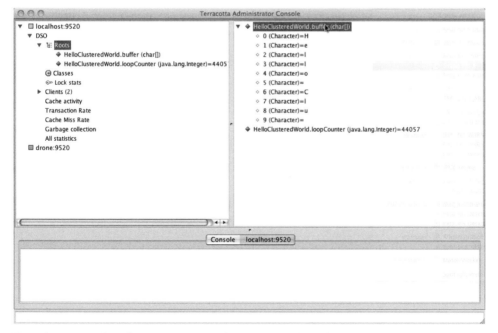

Figure 3-3. *Using the administrator console to examine shared objects*

As the program runs, you can click Refresh in the context menu for any point in the object graph to have that segment of the graph updated with a current snapshot. Do that a few times while HelloClusteredWorld is running, and you will see the contents of the character buffer fill up, get cleared, and fill up again. Likewise, you can watch the value of the loopCounter field increment.

The next item down from the Roots control displays the number of instances of each class that has been added to the cluster. In this example, nothing is displayed because HelloClusteredWorld doesn't actually share any objects—only primitives: a character array and an int.

The "Lock profiler" item allows you to turn on lock statistics gathering. If you enable lock statistics and click the server, you can see the locks on the buffer character array (denoted by "[C") and the loopCounter int are requested by each client as it goes through the while loop (there's an implicit lock acquisition when a root is accessed—nonroot fields do not require that implicit lock acquisition).

The Clients control displays information about currently connected client JVMs. If you still have your two instances of HelloClusteredWorld running, you should see two entries. Each entry can be expanded to display host and port information, as well as per-client graphs of client-side cache flush and fault rates, and the per-client transaction rate. The same cache and transaction rate statistics for the cluster as a whole can be viewed beneath the Clients control.

The "Garbage collection" item shows the statistics on executions of the Terracotta distributed garbage collector.

High Availability

Now that we've got a cluster up and running, let's see what happens when we start turning off and restarting parts of the cluster. First, let's try to kill the server while the two clients are running. You can do this by causing the server process to exit (for example, if you started it from a Unix-style command line, you can type Ctrl+C in the terminal you ran the server in).

When the Terracotta server process exits, you should see the clients halt. This happens because the thread that is in the while loop requests a clustered lock, but the server can't receive the lock request because it isn't running. What you aren't seeing in the standard output (but you can see in the client logs) is that the clients are continually trying to reconnect to the Terracotta server and being rebuffed because the server still isn't running.

If we had configured redundant Terracotta servers, killing the active server would have caused one of the passive secondary servers to automatically take over as the primary active server. For simplicity, we have only configured one server, but we can simulate this failover behavior by starting the server again the same way we started it the last time. Once the new server instance starts up, the clients will automatically reconnect and resume where they left off.

Heap Durability

Next, try killing all of the HelloClusteredWorld instances. Without Terracotta, the next time you start the program, it will start from the beginning. With Terracotta, however, when you kill all of the HelloClusteredWorld instances and start a new one, instead of starting from the beginning, the application will start *where it left off* in whatever state loopCounter and buffer were in when you killed the last HelloClusteredWorld instance. This is because the state of the clustered heap and, therefore, the state of loopCounter and buffer are maintained across JVM invocations.

In fact, the heap is maintained even if you shut down all of the `HelloClusteredWorld` instances *and* the Terracotta server, power down the machines they are running on (or, for example, your laptop), take the machines apart, and store them for ten years. If, after ten years, you reassemble the machines, plug them all back in, power them up, and start up the cluster again, your Terracotta-enabled Java program will resume operation exactly where it left off when you shut it down a decade ago.

Step-by-Step Hello Clustered World in Eclipse

Now that we've built up a simple Terracotta-enabled program and clustered it from scratch, let's see how the Terracotta Eclipse plug-in can make this process considerably easier. If you don't already have Eclipse, you can download it from `http://www.eclipse.org/`. Once you have Eclipse installed and running, you can install the Terracotta Eclipse plug-in (not included with the Terracotta download by default). Detailed installation instructions can be found online at `http://www.terracotta.org/confluence/display/howto/Eclipse+Plugin+Quick+Start`.

With the Terracotta Eclipse plug-in installed, create a new Terracotta project called `hello_clustered_world_eclipse` in your workspace by selecting File ➤ New ➤ Project, as shown in Figure 3-4.

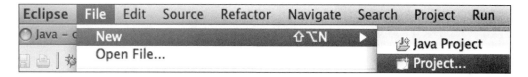

Figure 3-4. *Creating a new Eclipse project*

When the Project dialog box appears, choose Terracotta DSO Project, as shown in Figure 3-5, and name it "hello_clustered_world_eclipse" (actually, you can give it whatever name you want).

Figure 3-5. *Eclipse project browser*

Once the project has been created, create a new class called `HelloClusteredWorld` in the default package, and paste the source code from the last exercise into it. Now that we have the code in place, the Eclipse plug-in makes configuring and launching very simple.

To configure the roots, right-click each root field and, in the Terracotta context menu, declare it to be a shared root, as shown in Figure 3-6.

Figure 3-6. *Marking objects as Terracotta roots with Eclipse*

Once you've configured the root fields, you should see an adornment in the left gutter of the editor that looks like a little object graph.

Next, configure the main method for locking by right-clicking the method name and choosing Autolock from the Terracotta context menu, as shown in Figure 3-7.

Terracotta	▶	Method main	▶	Autolock
Run As	▶	Fields		Name Locked

Figure 3-7. *Using Eclipse to mark methods and classes as locked in Terracotta*

That's it for the configuration. Now, let's run it normally, without Terracotta, to make sure things are working properly. Go to the Run menu, and choose Run. You should see the familiar `HelloClusteredWorld` output.

When we're sure everything is working properly, it's time to run the Terracotta server. Make sure no other Terracotta servers are running (for example, the one you started from the command line in the previous exercise), and choose the localhost server in the Terracotta menu, as shown in Figure 3-8.

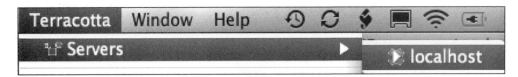

Figure 3-8. *Starting the Terracotta server inside Eclipse*

With the server running, we can start some clients. To configure a run profile for a Terracotta-enabled `HelloClusteredWorld` instance, choose Open Run Dialog from the Run menu, and double-click Terracotta DSO Application, as shown in Figure 3-9.

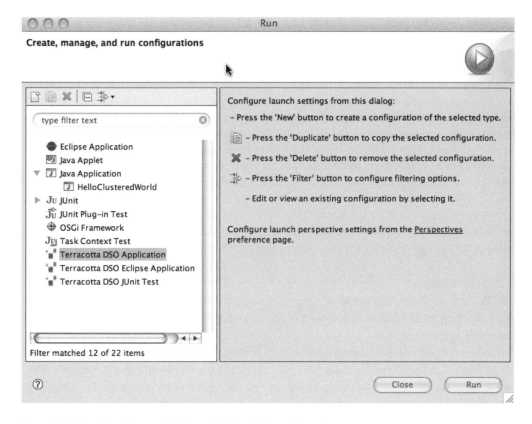

Figure 3-9. *Running the application with the Terracotta nature*

When the run profile is created, click the Run button. Eclipse will launch a fully configured, Terracotta-enabled instance of `HelloClusteredWorld` that will connect to the running server. You should see the familiar `HelloClusteredWorld` output. If you choose Run again from the Run menu, a second clustered instance of `HelloClusteredWorld` will start, and you will see the output of each start to advance two letters each cycle instead of one.

Implications for Every Developer

`HelloClusteredWorld` helps make clear to you how Terracotta works, but the application also does something else. It illustrates that the rules for clustering are changing. In Chapter 1, you learned that the power of clustering infrastructure is that an application can be simultaneously scalable, available, and simple. `HelloClusteredWorld` has shown two of these dimensions. The first dimension is scalability. Two JVMs working together each do half the work of building the buffer. The two together complete the message "Hello Clustered World!" in half the time too. Three JVMs would each do a third of the work, and the buffer would be populated in one third the time. In generic terms, the application throughput increases because it takes one-*n*th the time for *n* servers to complete the task at hand versus a single JVM.

The application also illustrates simplicity through transparency. The application might be considered unclusterable or very much a silo with respect to the fact that it is not multi-threaded and there is no upfront value in clustering such a simple application. At run time, it was possible to express a value-added notion of scale out to `HelloClusteredWorld`, nonetheless.

Last, we left the exercise of attempting to stop and restart the application to you, but you will learn in Chapter 4 that the `buffer` and the `loopCounter` variables persist across JVM processes as well as across application invocations. In other words, if the `loopCounter` were to reach 27 before we kill the Java process, the next time `HelloClusteredWorld` is invoked using `dso-java.sh`, the application would start with `loopCounter` at 27, not 0. `HelloClusteredWorld` is highly available and restartable as a result of running inside Terracotta's clustering infrastructure.

The power shown in Hello Clustered World can be extended into most Java applications we write. Since Terracotta is capable of clustering any heap-level objects and thread coordination, most applications can leverage the technology service.

■**Note**   Terracotta is a pure Java solution and uses only Java inside the Terracotta server process as well as the Java boot class loader and libraries used by the application's JVM. Terracotta cannot cluster objects that mutate system-level resources. System-level resources in Terracotta's definition include sockets, files, devices, and operating system constructs such as pipes or shared memory. Terracotta also cannot see inside JNI libraries. An application can use any of these technologies in the presence of Terracotta. Terracotta simply cannot see and thus is not able to hook into changes these technologies can apply to heap memory.

Summary

With Terracotta, simple, scalable, highly available object sharing is now available for enterprise applications running in a JEE container without the express need for object-relational mappers or bean-style programming. The same is true for applications running in a JSE container. The power can be delivered for frameworks downloaded from open source vendors and creators. Terracotta can cluster Java applications purchased from third parties, even if the original software vendor hasn't thought about scale out. And, as in `HelloClusteredWorld`, we can now cluster a simple Java `main()` run at the command line.

The ability to extract ourselves from scalability and availability concerns in an otherwise unclustered application saves money and time too. Developers have traditionally lived with clustering and scalability tightly coupled to business logic, as you have seen in this chapter. This tight coupling puts a burden on developers, starting in design and continuing long after application deployment. Specifically, without Terracotta, developers and architects have to select JDBC, JMS, or similar technologies for serializing and moving bytes between processes. During development, these technologies get integrated into the business logic. And during QA, the application must be tested in a clustered manner. Testing is quite challenging, because JVMs must be pushed hard to find bottlenecks in the replication logic, and workload must spread across JVMs attempting to update the same objects before we can be sure there are no race conditions or transactional issues with our application.

The Java runtime environment gained traction, in part, because of reasonably rapid development cycles offered by the language. It also gained traction because it can deliver on the promise of "write once, run anywhere." Terracotta is taking this promise one step further in asserting that spreading an application across JVMs should be a run-time decision. With Terracotta, developers avoid hard-coded clustering techniques. As a result, an operations team gets to decide if it wants an eight-CPU machine with 12 gigabytes of RAM or eight dual-core machines each with 2 gigabytes of RAM.

Chapter 4 will take the concepts and terminology introduced in Chapter 3 to the next level; by the end of that chapter, you will be able to cluster any POJO you write yourself. From Chapter 5 on, we will use the core concepts behind POJO clustering to cluster the objects inside popular frameworks such as Hibernate and Spring.

■ ■ ■

POJO Clustering

In the last chapter, you got some hands-on experience with Terracotta by building and running `HelloClusteredWorld`. Now that you've gotten your feet wet, it's time to introduce some major concepts that we have only briefly mentioned so far.

There are three broad concepts we need to discuss to help you understand how Terracotta works under the hood. The first is how Terracotta handles Java objects and the virtual heap. The second is how Terracotta manages the coordination of threads between JVMs and the changes threads make to objects on the virtual heap. The third major concept we'll introduce here is transparency and how Terracotta extends the existing semantics of your application to introduce clustering behavior at run time.

Armed with these crucial Terracotta concepts, we'll extend the hands-on experience you got with `HelloClusteredWorld` and walk through a more complex example of how Terracotta can transform a simple POJO application into a highly available, multi-JVM, scaled-out application.

All About Objects and Roots

In `HelloClusteredWorld`, we talked briefly about roots and how to configure them. You can think of a root as the top-level object in a clustered object graph—all objects referenced by the root object—on the virtual heap; in a sense, it's where Terracotta starts. A root is any field in any class that you declare in the Terracotta configuration as the beginning of a clustered object graph.

The first time you assign a value to a field declared as a root, Terracotta goes through the process of turning that object into a root. Terracotta traverses the object graph, transforming each of those objects, including the root itself, into a clustered object (more on what a clustered object is follows).

Roots are declared in the Terracotta configuration by name. You may create as many roots as you want (although, there is seldom need for more than a few). Additionally, the same root may be assigned to more than one field. When two different fields are assigned the same root, they are made by Terracotta to refer to the same clustered object graph.

A `<root>` stanza in the Terracotta configuration looks like this:

```
<roots>
  ...
  <root>
    <field-name>my.package.MyClass.myRootField</field-name>
    <root-name>my_root_name</root-name>
```

```
    </root>
    ...
</roots>
```

The `<root-name>` element is optional. If you don't specify a name, the field name is used implicitly as the root name. Here is an example where the same logical root is assigned to two separate fields:

```
<roots>
  <root>
    <field-name>demo.jtable.Main.model</field-name>
    <root-name>jtable_model</root-name>
  </root>
  <root>
    <field-name>demo.jtable.Roots.model</field-name>
    <root-name>jtable_model</root-name>
  </root>
</roots>
```

Fields that are declared as roots assume special behavior. This is the one area of Terracotta that diverges significantly from regular Java semantics.

- The first time a root is assigned by a JVM (which assigns it for the lifetime of the cluster), the root is created in the Terracotta cluster, and the object graph of the object assigned to the root field becomes the object graph of that logical root.

- Once assigned, the value of a root field may never be changed. After the first assignment, all subsequent assignments to fields declared to be that root are ignored. If a root is a Terracotta literal (more on literals later), the value of the primitive may be changed, but if the root is an object, the reference to that object may not be changed.

- The top-level object that represents the root object will never be collected by the Terracotta distributed garbage collector.

Because roots are durable beyond the scope of a single JVM's life cycle, they are sometimes called superstatic (that's just a name the creators of Terracotta made up). Static field references have the same life cycle as the classes they are declared in. Roots, which are superstatic, have the same life cycle as the virtual heap. This is true no matter what the scope modifier of the root field is. If a static field is declared to be a root, that static field will assume a superstatic life cycle. Likewise, if an instance field is declared to be a root, that instance field will assume the same superstatic life cycle. This can have a significant effect on code written with respect to root objects and can cause some astonishment if the behavior of Terracotta with respect to roots is not well understood.

While the reference of the root field itself cannot be changed, the object graph of that root object can. Typically, data structures like `Map`, `List`, and other `Collection` objects are chosen as root objects—although any portable object can be declared a root (more on object portability later). While the assignment of a `Map`, say, to a root field cannot be changed, the contents of that `Map` may be changed.

Clustered Objects

As we just mentioned, when a root field is first assigned, the Java object assigned to that field and all objects reachable by reference from that object become clustered objects. When an object becomes clustered, all of its field data is collected and stored in the Terracotta virtual heap. That object is also assigned a clusterwide unique object ID that is used to uniquely identify the object in the Terracotta virtual heap (and is, in fact, the key under which that object's data is stored in the disk-backed object store in the Terracotta server). At the appropriate time, all of this object data is sent to the Terracotta server, and thereafter, it is managed by Terracotta as a clustered object.

An object's data is composed of the values of that object's reference fields and its literal fields. Reference fields are references to other Java objects. The value of reference fields is the clusterwide object ID of the object that field refers to. Literal fields are those fields of an object that aren't reference fields—that is, fields whose type is not treated by Terracotta as an object. A Terracotta literal is similar to (but not exactly the same as) a Java primitive. They include the Java primitives as well as other types that are treated specially by Terracotta.

An object becomes clustered when it becomes referenced by any clustered object, unless that reference is transient (more on transience later). In fact, just like when a root is created, when an object becomes clustered, its entire object graph is traversed and all of its nontransient references are transformed into clustered objects. In that sense, root creation is a special case of clustered object creation. Once an object becomes clustered, it is always a clustered object and survives on the virtual heap until it becomes garbage collected by the Terracotta distributed garbage collector in the Terracotta server.

A NOTE ABOUT CLASSLOADERS

In Java, the identity of an object's class is tied to its `ClassLoader`. A class loaded by one `ClassLoader` is not the same as a bytecode-identical class loaded by a different `ClassLoader`. This means that an object instantiated in one `ClassLoader` context is not actually an object of the same class as an object instantiated in another `ClassLoader`. Even though their classes seem identical, they are actually objects of different classes. There is guaranteed to be one and only one instance of a particular clustered object per `ClassLoader` per JVM.

This has the side-effect that clustered objects are tied to the `ClassLoader` in which they were created and cannot cross `ClassLoader` boundaries. For example, a clustered object created in the context of the default `ClassLoader` in one JVM cannot be instantiated in the context of the `ClassLoader` of a web application (in most containers, each web application has its own `ClassLoader`; this allows, among other things, the dynamic reloading of JSP classes, for example). An attempt to instantiate Terracotta objects in a `ClassLoader` context different from that in which they were created will result in a `ClassCastException`.

Virtual Heap and Memory Management

The content of the Terracotta virtual heap is the set of all shared objects extant in the cluster. Because the virtual heap's state (i.e., the current values of every clustered object's fields) is managed by the Terracotta server, the Terracotta client libraries running in your application JVMs are free to manipulate the physical heap in the client JVMs. This means that not every object on the virtual heap needs to be instantiated in any JVM. Terracotta can load an object from the server automatically as it is needed by your application. When you traverse a reference to a clustered object that isn't currently instantiated on the local physical heap, Terracotta will automatically request that object's data from the Terracotta server, instantiate it on the local heap, and wire up the reference you are traversing, and your application will be none the wiser.

Likewise, Terracotta can artificially add null references to clustered objects as memory pressure increases, which lets arbitrarily large clustered object graphs fit within a constrained physical heap space. This ability to flush and fault objects to and from the Terracotta server is the virtual part of the Terracotta virtual heap. Just like the virtual memory subsystem of a modern operating system swaps the contents of physical memory back and forth between disk and RAM, letting the programs on your computer behave as if they had unlimited physical memory, the Terracotta virtual memory subsystem lets your application behave like it has an unlimited physical Java heap.

Distributed Garbage Collection

The Terracotta server has a distributed garbage collector that will remove clustered objects that are no longer referenced. This happens so the virtual heap doesn't fill up the disk under the Terracotta server with object data that is no longer needed. In order for a clustered object to be eligible for garbage collection, it must not be reachable from any root (i.e., must not be part of a root's object graph), and it must not be resident in the heap of any client JVM. When the distributed garbage collector finds objects that are eligible for collection, it removes them from the server and from the server's persistent storage.

Managing Object Changes and Coordinating Threads

Just like objects shared between threads in a single JVM, access to Terracotta clustered objects by threads in different JVMs must be coordinated so that threads don't unexpectedly overwrite each other's changes and so that changes are reliably applied where they need to be. To do this, Terracotta takes further cues from the existing architecture of the JVM.

In the JVM, object data is protected from concurrent thread execution by synchronizing access to certain critical areas of code through the use of mutexes. Before a thread may enter such a critical code section—signified by a synchronized block—it must first acquire a mutual exclusion lock that serializes access to that code section. No two threads may execute the code in a synchronized block at the same time.

In addition to providing serialized access to critical code sections, the lock acquisition and subsequent lock release of synchronized code blocks provide another crucial function for the consistency of object data: they serve as transaction boundaries between which changes made to objects by a thread are batched and ordered. When a thread acquires an object's lock—also known as its monitor—there are certain guarantees about the visibility of changes made to objects by other threads (there is actually no relation between an object's lock and the changes that can be made under that lock; the fact that locks are associated with objects is essentially syntactic sugar). The JVM ensures that the state of all objects visible to a thread that has acquired a particular lock reflects all of the changes to those objects made under the scope of that same lock by all other threads.

Another thread-related function connected to locking provided by the JVM is the wait() and notify() facility. An object that holds a lock on an object may call the wait() method on that object, which will cause that thread of execution to pause. That thread will remain paused until either a specified time interval has passed or until another thread calls notify() or notifyAll(). When a waiting thread is notified, it is placed back into contention for the lock on the object in question. Thread coordination to perform all sorts of time- and sequence-sensitive operations can be programmed using just the concurrency primitives, synchronized(), wait(), and notify(). Over time, these concurrency concerns have been encapsulated into standard Java libraries, most notably the java.util.concurrent package (which, incidentally, can also be clustered by Terracotta).

Terracotta provides exactly the same access serialization, coordination, and visibility guarantees to threads in different JVMs as the JVM itself provides to threads within the same JVM. The facilities that Terracotta uses to provide these guarantees take the form of locks and transactions.

Locks

Terracotta extends the built-in locking semantics of the JVM to have a clusterwide, cross-JVM meaning. Clustered locking is injected into application code based on the <locks> section of the Terracotta configuration file. Each lock configuration stanza uses a regular expression that matches a set of methods. The locking that Terracotta injects into that set of methods is controlled by further configuration options specified in the lock configuration stanza.

We did some lock configuration in the last chapter for HelloClusteredWorld. There, we had a lock configuration stanza that looked like this:

```
<locks>
  <autolock>
    <lock-level>write</lock-level>
    <method-expression>void HelloClusteredWorld.main(..)</method-expression>
  </autolock>
</locks>
```

This configuration stanza tells Terracotta to look for methods in your code that match the method expression. The method expression is expressed in a pattern selection language developed by AspectWerkz, a pioneering aspect-oriented programming (AOP) framework. This pattern selection language allows you to specify particular sections of your code. In AOP parlance, this is known as a join point. Using this expression language, you can precisely specify how Terracotta should treat the locking in your code. For a complete reference to the AspectWerkz pattern language, see http://www.terracotta.org/confluence/display/docs1/AspectWerkz+Pattern+Language.

Let's use the main() method in our familiar HelloClusteredWorld program to discuss the effect of each lock configuration option. For convenience, we'll reiterate it here:

```
public static void main( String args[] ) throws Exception {
    while( true ) {
      synchronized( buffer ) {
        int messageIndex = loopCounter++ % length;
        if(messageIndex == 0) java.util.Arrays.fill(buffer, '\u0000');

        buffer[messageIndex] = message.charAt(messageIndex);
        System.out.println( buffer );
      }
      Thread.sleep( 100 );
    }
}
```

Autolocks and Named Locks

A lock stanza must be specified as either a named lock or an autolock. Methods that match an autolock stanza are augmented by Terracotta to acquire a clusterwide lock on a clustered object wherever there is synchronization on that object. You can think of autolocks as an extension of a method's existing Java synchronization to have a clusterwide meaning. The configuration for HelloClusteredWorld uses an autolock that tells Terracotta to inspect the main() method for synchronization. In this case, the synchronization on the buffer field is augmented by Terracotta to have a clusterwide effect.

Unlike autolocks, named locks function only at method entry and exit. This means that, for methods that match a named lock configuration stanza, a thread must first acquire the lock of that name from the Terracotta server before being allowed to execute that method. As a result, named locks are very coarse grained and should only be used when autolocks are not possible. Had we chosen to use a named lock for HelloClusteredWorld, only one thread in the entire cluster would have been allowed into the main() method at a time. The effect would be to allow the first JVM to execute the main() method. Thereafter, any JVM that joins the cluster would block at the entrance to the main() method attempting to acquire the named lock. Since the main() method never exits, all except the first JVM would block indefinitely or until the first JVM was terminated, at which point another JVM would be granted the lock and be allowed into the main() method.

Autolocks can provide considerably more concurrency than named locks, but autolocks only acquire a lock if the object being synchronized on is a clustered object. In automatically locked methods, if the object being synchronized on is not a clustered object, then only the local JVM lock is acquired. For example, if an object of type product is clustered, maintains a reference to objects of type productprice, and you exclude the productprice object from instrumentation, product will not be updated across a cluster of JVMs when methods in the productprice class are invoked.

Autolocks applied to methods that have no synchronization in them will have no clustered locking. Also, methods that match a lock stanza but do not belong to a class included in the set of classes configured for instrumentation by Terracotta will have no clustered locking behavior. Such methods are invisible to Terracotta (more on class instrumentation later).

Lock Level

Another configuration option in the lock configuration stanza is the lock level. Unlike Java, Terracotta locks come in four levels:

- `write`

- `synchronous-write`

- `read`

- `concurrent`

Write locks are mutual exclusion locks that act like regular Java locks. They guarantee that only one thread in the entire cluster can acquire that lock at any given time.

Synchronous write locks add the further guarantee that the thread holding the lock will not release the lock until the changes made under the scope of that lock have been fully applied and acknowledged by the server.

■**Caution** While synchronous-write locking sounds like a good idea for guaranteed transactions, the overhead is high. The JVM holding the lock will be blocked while the Terracotta server receives acknowledgement from all other JVMs and while the server flushes the change to disk. Normally, Terracotta allows threads to continue and asynchronously waits for acknowledgement, so the performance difference will be large.

Read locks allow multiple reader threads to acquire the lock at a time, but those threads are not allowed to make any changes to clustered objects while holding the read lock. No thread may acquire a write lock if any thread holds a read lock. No thread may acquire a read lock if any thread holds a write lock. If a thread attempts to make modifications while holding a read lock, Terracotta will cause an exception to be thrown.

If, however, it crosses another lock acquisition boundary on the same lock (e.g., a synchronization on the same object), but that new lock acquisition boundary is configured to be a write lock, that thread will try to upgrade its lock from a read lock to a write lock and will not be allowed to proceed until it acquires that upgraded write lock. Read locks offer a significant performance advantage over write locks when multiple threads concurrently execute code that does not modify any clustered objects.

Concurrent locks are always granted. They do not protect critical code sections and serve only as transaction boundaries. Changes made within the scope of a concurrent lock are applied automatically, but there is no guarantee about the order in which transactions created in the scope of concurrent locks in different threads are applied. Nor is there a guarantee that changes from other threads are not being received and applied to heap while inside the lock. You should only use concurrent locks when you care about neither potential write-write conflicts between threads nor about dirty reads. Concurrent locks are best when every JVM is guaranteed to work on different objects from any other JVM yet Terracotta is in use for things like master/worker relationship (see Chapter 11).

Distributed wait() and notify()

A thread that holds the clustered lock for a clustered object may call wait() on that object. This will cause the thread to commit the current Terracotta transaction, release the clustered lock, and pause execution. Any other thread in the cluster that holds the clustered lock on that object may call notify() on that object. The Terracotta server will select a waiting thread (in the case of a notify() call) or the set of all waiting threads (in the case of a notifyAll() call) and ensure that the appropriate waiting threads throughout the Terracotta cluster are notified. Any thread that is notified will contend for the clustered lock and resume execution when granted that lock.

Transactions

Terracotta batches changes made to objects into sets called transactions. A Terracotta transaction is bounded by the acquisition and later release of a lock. When a thread acquires a clustered lock, a Terracotta transaction is started for that thread, and all changes to clustered objects made by that thread within the scope of that lock are added to that transaction. When the lock is released, the Terracotta transaction is committed, meaning that it is sent to the Terracotta server. (It might not be sent immediately; Terracotta optimizes the conversation between clients and the Terracotta server by batching transactions when possible.)

Transactions are applied in order to preserve the "happens before" relationship discussed in Chapter 1. When a lock is acquired, Terracotta guarantees that all of the transactions made under the scope of that lock in every JVM in the Terracotta cluster are applied locally on the heap of the acquiring thread. This ensures that threads always see a consistent view of clustered objects.

All changes to clustered objects must happen within the context of a Terracotta transaction. This means that a thread must acquire a clustered lock prior to modifying the state of any clustered objects. If a thread attempts to modify a clustered object outside the context of a Terracotta transaction, a runtime exception will be thrown.

A special case of this is worth mentioning, because it is not obvious. If a thread synchronizes on an object that is not yet clustered, that thread does not acquire a clustered lock and does not start a Terracotta transaction. That thread may not make modifications to any shared objects, even if the object the thread has synchronized becomes shared within the scope of that synchronization.

Distributed Method Invocation

Terracotta provides a facility for causing methods on shared objects to be called wherever they are resident in the cluster. This facility is called Distributed Method Invocation (DMI). An invocation of a method declared as a distributed method on a clustered object will trigger that same method invocation on all the instances of that object that happen to be currently instantiated on the heap of any JVM in the cluster.

It is important to note that distributed methods work in the context of a shared instance that defines that method. There are also no guarantees about when the distributed methods will be executed. Likewise, there are no guarantees about which JVMs that method will be executed on, since whether or not the method is executed is contingent on whether or not the object in question in currently on the heap of a JVM.

DMI is a useful mechanism for implementing a distributed listener model. It is not, however, a good way to coordinate actions or share data between threads in different JVMs. For those purposes, the `java.util.concurrent` package is a much better fit.

Transparency and Bytecode Instrumentation

So far, we have discussed how Terracotta augments your application code to give it cluster-wide meaning, but we haven't discussed exactly how this happens. The essential mechanism behind Terracotta's transparency is bytecode instrumentation. Java classes are compiled down to bytecode instructions that must be loaded by the JVM before new instances of those classes may be created. That process of loading the bytecode gives Terracotta an opportunity to inspect and manipulate the bytecode of your classes prior to being used in your application. These techniques were first developed to enable AOP and are currently in widespread use in frameworks like Spring.

Terracotta can be configured to instrument all or just a subset of the classes loaded into the JVM. You can elect to instrument all classes to make sure that Terracotta can see into everything your business logic does to memory at runtime. For performance reasons, however, it is often beneficial to restrict the set of classes that Terracotta instruments to only those that you know will interact with clustered objects. Just remember that if a class isn't instrumented, it is essentially invisible to Terracotta. Any changes to clustered objects made by a class that isn't instrumented will not be reflected in the cluster.

It is also important to note that the code of a class may manipulate clustered objects even if no instances of that class are themselves clustered. This means that the set of classes that you must instrument is not just the set of classes whose objects may become clustered, but rather, the set of classes that manipulate shared objects.

The set of classes instrumented is determined by the `<instrumented-classes>` section of the Terracotta configuration. In `HelloClusteredWorld`, we configured Terracotta to instrument every class. To narrow the set of instrumented classes, you can modify the class selection expression in the `<include>` or `<exclude>` stanzas. Like the method expression you saw in the previous section on locks, the class expression is part of the AspectWerkz join point, selection pattern language.

The `<include>` and `<exclude>` stanzas are evaluated bottom up according to the order in the Terracotta configuration file. The first pattern that matches will determine whether the class will or will not be instrumented. If no patterns match, the class will not be instrumented. Using a combination of `<include>` and `<exclude>` class expressions, you can pick out exactly the set of classes that you want included for instrumentation.

```
<instrumented-classes>
  <include>
    <class-expression>com.mycompany.pkga.*</class-expression>
  </include>

  <exclude>com.mycompany.pkga.subpkg.*</exclude>

  <include>
    <class-expression>com.mycompany.pkgb.*</class-expression>
  </include>
</instrumented-classes>
```

In the preceding example, every class in the package com.mycompany.pkgb and in every package under it will be instrumented. However, no class in com.mycompany.pkga.subpkg or in any package under it will be instrumented. But, every class in the package com.mycompany.pkga and in every package under it *except* com.mycompany.pkga.subpkg and below will be instrumented. You may also use class name patterns as well as package patterns to fine-tune the set of included classes.

■**Note** Some classes are automatically instrumented by Terracotta. These classes are placed automatically in the Terracotta boot JAR when the boot JAR is created.

Portability

Terracotta can cluster most Java objects, but there are limits to what you can add to a Terracotta cluster. An object that can be clustered by Terracotta is called portable. For any object to be portable, its class must be instrumented.

Instances of most instrumented classes are portable, but there are a few constraints on portability. Some objects are inherently nonportable, because they represent JVM-specific or host-machine-specific resources that don't make sense in a clustered context. Some file-system-related classes such as java.io.FileDescriptor are examples of host-machine-specific resources that are inherently nonportable. Instances of java.lang.Thread and java.lang.Runtime are examples of JVM-specific resources that are inherently nonportable.

Other nonportable objects are instances of classes that extend inherently nonportable classes, uninstrumented classes, or classes of logically managed objects (more on logically managed objects later).

Boot JAR Classes

Most classes may be instrumented at class load time if you need them to be. Some classes, however, are loaded too early in the life cycle of the JVM for Terracotta to hook into their loading process. Such classes cannot be instrumented at load time but must instead be preinstrumented and placed in a special JAR file that is then prepended to the boot classpath.

Some of the classes in the boot JAR are placed there automatically by Terracotta. Other classes may be added to the boot JAR by augmenting the Terracotta configuration to include them in the boot JAR section of the Terracotta configuration and then running the make-boot-jar script in the bin directory of the Terracotta installation.

The location of the boot JAR must be passed in as a JVM argument to the java command when you start your application. You can run the dso-env script in the bin directory of the Terracotta installation to see how to add the boot JAR to your JVM arguments.

Physically vs. Logically Managed Objects

Most objects are managed by moving their field data around the Terracotta cluster. These classes of objects are described as physically managed because Terracotta records and distributes changes to the physical structure of the object. When a field of a physically managed object changes, the new value of the field is sent to the Terracotta server and to other members of the Terracotta cluster that currently have the changed object in memory.

Some classes of objects are not shared this way, however. Instead of moving the physical structure of such objects around, we record the methods called on those objects along with the arguments to those method calls and then replay those method calls on the other members of the Terracotta cluster. These classes of objects are described as logically managed, because Terracotta records and distributes the logical operations that were performed on them rather than recording the changes to their internal structure.

Terracotta uses logical management either for performance reasons or because a class's internal structure is JVM specific. For example, classes that use hashed structures such as java.util.Hashtable, java.util.HashMap, or java.util.HashSet are logically managed. The hashcodes used to create the internal structure of these classes are JVM specific. If an object that has a structure based on JVM-specific hashcodes were physically managed, its structure on other JVMs in the Terracotta cluster would be incorrect and nonsensical, since the hashcodes would be different on those other JVMs.

Other classes are logically managed, because changes to them can involve wholesale shifts in their internal structure. While those shifts in memory happen with acceptable latency, they would cause a flurry of clustered object changes in the cluster. This happens when, for example, an array-backed List is rebalanced or reordered. Rather than mirroring the exact internal structure of such objects, Terracotta keeps track of the methods that are called. The object may be brought up to date by replaying the method call sequence, which updates the internal data structures inside the object in memory.

Nonportable and Logically Managed Classes

You saw previously that classes with a nonportable class in their type hierarchy are not portable. Subclasses of uninstrumented classes fall into this category, as do subclasses of inherently nonportable classes like java.lang.Thread.

While logically managed classes are themselves portable, there are some restrictions on the portability of classes that have logically managed classes in their type hierarchy. This stems from the technical details of the Terracotta implementation of logically managed classes.

If the subclass of a logically managed class has declared additional fields, that class is not portable if

- It directly writes to a field declared in the logically managed superclass.

- It overrides a method declared in the logically managed superclass.

If you find that a class is nonportable because it inherits from a class that is nonportable because it hasn't been instrumented, you can modify the Terracotta configuration to include all of the classes in the type hierarchy for instrumentation. However, if you find that a class is not portable because of the other inheritance restrictions, you must refactor the class you want to make portable so that it does not violate the inheritance restriction.

Portability Contexts

There are a number of contexts in which objects become shared by Terracotta. In each of these contexts, the portability of the objects that are about to be shared is checked. If there is a portability error, Terracotta throws an exception.

Field Change

When a field of an object that is already shared changes, the object being newly assigned to that field is checked for portability. If that object is not portable, Terracotta throws a portability exception.

If the newly referenced object is itself portable, its object graph is traversed. If any object reachable by the newly reference object is not portable, Terracotta throws a portability exception.

Logical Action

Methods called on logically managed objects that change the state of that object are termed logical actions. When such a method is called, the arguments to that method are checked for portability. If any of those objects are not portable, Terracotta throws a portability exception.

If the argument objects themselves are portable, their object graphs are traversed. If any object reachable by the argument objects is not portable, Terracotta throws a portability exception.

Object Graph Traversal

When an object becomes shared via any of the mechanisms just discussed, including joining the graph of another shared object through field assignment or by becoming the argument to a logically shared action, Terracotta traverses all of the objects reachable in that object's graph. During that traversal, if any nonportable object is encountered, Terracotta throws a portability exception.

Transient Fields and On-Load Behavior

If the field of an object that you want to cluster is not portable, you have two options:

- Refactor the code so as to remove the nonportable field.

- Declare the field transient.

A transient field in Terracotta is similar to a transient field in Java: it is ignored during object graph traversal when an object graph is being shared. You can declare a field as transient in the Terracotta configuration like so:

```
<transient-fields>
  <field-name>com.mycompany.pkga.MyClassOne.fieldA</field-name>
  <field-name>com.mycompany.pkgb.subpkg2.fieldB</field-name>
</transient-fields>
```

You can also declare a field transient by setting the `<honor-transient>` option in the class instrumentation section of the Terracotta configuration. Any classes that match an `<include>` stanza where `<honor-transient>` is specified will be inspected for the `transient` keyword in the Java language. Any field marked as transient in source code will be honored as transient by Terracotta.

```
<instrumented-classes>
  <include>
  <honor-transient>true</honor-transient>
  <class-expression>com.mycompany.pkga.*</class-expression>
  </include>
...
</instrumented-classes>
```

Initializing Transient Fields on Load

Since transient fields are ignored by Terracotta, you must take care to initialize them after they have been instantiated on other JVMs. When an object is materialized on a JVM by Terracotta, any transient reference fields will be `null`, and transient primitive fields will be their default values.

Terracotta offers two facilities to initialize those fields to their proper values. In the Terracotta configuration, you can specify a method to be called when an object is materialized on the heap of a JVM. That method should contain the proper initialization code. Alternatively, you can write BeanShell script directly into the configuration file that will be executed when the object is loaded.

The following configuration snippet declares an initialization method. It instructs Terracotta to invoke `com.mycompany.pkga.MyClass.myMethod()` whenever a clustered instance of `com.mycompany.pkga.MyClass` is loaded in a JVM.

```
<instrumented-classes>
  <include>
    <class-expression>com.mycompany.pkga.MyClass</class-expression>
    <on-load>
      <method>myMethod</method>
    </on-load>
  </include>
...
</instrumented-classes>
```

The following configuration snippet declares some BeanShell script to be invoked whenever a clustered instance of `com.mycompany.pkga.MyClass` is loaded in a JVM:

```
<instrumented-classes>
  <include>
    <class-expression>com.mycompany.pkga.MyClass</class-expression>
    <on-load>
      <execute><![CDATA[self.myTransientField = new ArrayList();]]></execute>
    </on-load>
```

```
    </include>
...
</instrumented-classes>
```

More information on BeanShell scripting may be found at `http://www.beanshell.org/`.

Clustered POJOs Step by Step

Now that you've been introduced to some of the major concepts of Terracotta, we are ready to discuss POJO clustering in depth and what it means for your application. The definition of a POJO is quite contentious. Rebecca Parsons originally defined POJO. Later, on the definition, Fowler wrote:

> *"I've come to the conclusion that people forget about regular Java objects because they haven't got a fancy name—so while preparing for a talk Rebecca Parsons, Josh Mackenzie, and I gave them one: POJO (Plain Old Java Object). A POJO domain model is easier to put together, quick to build, can run and test outside of an EJB container, and isn't dependent on EJB (maybe that's why EJB vendors don't encourage you to use them)."*

—Martin Fowler (`http://www.martinfowler.com/isa/domainModel.html`)

POJO is essentially a feeling more than a specification. What is certain is that a developer knows when he is writing POJOs and when he is not.

Terracotta enables a POJO programming model when running applications in a cluster. The model is represented by the ability to honor the Java Memory Model as well as the language semantics. Specifically, POJO clustering implies that object identity is preserved across JVMs. Clustered POJOs are, in a fundamental way, the *same* object in different JVMs, not merely copies or clones that have the same data. A POJO should be able to simultaneously reside in two separate object graphs without ending up cloned into one of them.

A Java developer should be able to synchronize access to a POJO using the `synchronized` keyword. POJO clustering is the basis of Terracotta's ability to cluster many frameworks. Community members have built prototypes for Scala, JRuby, Quercus, and Groovy clustering. These technologies were not implemented with clustering in mind, but as long as the clustering honors the language specification and developer contract (preserving threading semantics and object identity), these technologies needn't think about clustering.

In Chapters 5 and on, you will see a number of use cases that demonstrate Terracotta adapted for a particular technology. But, under the covers, Terracotta is a generic technology that can be applied to any distributed computing task. The core Terracotta technology makes POJOs available across JVM instances as if they all shared a massive distributed heap. In the rest of this chapter, we will address how POJO clustering works and can be used under many use cases. With this knowledge, you can better understand subsequent chapters, and you can build your own prototypes or production applications using frameworks Terracotta has yet to support.

What Do We Mean by POJO?

To understand what POJO clustering is, let's first describe exactly what we mean by POJO. We use the term "POJO" to mean a plain Java object that lives on the heap of your JVM and doesn't need any extra framework or component trussing to enable the functionality it is intended to provide.

The essential feature of a POJO is that it actually lives on the heap of the JVM and that it can be treated as a regular Java object without any surprising side effects. References to a POJO should be plain references such that comparisons to them with the == operator evaluate to true. You should be able to modify the fields of a POJO through the normal access (.) operator (e.g., foo.bar = baz) without having to later call some commit or put-back operation (e.g., session.setAttribute("foo", foo)). You should be able to put a POJO into a data structure (like a Map) and get it out again without being handed back a copy of the object. You should also be able to execute concurrency operations (e.g., synchronized, wait(), and notify()) on a POJO and have them do what you expect.

Traditionally, POJOs are used until the data they represent needs to be externalized outside the boundaries of a single JVM's heap. For example, if you want to store the data represented by an object to a database, you might use EJBs or an object-relational framework like Hibernate to manage the persistence for you. Or, if you want to send messages between JVMs, you might use JMS or RMI. In all of these cases, a significant amount of framework trussing supports the externalization of object data off the local heap, and the objects involved can't be called POJOs. Interactions with these externalized objects are framework dependent and sometimes complicated, and they always need to be treated in special ways.

What's a Clustered POJO?

Given this understanding of POJOs, what, then, is a clustered POJO? For Terracotta, a clustered POJO is an object that has all of the qualities of a regular POJO plus the additional feature that it lives on a virtual heap shared by all the JVMs in the cluster.

A clustered POJO, first and foremost, should be a first-class object with a unique identity on the clustered heap. This means that references to it should be plain references such that comparisons to them with the == operator evaluate to true. There should be no object cloning, either explicitly through the Java object cloning mechanism or implicitly through data copying or object serialization. Therefore, you should be able to put a clustered POJO into a data structure and get it out again without being handed back a copy of the object. All references to a POJO, clustered or not, should point to exactly the same object on the heap.

If synchronized properly, object modifications should be visible across threads on multiple JVMs sharing the same virtual heap exactly as those modifications are visible across threads on the same JVM sharing the same physical heap.

You should also be able to execute concurrency operations (e.g., synchronized, wait(), and notify()) on a clustered POJO and have them behave across threads on multiple JVMs sharing the same virtual heap exactly as they do across threads in the same JVM sharing the same physical heap.

Since the scope and life cycle of a clustered POJO are beyond those of any specific JVM, the virtual heap on which clustered POJOs live should be persistent beyond the life cycle of any particular JVM. That means that clustered POJOs are durable and, unlike nonclustered POJOs, they don't disappear when any number of JVMs shut down.

Why Clustered POJOs?

Essentially, the motivation behind using a clustered heap is simplicity. Using a virtual heap lets you focus on the logic of your application without the architectural and semantic distortions inherent with explicit object externalization. Every other attempt to provide object durability and/or inter-JVM communication presents object modification and cross-JVM message passing as an explicit API that is inextricably embedded in your application code.

A great deal of effort has been put in to making Java applications enterprise class, meaning that they have very high uptimes, handle data reliably, and scale properly to keep perceived latency minimal regardless of user load. To provide enterprise-class functionality, two features are required that are not provided by the JVM:

- Durability and portability of object data

- Cross-JVM thread communication

Durability and portability of object data is required for reliability and high availability. Reliable data handling requires that application data be durable. Since the Java heap is not durable, object data must be externalized to a durable store.

For an application to be highly available, it must either run on highly available hardware or be deployable redundantly on commodity hardware. This latter path has traditionally been chosen by Java enterprise architects to provide high availability for a number of reasons, not the least of which is that it can be extended to yield scalability by elastically adding (or removing) commodity hardware to fit user demand, theoretically keeping latency stable. As discussed earlier, this scale-out architecture requires that at least some of the running state of an application instance be externalized so that, should one application instance fail or be taken offline, another may seamlessly take its place, picking up from where it left off. Durability and portability of object data are, therefore, required to maintain application state in a scaled-out architecture.

Once an application is deployed in a scaled-out architecture, there inevitably arises the need for inter-JVM communication and coordination for one reason or another. Typical examples are cache flushing or expiration and administrative functionality. More advanced architectures, such as the master/worker form of workload distribution discussed in Chapter 11, are explicitly designed to take advantage of multiple JVM deployment footprints and require robust and flexible inter-JVM communication and coordination.

These twin features, durability and portability of object data and cross-JVM thread communication, have been backfilled into the Java execution environment in a number of more or less sophisticated ways since Java's inception. The core of many such technologies is object serialization, the most basic way to externalize object data. Once an object graph is serialized, it may then be exported to a durable store such as a file or a database or across a network to another JVM.

Based on this core feature, extra scaffolding has been built up to provide more sophisticated persistence handling (e.g., EJBs or object-relational mapping engines like Hibernate), or to provide inter-JVM communication (e.g., RMI or JMS) and data sharing.

In conceiving Terracotta, the creators noticed that most of the features provided by explicit object durability and inter-JVM communication frameworks could be provided much more simply if existing facilities already found in the JVM were extended to allow the participation of threads not in the same JVM. The JVM already has a notion of local and remote objects: thread memory and main memory (heap). Likewise, it already has a notion of inter-process communication and coordination: the thread-level concurrency primitives `synchronized`, `wait()`, `notify()`, and `join()`.

Adding a durable object store in the form of an extended, network-attached virtual heap and extending the meaning of the concurrency primitives to apply to all threads in all participating JVMs provides the twin enterprise features of object durability and portability and inter-JVM communication and coordination in a way that looks remarkably similar, if not identical in all cases, to Java code written with only one JVM in mind.

By injecting distributed computing into the existing facilities provided by the JVM, we have extracted much of the complexity of distributed computing from application-level code where explicit enterprise frameworks have traditionally forced it to live. Instead, distributed computing becomes an inherent feature of the JVM rather than an explicit problem to be solved inside the application.

An Example of Clustered POJOs

To explore the simplicity of using clustered POJOs, let's look at an in-depth example. This example is a simplified version of a retail system with a catalog of products that can be added to a shopping cart by a customer. At any time, an operator may view any or all of the active shopping carts. The sample code is written using simple Java data structures. Some of the problem domain is idealized for simplicity. For example, the business data encapsulated in the product, catalog, customer, and order classes in a real system would likely be backed by a relational database and perhaps be fronted by an object-relational system like Hibernate, as described in Chapter 6. The transient shopping cart data, though, might very well be best expressed purely as simple Java objects with no backing system of record.

The Example Classes

There are six important classes in this system:

- `ProductImpl`

- `Catalog`

- `ShoppingCartImpl`

- `ActiveShoppingCarts`

- `Roots`

- `Main`

The code is displayed in Listings 4-1 through 4-8, but it may also be retrieved from `http://www.apress.com`.

The ProductImpl Class

The `ProductImpl` class, shown in Listing 4-1, contains data about a particular product: the product name, the SKU, and the price. Products are kept in a `Catalog` that maps the SKU of the product to a product object. It implements a simple `Product` interface.

Listing 4-1. *The ProductImpl Class*

```java
package example;

import java.text.NumberFormat;

public class ProductImpl implements Product {
  private String name;
  private String sku;
  private double price;

  public ProductImpl(String sku, String name, double price) {
    this.sku = sku;
    this.name = name;
    this.price = price;
  }

  public String getName() {
    return this.name;
  }

  public String getSKU() {
    return this.sku;
  }

  public String toString() {
    NumberFormat fmt = NumberFormat.getCurrencyInstance();
    return "Price: " + fmt.format(price) + "; Name: " + this.name;
  }

  public synchronized void increasePrice(double rate) {
    this.price += this.price * rate;
  }
}
```

We also have a NullProduct class, shown in Listing 4-2, that represents an unknown product.

Listing 4-2. *The NullProduct Class*

```java
package example;

public class NullProduct implements Product {

  public void decrementInventory(int count) {
    return;
  }
```

```
  public String getName() {
    return "NULL";
  }

  public String getSKU() {
    return "NULL";
  }

  public void increasePrice(double hike) {
    return;
  }
}
```

The Catalog Class

The Catalog class, shown in Listing 4-3, can be used to display products and to look them up by SKU, so they may be placed in a shopping cart.

Listing 4-3. *The Catalog Class*

```
package example;

import java.util.ArrayList;
import java.util.HashMap;
import java.util.Iterator;
import java.util.Map;

public class Catalog {

  private final Map<String, Product> catalog;

  public Catalog() {
    this.catalog = new HashMap<String, Product>();
  }

  public Product getProductBySKU(String sku) {
    synchronized (this.catalog) {
      Product product = this.catalog.get(sku);
      if (product == null) {
        product = new NullProduct();
      }
      return product;
    }
  }

  public Iterator<Product> getProducts() {
    synchronized (this.catalog) {
```

```
      return new ArrayList<Product>(this.catalog.values()).iterator();
    }
  }

  public int getProductCount() {
    synchronized (this.catalog) {
      return this.catalog.size();
    }
  }

  public void putProduct(Product product) {
    synchronized (this.catalog) {
      this.catalog.put(product.getSKU(), product);
    }
  }
}
```

The ShoppingCartImpl Class

The ShoppingCartImpl class, shown in Listing 4-4, contains a list of products that a shopper has browsed and tentatively wants to purchase. The ShoppingCart interface is, again, very simple with no surprises.

Listing 4-4. *The ShoppingCartImpl Class*

```
package example;

import java.util.Iterator;
import java.util.LinkedList;
import java.util.List;

public class ShoppingCartImpl implements ShoppingCart {

  private List<Product> products = new LinkedList<Product>();

  public void addProduct(final Product product) {
    synchronized (products) {
      this.products.add(product);
    }
  }

  public String toString() {
    final StringBuffer buf = new StringBuffer();
    synchronized (this.products) {
      int count = 1;
      for (Iterator<Product> i = this.products.iterator(); i.hasNext();) {
        buf.append("\titem " + count + ": " + i.next() + "\n");
```

```
      }
    }
    return buf.toString();
  }

}
```

The ActiveShoppingCarts Class

The ActiveShoppingCarts class, shown in Listing 4-5, is a companion to the ShoppingCartImpl class that does some bookkeeping about active shopping carts.

Listing 4-5. *The ActiveShoppingCarts Class*

```
package example;

import java.util.LinkedList;
import java.util.List;

public class ActiveShoppingCarts {

  private final List<ShoppingCart> activeShoppingCarts =
    new LinkedList<ShoppingCart>();

  public void addShoppingCart(ShoppingCart cart) {
    synchronized (activeShoppingCarts) {
      this.activeShoppingCarts.add(cart);
    }
  }

  public List getActiveShoppingCarts() {
    synchronized (this.activeShoppingCarts) {
      List<ShoppingCart> carts =
        new LinkedList<ShoppingCart>(this.activeShoppingCarts);
      return carts;
    }
  }
}
```

The Roots Class

The Roots class, shown in Listing 4-6, for purposes of encapsulation, holds references to the roots of the clustered object graphs that are used by this application. It isn't a requirement to put the root fields in a special class, but it's convenient for this example.

Listing 4-6. *The Roots Class*

```java
package example;

import java.util.concurrent.CyclicBarrier;

public class Roots {
  private final CyclicBarrier barrier;
  private final Catalog catalog;
  private final ActiveShoppingCarts activeShoppingCarts;

  public Roots(CyclicBarrier barrier, Catalog catalog, ActiveShoppingCarts
                     activeShoppingCarts) {
    this.barrier = barrier;
    this.catalog = catalog;
    this.activeShoppingCarts = activeShoppingCarts;
  }

  public ActiveShoppingCarts getActiveShoppingCarts() {
    return activeShoppingCarts;
  }

  public CyclicBarrier getBarrier() {
    return barrier;
  }

  public Catalog getCatalog() {
    return catalog;
  }
}
```

The Main Class

The Main class, shown in Listing 4-7, illustrates how the classes in Listings 4-1 through 4-6 might be used in a multithreaded environment. It assumes two threads enter the run() method, and at various points, they use a threading construct built in to the language to coordinate with each other. This threading construct is called a CyclicBarrier—available in the util.Concurrent library in the core JDK. It is a simple class that hides the threading logic required to get any number of threads to wait for each other at the exact same point in a method before continuing. A barrier can be thought of as a gate that all threads have to meet in front of before the gate opens and all threads move through.

Listing 4-7. *The Main Class*

```java
package example;

import java.util.Iterator;
import java.util.concurrent.CyclicBarrier;
```

```java
public class Main implements Runnable {

  private final CyclicBarrier barrier;
  private final int participants;
  private int arrival = -1;
  private Catalog catalog;
  private ShoppingCartFactory shoppingCartFactory;
  private ActiveShoppingCarts activeCarts;

  public Main(final int participants, final CyclicBarrier barrier,
                  final Catalog catalog,
                  final ActiveShoppingCarts activeCarts,
                  final ShoppingCartFactory shoppingCartFactory) {
    this.barrier = barrier;
    this.participants = participants;
    this.catalog = catalog;
    this.activeCarts = activeCarts;
    this.shoppingCartFactory = shoppingCartFactory;
  }

  public void run() {
    try {
      display("Step 1: Waiting for everyone to arrive.  I'm expecting " +
                  (participants - 1) + " other thread(s)...");
      this.arrival = barrier.await();
      display("We're all here!");

      String skuToPurchase;
      display();
      display("Step 2: Set Up");
      boolean firstThread = arrival == (participants - 1);

      if (firstThread) {
        display("I'm the first thread, so I'm going to populate the catalog...");
        Product razor = new ProductImpl("123", "14 blade super razor", 12);
        catalog.putProduct(razor);

        Product shavingCream = new ProductImpl("456",
                                              "Super-smooth shaving cream",
                                              5);
        catalog.putProduct(shavingCream);

        skuToPurchase = "123";
      } else {
        skuToPurchase = "456";
      }
```

```
        // wait for all threads.
        barrier.await();

        display();
        display("Step 3: Let's do a little shopping...");
        ShoppingCart cart = shoppingCartFactory.newShoppingCart();

        Product product = catalog.getProductBySKU(skuToPurchase);
        display("I'm adding \"" + product + "\" to my cart...");
        cart.addProduct(product);
        barrier.await();

        display();
        display("Step 4: Let's look at all shopping carts in all JVMs...");
        displayShoppingCarts();

        display();
        if (firstThread) {
          display("Step 5: Let's make a 10% price increase...");
          for (Iterator<Product> i = catalog.getProducts(); i.hasNext();) {
            Product p = i.next();
            p.increasePrice(0.1d);
          }
        } else {
          display("Step 5: Let's wait for the other JVM to make a price change...");
        }
        barrier.await();

        display();
        display("Step 6: Let's look at the shopping carts with the new prices...");
        displayShoppingCarts();

      } catch (Exception e) {
        throw new RuntimeException(e);
      }
    }

    private void displayShoppingCarts() {
      StringBuffer buf = new StringBuffer();
      for (Iterator<ShoppingCart> i = activeCarts.getActiveShoppingCarts().iterator();
           i.hasNext();) {
        ShoppingCart thisCart = i.next();
        buf.append("==========================\n");
        buf.append("Shopping Cart\n");
        buf.append(thisCart);
      }
```

```
    display(buf);
  }

  private void display() {
    display("");
  }

  private void display(Object o) {
    System.err.println(o);
  }

  public static void main(String[] args) throws Exception {
    int participants = 2;
    if (args.length > 0) {
      participants = Integer.parseInt(args[0]);
    }

    Roots roots = new Roots(new CyclicBarrier(participants), new Catalog(),
                            new ActiveShoppingCarts());

    if (args.length > 1 && "run-locally".equals(args[1])) {
      // Run 'participants' number of local threads. This is the non-clustered
      // case.
      for (int i = 0; i < participants; i++) {
        new Thread(new Main(participants, roots.getBarrier(), roots.getCatalog(),
                       roots.getActiveShoppingCarts(),
            new ShoppingCartFactory(roots.getActiveShoppingCarts()))).start();
      }
    } else {
      // Run a single local thread. This is the clustered case. It is assumed
      // that main() will be called participants - 1 times in other JVMs
      new Main(participants, roots.getBarrier(), roots.getCatalog(),
                   roots.getActiveShoppingCarts(),
          new ShoppingCartFactory(roots.getActiveShoppingCarts())).run();
    }

  }

}
```

The Main class uses the ShoppingCartFactory class, which is shown in Listing 4-8.

Listing 4-8. *The ShoppingCartFactory Class*

```
package example;

public class ShoppingCartFactory {
```

```
  private final ActiveShoppingCarts activeShoppingCarts;

  public ShoppingCartFactory(final ActiveShoppingCarts activeCarts) {
    this.activeShoppingCarts = activeCarts;
  }

  public ShoppingCart newShoppingCart() {
    ShoppingCart shoppingCart = new ShoppingCartImpl();
    activeShoppingCarts.addShoppingCart(shoppingCart);
    return shoppingCart;
  }
}
```

Clustering Requirements for the Example

Out of the box, this code works fine in the context of a single JVM. Multiple threads interact with Catalog, Product, ShoppingCart, Customer, and Order objects as simple POJOs and can coordinate with each other, if need be, using standard Java library java.util.concurrent classes, namely CyclicBarrier.

If this were more than just a sample application, however, we would want to deploy it on at least two physical servers for high availability with the option to add additional servers for scalability as usage increases over time. Adding servers causes a number of requirements to emerge that don't exist in the single JVM deployment scenario:

- All active shopping carts should be available in all JVMs, so a browsing customer's requests can be sent to any of the servers without losing the items in that customer's shopping cart.

- A view on all the active carts will require access to all active carts in every JVM.

- Thread interaction expressed in the example code by using CyclicBarrier must be extended to threads in multiple JVMs.

If the Catalog data becomes large enough, it might not fit comfortably in RAM. It could be retrieved as needed from the product database, but the database will be a bottleneck. If caching is used to alleviate the database bottleneck, each JVM will need access to that cache. To avoid critical spikes in database usage, the cache should be loaded once from the database and shared among the JVMs rather than loaded separately by each JVM.

All of the requirements introduced by deploying the application in a cluster can be met by using Terracotta with a small amount of configuration and no code changes. Let's take a quick look at what the configuration looks like to make this happen.

Configuration for the Example

The first configuration step is to determine which objects in the application should be shared by the cluster. These shared object graphs are specified by declaring specific variables to be roots. Every object reachable by reference from a root object becomes a shared object available to all JVMs, clusterwide. In our example so far, we have three roots, all of them declared in the Roots class. This is specified in the Terracotta configuration like so (again using the config-examples/tc-config-pojo.xml file as a base):

```
<roots>
  <root>
    <field-name>example.Roots.barrier</field-name>
  </root>
  <root>
    <field-name>example.Roots.catalog</field-name>
  </root>
  <root>
    <field-name>example.Roots.activeShoppingCarts</field-name>
  </root>
</roots>
```

The next configuration step is to determine which classes should have their bytecode instrumented at load time. The class of any object that is to become part of a shared object graph must have its bytecode instrumented by Terracotta when the class is loaded. This instrumentation process is how the transparent clustering capabilities of Terracotta are injected into the application. For this example, all we have to do is include everything in the example.* package. The CyclicBarrier class is automatically included by Terracotta because it is part of a core set of Java library classes that are required to be instrumented. The <instrumented-classes> configuration section looks like this:

```
<instrumented-classes>
  <include>
    <!--include all classes in the example package for bytecode instrumentation-->
    <class-expression>example..*</class-expression>
  </include>
</instrumented-classes>
```

The final configuration step is to determine which methods should have cluster-aware concurrency semantics injected into them. For the purposes of this example, we will use a regular expression that encompasses all methods in all included classes for automatic locking:

```
<locks>
  <autolock>
    <method-expression>void *..*(..)</method-expression>
    <lock-level>write</lock-level>
  </autolock>
</locks>
```

This configuration will instruct Terracotta to find all synchronized methods and blocks and all calls to wait() and notify() in the methods of every class that is instrumented and augment them to have a clusterwide meaning.

Running the Example

Once the configuration is complete, running the application in a cluster can be done from the command line or from the Eclipse plug-in. If you are not using Eclipse, you must compile the project first, like so (assuming your current working directory is the top-level project directory):

```
%> javac -d classes src/example/*.java
```

Once the project is compiled, start the Terracotta server. To start the server from the command line, use the start-tc-server script. You can specify the configuration file explicitly using the -f flag. If you don't specify the location of the configuration file, the server will look for a file called tc-config.xml in the current working directory.

The command line to start the server with an explicit path to the Terracotta configuration file looks something like this:

```
%> /usr/local/terracotta/bin/start-tc-server.sh -f /path/to/tc-config.xml
```

To start the server with an implicit path to the Terracotta configuration file, change directories to the top-level directory of the example project. The top-level project directory contains the tc-config.xml file. You may then execute the following command:

```
%> /usr/local/terracotta/bin/start-tc-server.sh
```

In Eclipse, the server can be started from the Terracotta menu, using the Start Terracotta Server command. Once the server is started, the instances of your application can be started. For this example, we must run the Main class in two JVMs, so you will need to invoke Java twice. Depending on your operating system and Terracotta installation directory, your command line will look something like this (again, assuming that you run the command from the top-level project directory):

```
%> java -Xbootclasspath/p:/usr/local/terracotta/bin/../lib/dso-boot/dso-boot-
hotspot_osx_150_13.jar  -Dtc.install-root=/usr/local/terracotta/bin/..
-Dtc.config=./tc-config.xml -cp classes example.Main
```

To determine the Terracotta-specific JVM arguments, you can use the output of the dso-env script. Alternatively, you can invoke Java using the dso-java script instead of the java command. The dso-java script will supply the proper JVM arguments and invoke the java command for you:

```
%> /usr/local/terracotta/bin/dso-java.sh -cp classes example.Main
```

In Eclipse, you can start the Main program as a Terracotta-enabled application as shown in Figure 4-1.

Figure 4-1. *Running a Terracotta-enabled application in Eclipse*

When the first application instance is started, you should see something like this in the output console:

```
2007-01-18 15:49:42,204 INFO - Terracotta, version 2.6 as of 20080415-071248.
2007-01-18 15:49:42,811 INFO - Configuration loaded from the file at
'/Users/orion/Documents/workspace/TerracottaExample/tc-config.xml'.
2007-01-18 15:49:42,837 INFO - Log file:
'/Users/orion/Documents/workspace/TerracottaExample/terracotta/client-
logs/terracotta-client.log'.
Waiting for everyone to arrive.  I'm expecting 1 other thread(s)...
```

This indicates that the main thread in the first instance is blocking at `barrier.await()`. The barrier field is an instance of `java.util.concurrent.CyclicBarrier`. It is designed to coordinate the arrival of a specified number of threads at a certain point such that no thread is allowed to proceed until all expected threads have arrived. Every thread that calls the method `java.util.concurrent.CyclicBarrier.await()` will block until the specified number of threads has arrived at the barrier point. Once the expected number of threads has called `await()`, all the threads blocking on `await()` will be allowed to proceed through the `await()` method. After the expected number of threads passes through the `await()` barrier, the barrier is reset so that subsequent calls to `await()` will be blocked until the expected number of threads calls `await()` again. This is why it's called a cyclic barrier: once the barrier is released, it recycles back to its initial state.

■**Note** An in-depth discussion of inter-JVM thread coordination techniques using both basic concurrency primitives and the `java.util.concurrent` library follows in Chapter 10.

Since the barrier is a shared object, the main thread will be blocked until another thread in either this JVM or another JVM in this Terracotta cluster calls `barrier.await()`. Then, both threads will be allowed to proceed. This will happen if we start up another application instance. Once the second application instance is started, you should see something like the following output in the consoles (you might see slightly different output depending on the order in which the threads reach the various barrier points):

```
Step 1: Waiting for everyone to arrive.  I'm expecting 1 other thread(s)...
We're all here!

Step 2: Set Up
I'm the first thread, so I'm going to populate the catalog...

Step 3: Let's do a little shopping...
I'm adding "Price: $12.00; Name: 14 blade super razor" to my cart...
```

```
Step 4: Let's look at all shopping carts in all JVMs...
============================
Shopping Cart
   item 1: Price: $12.00; Name: 14 blade super razor
============================
Shopping Cart
   item 1: Price: $5.00; Name: Super-smooth shaving cream


Step 5: Let's make a 10% price increase...

Step 6: Let's look at the shopping carts with the new prices...
============================
Shopping Cart
   item 1: Price: $13.20; Name: 14 blade super razor
============================
Shopping Cart
   item 1: Price: $5.50; Name: Super-smooth shaving cream
```

In the console output of the other application instance, you should see something like
this:

```
Step 1: Waiting for everyone to arrive.  I'm expecting 1 other thread(s)...
We're all here!

Step 2: Set Up

Step 3: Let's do a little shopping...
I'm adding "Price: $5.00; Name: Super-smooth shaving cream" to my cart...

Step 4: Let's look at all shopping carts in all JVMs...
============================
Shopping Cart
   item 1: Price: $12.00; Name: 14 blade super razor
============================
Shopping Cart
   item 1: Price: $5.00; Name: Super-smooth shaving cream


Step 5: Let's wait for the other JVM to make a price change...

Step 6: Let's look at the shopping carts with the new prices...
============================
Shopping Cart
   item 1: Price: $13.20; Name: 14 blade super razor
============================
```

```
Shopping Cart
   item 1: Price: $5.50; Name: Super-smooth shaving cream
```

What Just Happened

In step 1, the two threads in the different application instances were waiting for each other to start and arrive at the same rendezvous point. In step 2, the first thread created Product objects and added them to the clustered Catalog. In step 3, each thread pulled a Product object out of the clustered Catalog by SKU—notice that the products added by the first thread in one JVM are automatically available in the Catalog in the other JVM. In step 4, both threads iterate over all of the active shopping carts in all JVMs and print the contents. In step 5, the first thread made a ten percent price increase by iterating over all of the Product objects in the Catalog while the second thread blocks. In step 6, both threads display all of the active shopping carts—notice that the price increase was applied in one thread by manipulating the Catalog, and the new prices were automatically reflected in all of the ShoppingCart objects in both JVMs.

All of the clustered objects can be viewed in real time in the Terracotta administration console. Each root can be viewed as a tree of primitives and references. Figure 4-2 is a view of the Catalog.

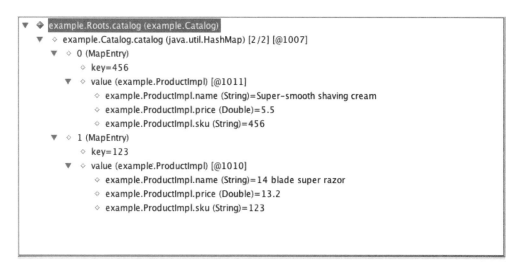

Figure 4-2. *A runtime view of a Product object in the Terracotta administration console*

You can see the Product objects inside the catalog HashMap. In Figure 4-3, you can see those same Product objects referenced by the ShoppingCart objects as well.

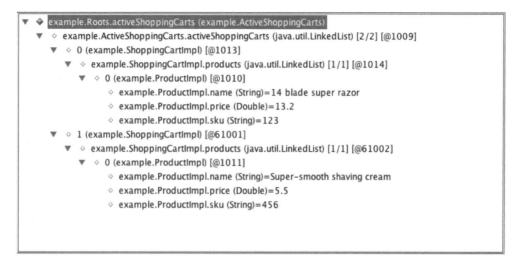

Figure 4-3. *A runtime view of the ActiveShoppingCarts object graph in the Terracotta administration console*

This view shows the `Product` objects referenced by the `LinkedList` inside the `ShoppingCart`.

If you run the example a second time, you will see the effect of a durable heap. The example is designed to run in pairs of executions; by default, the `CyclicBarrier` defined in the `Roots` class is set to block at `await()` until two threads arrive. After the second thread arrives, the `CyclicBarrier` is reset so that the example can be run with two new invocations of `Main.main()`. When you run the example a second time with a new pair of JVM invocations, you will notice that the prices of the items maintain the ten percent price increase from the last invocation.

What the Example Shows

This example exercises many of the strengths and features of Terracotta, the first being basic object sharing. By declaring shared roots in the `Roots` class, Terracotta automatically makes all objects referenceable from those root objects shared objects available to every connected JVM.

The shared `Catalog` object is essentially a shared `Map` of SKUs mapped to `Product` objects. `Product` objects can be added and removed from the `Catalog` simply by adding or removing them from the shared `Map`. The `ActiveShoppingCarts` object is essentially a shared `List` of `ShoppingCart` objects that provides a global view of all currently active shopping carts. Bookkeeping active shopping carts is as simple as modifying the list, and viewing the active shopping carts is as simple as iterating over the list. The power of Terracotta here comes from being able to express business policy in simple Java, while at the same time, that expression of business policy is available clusterwide and persistent.

In step 5, a ten percent price increase was placed into effect across all products simply by iterating over all of the `Product` objects and updating their prices. That change is automatically visible to any JVM that has a reference to a `Product` object. This highlights two essential characteristics of Terracotta: object identity and fine-grained change management.

■**Caution** This example is meant to illustrate the transparency and simplicity of Terracotta clustering. It is not performance-optimized. Iterating over a clustered collection will force all clustered objects into a single thread in one JVM and, thus, does not perform well.

In an application running on a single JVM, coding a business rule like this in such a way is rather obvious. All references to a `Product` object point to the same object on the heap (the heap provides object identity); any modifications to that object are trivially made visible to every thread with a reference to that object. But, because the JVMs in a multitier, scaled-out architecture don't share the same heap, object identity is broken, making changes to business data by simple reference traversal impossible.

Typically, to make a price change visible across multiple machines in an enterprise Java application, you would have to send messages around the cluster or flush a database cache and force a reload or perform some similar behavior. And, at each JVM, you would have to make sure that all of the appropriate `Product` objects were updated accordingly.

Without Terracotta, most enterprise Java frameworks force on you the notion of a management context from which objects are checked in and out. The manager gives application threads copies of business entities so that multiple threads can work separately from each other and any exceptions at runtime cannot corrupt the manager's internal copy of objects and data. Basically, heap can't be trusted to be consistent across all instances of the application, so copies and managers are used instead. Enterprise software developers are so used to being abused by this problem that they don't think twice about being forced to discard nice, clear object-oriented code in favor of a complex data externalization framework to keep all of the heaps in sync. When you can't trust your objects, you can't write simple code.

With Terracotta, you get all of that nice, clean object-oriented code back, because Terracotta handles the data externalization and synchronization transparently. Terracotta effectively provides a shared heap that all JVMs can trust. A perusal of the example code will show that any given `Product` object may be referenced in a number of different places: in the `Catalog` map as well as in users' `ShoppingCart` objects. As you have seen from the price increase operation, an update made to a `Product` object by traversing any of these references is automatically visible across the entire cluster, just as it was made visible to all threads in the same JVM. This is possible precisely because object identity is preserved.

Because object identity is preserved across JVMs, it's safe again to make changes to business data by simple reference traversal in an enterprise Java application, while achieving the availability and scalability characteristics provided by a multi-JVM scale-out architecture.

Another important and related feature of Terracotta highlighted by the price increase example is fine-grained change management. On a trusted heap, making a change to a product object is as simple as updating the appropriate field. Unfortunately, the externalization frameworks imposed by traditional enterprise Java programming usually rely on some form of whole-object serialization or, in the worst case, whole-object-graph serialization, replication, and synchronization. This means that a change to a single field of an object usually requires much more than just that field to be moved around the network and patched on each JVM.

Terracotta, on the other hand, can make the same surgical field modification that normally happens in Java on a single JVM's heap happen in a shared heap without resorting to object or whole-graph serialization. And, because the Terracotta server knows which JVMs have which portions of the shared heap, it can efficiently send only the necessary changes tailored for each JVM. Terracotta's fine-grained field-level change management is the most efficient way to keep the shared heap synchronized.

Summary

We've covered a lot of ground in this chapter. First, we introduced the major concepts that make Terracotta work. Then, we showed how those concepts are brought to bear in actual code. By now, the power of Terracotta that you glimpsed in `HelloClusteredWorld` should be taking shape in your mind. What it means to be able to write plain Java that works across JVMs should be getting clearer.

Remember that how you use Terracotta, like Java itself, is limited only by your imagination. Terracotta was developed with the problems of scalability and high availability in mind, and we will introduce you to many of the solutions to these problems that Terracotta provides. But in all likelihood, many uses exist for a transparent and durable virtual JVM heap that nobody has thought of yet.

Now that you are armed with the conceptual and practical understanding of what Terracotta is and how it works, the following chapters will explore how Terracotta can be used in a number of specific problem domains.

CHAPTER 5

▪▪▪

Caching

A cache provides temporary storage of data that can be accessed faster than it can be computed or obtained from a more authoritative source. In the first case, values that are expensive to compute are remembered to avoid performing the computation repeatedly. In the second case, values are remembered to avoid obtaining them from a much slower or more expensive source such as a database, a remote source, or a file system.

In this chapter, we will examine the many ways caching can help and hurt your application. We will then examine how Terracotta can address some of the common problems with caching and how to extend the benefits of caching to distributed systems. Finally, we will look at examples of caching using basic Java data structures and also with sophisticated open source caching libraries like Ehcache.

The Pain of Caching

While caching is an invaluable tool for reducing latency or relieving load from an overburdened system of record, it does not provide its benefits without trade-offs, as anyone who has ever managed a cache can attest. The trade-offs are generally various flavors of the following:

- *Space for time*: The cached data must be stored in an accessible location (e.g., RAM or local disk) for some period of time. The cost of space in that accessible location must be balanced against the cost of going to the source for the result.

- *Freshness*: Since the cache is not the authoritative source of the data, its usefulness is relative to how fresh the data is, how important that freshness is, and how hard it is to keep the cache fresh enough.

- *Complexity*: Managing the trade-offs of space and freshness introduces a degree of complexity that can quickly become unbearable.

Let's take a moment to walk through some of the most common ways that cache management can make the life of a cache maintainer painful.

The Pain of Large Data Sets

If the important part of your data set (the part that you use often enough to warrant caching) fits into available RAM and it changes slowly enough so that freshness is not an issue, caching can be as simple as storing computed results in a map by some unique identifier, occasionally invalidating cache entries as they grow stale. However, caches have a habit of outgrowing the boundaries of available RAM. When that happens, you have a few choices:

- Buy more RAM. This works up to a point, but there's a hard limit on how much RAM you can install or is addressable by your operating system. In a JVM, very large heaps can also present significant garbage collection tuning challenges. Suffice it to say that buying more RAM isn't always the best or even a viable option.

- Purge less important cache entries even though they are still valid to make room for the more important entries. This can reduce the effectiveness of your cache to the point of making the cache useless. If the miss rate is high enough, your cache may end up thrashing—continually purging and reloading entries—so that the overhead of maintaining the cache actually makes things worse.

- Spill the cache to disk or a networked cache server. This is more sophisticated, but your cache implementation must support it. If you require this sophisticated functionality of your cache and you are using a homegrown implementation that started out life as a simple map, it's probably time to swap it for an existing cache implementation that does this kind of thing already. Unless you are in the business of writing a cache implementation, you shouldn't extend your homegrown cache to provide these more sophisticated features, or you will end up in the business of writing and, worse, *maintaining* a cache implementation whether you like it or not.

The Pain of Staleness

Keeping a cache up to date is another common problem of cache maintenance. If you're lucky, you'll be caching data that doesn't change much. If not, you have to deal with keeping the cache entries fresh enough. "Fresh enough" is highly data dependent. Sometimes, you can get away with having some stale entries as long as they get updated eventually. In that case, you might be able to get away with an algorithm-based invalidation policy.

Often, though, the cached data *must* agree with the system of record at all times. This is common for financial and transaction data. The fresher the cache must be, the more constraints exist on the implementation. Maintaining both freshness and a hit rate high enough to be worth using a cache at all may require extreme measures. How a cache is kept fresh is ultimately an architectural and business decision.

The Pain of Duplication

The many pains of caching become even worse if the same data source is cached in multiple locations, as is common in a scaled-out deployment where many instances of the same application all keep their own copies of the same cached data. As each new instance of the cache comes online, it must query the system of record to populate the cache with entries it doesn't have yet. As such, the protection provided by caching to the system of record is the reciprocal of the number of copies of the cache. Terracotta calls this the $1/n$ effect (pronounced "one-over-n"), where the effectiveness of a cache at protecting a precious data source is one over the number of copies of the cache.

Figure 5-1 demonstrates the $1/n$ effect: if there are n application servers, each application server must load the same data as it is requested, which causes *n–1* unnecessary cache loads.

Ultimately, this means that the cache efficiency can be no more than $1/n$ of its possible efficiency.

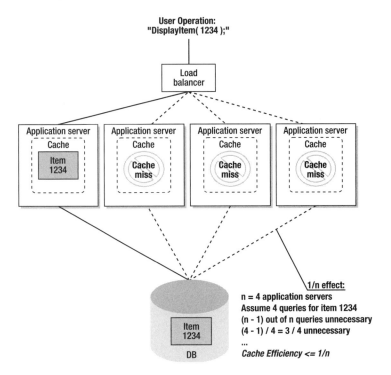

Figure 5-1. *The 1/n effect*

Keeping many copies of the same cached data up to date presents a similar problem, especially if, for example, the cache deployment uses network messages to send updates or invalidation messages. The number of update or invalidation messages is a multiple of the number of copies of the cache. As the number of instances of a scale-out deployment grows, the overhead of processing these cache messages can overwhelm the connecting network and the infrastructure used to send such messages.

Last but not least, operating many caches can lead to an administrative and tuning nightmare as the complexity of managing the state, freshness, and size of many caches mounts.

How Terracotta Can Help

The Terracotta virtual heap can help resolve the complexity and reduce the cost of caching along every painful dimension we have so far discussed. When a cache lives on the virtual heap, it is simultaneously available to every instance of the cache connected to the Terracotta cluster. This minimizes the $1/n$ effect, because each cache entry needs to be loaded only once for the entire cluster, not once per instance of the cache. And, because the Terracotta virtual heap is persistent, it survives application server restarts, avoiding the hit to the system of record such a restart would normally engender.

This is shown in Figure 5-2, where a load of the cache in the first application server will place the data in the Terracotta server. Subsequent reads in the other application servers of the same data causes the data to be paged in transparently from the Terracotta server, and the database does not need to be accessed.

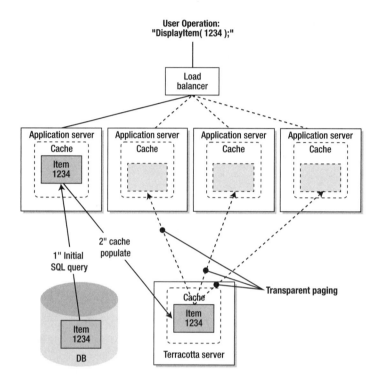

Figure 5-2. *Terracotta transparently pages Item1234 into cache only when the load balancer sends traffic to other application server instances.*

Similarly, the virtual heap removes the complexity of keeping a cache up to date across many instances of the cache. A single update to the cache in one server is automatically visible to every instance of the cache. Because such changes are ACID (see note), you can rely on the cache being up to date everywhere, even if your data is very sensitive data and *must* be accurate. And, because changes to the Terracotta virtual heap are already optimized to send only fine-grained changes to only the nodes that have the changed data resident in memory, you avoid sending the flurry of update messages that would otherwise occur.

■**Note** "ACID" is an acronym used to describe properties of a transaction; it stands for atomicity, consistency, isolation, and durability. Atomicity means that a transaction is either committed or rolled back, never partially committed. Consistency means that the integrity of the data store is maintained as invariant before, during, and after the transaction. Isolation means that one transaction in progress does not see the in-progress state of another transaction. Durability means that once a transactional commit has been acknowledged, it is saved and cannot be lost. In reality, some of these properties may be relaxed at the user's discretion to improve performance. For example, databases often allow you to choose your level of transaction isolation to improve concurrency and performance.

The problem of very large data sets is solved by Terracotta's built-in memory management capabilities, where the hottest data is kept in local heap but cooler cache entries are pushed and pulled automatically to and from the Terracotta server. This means that the entire cache can fit in the virtual heap, radically increasing the cache's effectiveness on large data sets, since you don't have to prematurely purge cache entries. Because the virtual heap is disk backed, your cache can grow to the size of available disk on the Terracotta server.

To see these pain-mitigating features in action, let's look at some real-world examples of caches and their Terracotta-enabled counterparts.

A Simple Example of Caching

A basic cache can be built just using a Map in Java. In this example, we use a simple HashMap to cache information about a user. Listing 5-1 shows the use of a Map as a cache of users (represented by a String) by identifier (represented by an Integer).

Listing 5-1. *Simple Map Example*

```java
package org.terracotta.book.caching.map;

import java.util.HashMap;
import java.util.Map;

public class UserCacheExample {
  private Map<Integer, String> userCache = new HashMap<Integer, String>();

  public String findUser(Integer id) {
    String user = cacheGet(id);
    if (user == null) {
      user = fetch(id);
      cachePut(id, user);
      System.out.println("\t- MISS");
    } else {
      System.out.println("\t- HIT");
```

```
    }
    return user;
  }

  private String cacheGet(Integer id) {
    synchronized (userCache) {
      return userCache.get(id);
    }
  }

  private void cachePut(Integer id, String user) {
    synchronized (userCache) {
      userCache.put(id, user);
    }
  }

  private String fetch(Integer id) {
    switch (id.intValue()) {
      case 0: return "Ari Zilka";
      case 1: return "Alex Miller";
      case 2: return "Geert Bevin";
      case 3: return "Taylor Gautier";
      case 4: return "Jonas Boner";
      default:
        throw new RuntimeException("Unknown id: " + id.intValue());
    }
  }

  public static void main(String arg[]) throws InterruptedException {
    UserCacheExample userCache = new UserCacheExample();
    for (int i = 0; i < 10; i++) {
      helpFind(i % 5, userCache);
    }
  }

  public static void helpFind(int id, UserCacheExample userCache) {
    System.out.print("Find " + id);
    userCache.findUser(id);
  }
}
```

In this program, the userCache attribute is a HashMap serving as a cache of users. The findUser() method takes a user identifier and looks up the name in the cache. If the user is not found, we must look up the real object (which we are mocking out with the fetchUser() method) and use it to populate the cache. We return the user that we found either in the cache or from the fetch and print to the console whether this find operation was a hit or a miss.

Since the Map in this program is not synchronized, we must protect access to the Map by synchronizing on the same Map instance when reading or writing to the cache.

Running this program will loop through all the user identifiers twice. On the first call to each, there will be a cache miss, and the cache will be populated. On the second time through the identifiers, all requests will be a hit as the cache is now fully populated. The output follows:

```
Find 0 - MISS
Find 1 - MISS
Find 2 - MISS
Find 3 - MISS
Find 4 - MISS
Find 0 - HIT
Find 1 - HIT
Find 2 - HIT
Find 3 - HIT
Find 4 - HIT
```

Distributed Caching

Distributed caching addresses the question of what we do when we run our application and share data across many nodes in a cluster. Further, suppose that we are not just storing these User objects but occasionally modifying them. In this scenario, when a particular User object is modified, the modified object needs to be replicated across the cluster. Depending on the nature of the data, it may be very important that the same User object is not modified at the same time in a different node.

There are a number of approaches taken to address these issues of replication and coherency. Often, replication is performed by notifying other nodes in the cluster that data in the cache has changed. This notification can happen over TCP, multicast, RMI, JMS, or other means. Each local cache must then listen for and apply remote changes by invalidating the local cache and/or reloading the value. A fully coherent cache is typically built using transactions and commit protocols.

Looking at our code example and considering these issues, it should be clear that no simple modification will allow us to turn our Map into a distributed Map. The changes required would be extensive, invasive, and substantially more complex than the existing code.

Transparent Distributed Caching

Fortunately, Terracotta provides transparent distributed shared objects and makes turning this example into a distributed cache a simple exercise. Because Terracotta is transparent (to the application), the code itself does not need to be modified. Instead, we create a Terracotta configuration file that specifies how the objects in this application should be clustered and locked. Then, when the application is run, the data can be accessed in every node of the cluster with no additional changes. Updates to the data on one node are automatically (and safely) made available on every node.

The complete configuration file is in Listing 5-2. We will examine each piece of the configuration in turn. A complete reference to the Terracotta configuration file may be found online at http://www.terracotta.org/confluence/display/docs1/Configuration+Guide+and+Reference.

Listing 5-2. *CacheUserExample Distributed Configuration*

```xml
<?xml version="1.0" encoding="UTF-8"?>
<con:tc-config xmlns:con="http://www.terracotta.org/config">
  <servers>
    <server host="%i" name="localhost">
      <dso-port>9510</dso-port>
      <jmx-port>9520</jmx-port>
      <data>terracotta/server-data</data>
      <logs>terracotta/server-logs</logs>
    </server>
  </servers>
  <clients>
    <logs>terracotta/client-logs</logs>
  </clients>
  <application>
    <dso>
      <instrumented-classes>
        <include>
          <class-expression>org.terracotta.book.caching.map.UserCacheExample
          </class-expression>
        </include>
      </instrumented-classes>
      <roots>
        <root>
          <field-name>org.terracotta.book.caching.map.UserCacheExample.userCache
          </field-name>
        </root>
      </roots>
      <locks>
        <autolock>
          <method-expression>
* org.terracotta.book.caching.map.UserCacheExample.cacheGet(..)
          </method-expression>
          <lock-level>read</lock-level>
        </autolock>
        <autolock>
          <method-expression>
* org.terracotta.book.caching.map.UserCacheExample.cachePut(..)
          </method-expression>
          <lock-level>write</lock-level>
        </autolock>
      </locks>
    </dso>
  </application>
</con:tc-config>
```

First, the `<servers>` and `<clients>` blocks will specify the ports and log files to use for the Terracotta server and clients.

Next, we must specify which classes need to be instrumented in our application. Instrumented classes will include any classes that are shared and any classes that hold clustered root objects. In our example, we simply instrument our single class.

Next, we specify the root objects that will be clustered. Any object attached to an object graph connected to the root will be clustered (several techniques exist for exclusion however). In our case, the `Map` field `userCache` will be clustered, so we declare it as a root. Once we declare the `userCache` as a root, all objects referred to by the `userCache` will become clustered objects.

Finally, we must specify the locking constraints around our clustered root. In our case, we want to automatically lock the two methods that access the cache. We will lock the `cacheGet()` method with a read lock (so multiple threads in the cluster can read simultaneously) and the `cachePut()` method with a write lock as it modifies the `Map`.

We can then start the Terracotta server using `start-tc-server.sh` and run the application again as a Terracotta Client application using `dso-java.sh`:

```
dso-java.sh –Dtc.config=tc-config.xml \
org.terracotta.book.caching.map.UserCacheExample
```

When we do this, we will see identical output to the simple caching example. But if we run it again, we'll see something different, which follows:

```
Find 0 - HIT
Find 1 - HIT
Find 2 - HIT
Find 3 - HIT
Find 4 - HIT
Find 0 - HIT
Find 1 - HIT
Find 2 - HIT
Find 3 - HIT
Find 4 - HIT
```

On the second run, we see that every user lookup is a cache hit. This happens because the cache is now shared and persistent due to the configuration we added. When the second client starts up, it has the ability to transparently load the cache objects from the Terracotta shared virtual heap. These objects are loaded on demand, and thus expensive calls to compute or retrieve the cache values are unnecessary.

You've seen in this example that it is quite easy to construct a single virtual machine application using a `Map` as a cache and then cluster or distribute that application using Terracotta by applying some external configuration. In many applications, this basic technique is sufficient to build distributed shared data structures. In others, you'll want a cache with more sophisticated behavior, cache eviction policies, and so on, and in that case, you can use popular open source cache frameworks with Terracotta integrated.

Caching with Maps

The JDK provides a range of map implementations that you can choose from when creating your application. This section will explore the available choices and the various trade-offs in both Java and Terracotta.

Unsorted Maps

In the JDK, your unsorted `Map` implementations include `Hashtable`, `HashMap`, `LinkedHashMap`, and `ConcurrentHashMap`.

- `Hashtable` is a legacy data structure, provided in the initial JDK and predating the modern Java Collections API. It should be considered a deprecated part of the JDK and is not recommended for use.

- `HashMap` is the most commonly used `Map` implementation. It is unsynchronized, so it should be not be used in concurrent (or distributed) code without external synchronization. `HashMap` stores its values in a single large table. When the internal table is updated, it must be locked for all users. This global locking can often become a performance bottleneck. Terracotta provides excellent support for `HashMap` but will face the same bottleneck in locking across the cluster on updates.

- `ConcurrentHashMap` is generally the best choice when sharing maps with Terracotta. The `ConcurrentHashMap` API is designed for concurrent use. The implementation uses internal locking, so calls to the map do not need external synchronization for safety. Internally, data is split across many tables (also called segments), and each segment can be locked individually. This generally yields far better performance under concurrent use than a normal `HashMap`, both in everyday Java and with Terracotta.

- `LinkedHashMap` is basically a `HashMap`, but one with an additional doubly linked list running through the entries. The linked list is usually used to track insertion order, although it can also be used to track usage of entries in the `Map`. This additional capability makes it easy to turn `LinkedHashMap` into a cache with LRU (least recently used) cache eviction semantics. At the time of this writing, `LinkedHashMap` is not supported by Terracotta.

The `Collections.synchronizedMap()` method can be used to wrap a synchronized thread-safe wrapper around an unsynchronized `Map` such as `HashMap` or `LinkedHashMap`. By default, Terracotta does not provide automatic locking on synchronized `Map` objects returned from this method, which gives you more freedom in distributed lock granularity. You can add locking support to the synchronized wrapper collections and legacy collections like `Hashtable` and `Vector` by using the autolocked collections Terracotta Integration Module, which is discussed later in this chapter.

Sorted Maps

The JDK also provides an interface for sorted maps (`SortedMap`), which is implemented by `TreeMap`. Terracotta fully supports this implementation (which is backed by a tree data structure), but unsorted `Map` will `get()` and `put()` faster than a `TreeMap`. This is consistent with the relative performance of `get()` and `put()` for `TreeMap` and `Map` in regular Java. Performance is slower because the data is stored in a tree that must be balanced on put and remove actions and traversed on a get action.

The `Collections.synchronizedSortedMap()` method can be used to wrap a synchronized thread-safe wrapper around an unsynchronized `SortedMap` like `TreeMap`. By default, Terracotta does not provide automatic locking on synchronized `Map` instances returned from this method, which gives you more freedom in distributed lock granularity. Again, you can add locking support by using the autolocked collections Terracotta Integration Module.

`ConcurrentSkipListMap` was added in Java 6 and provides a high-performance concurrent sorted `Map` implementation. However, it is implemented using lock-free algorithms, and these algorithms are much more difficult to efficiently port to distributed implementations. Terracotta does not yet support `ConcurrentSkipListMap`.

Autolocked Collections

When using shared collections with Terracotta, one of the keys to getting excellent performance is to optimize locking. Terracotta provides multiple lock levels, and in cases where only a read lock is required, using distributed read locks greatly improves performance.

By default, synchronized collections do not have Terracotta locking applied to them so that your application is free to decide the best way to lock access to a synchronized collection.

If you wish to provide locking at the same granularity as a normal, synchronized collection, Terracotta provides a Terracotta Integration Module (TIM) for autolocked collections that will do this.

The available autolocked collections follow:

- `tim-vector`: Automatically locks `java.util.Vector`

- `tim-hashtable`: Automatically locks `java.util.Hashtable`

- `tim-synchronizedcollection`: Automatically locks collections returned from `java.util.Collections.synchronizedCollection()`

- `tim-synchronizedmap`: Automatically locks collections returned from `java.util.Collections.synchronizedMap()`

- `tim-synchronizedset`: Automatically locks collections returned from `java.util.Collections.synchronizedSet()`

- `tim-synchronizedsortedmap`: Automatically locks collections returned from `java.util.Collections.synchronizedSortedMap()`

- `tim-synchronizedsortedset`: Automatically locks collections returned from `java.util.Collections.synchronizedSortedSet()`

Each of these autolocked collection modules specifies read and write locking appropriately on the synchronized collection. For example, getting an item from an autolocked synchronized `Map` will obtain a clustered read lock, whereas a `put()` will obtain a clustered write lock. This will yield better performance by requiring less exclusive locks for reads, allowing multiple concurrent readers in the cluster.

Downloading and Installing the Autolocked Collections TIM

To use the autolocked Collections TIM, you will first need to download and install it from the Terracotta Forge at `http://forge.terracotta.org`.

Note There are a variety of ways to install modules, depending on whether you want to install from source or binary and whether you want to load the module into your Terracotta installation or your own local repository. For this example, we'll assume you're going to download in the binary form and install it in your Terracotta installation. For more information, see the Terracotta Forge web site or Chapter 9.

To download the binary distribution for `tim-collections`, version 2.0.1, issue this command:

```
$ curl -o tim-collections-2.0.1-bin.zip \
http://forge.terracotta.org/\
projects/tim-collections/downloads/tim-collections-2.0.1-bin.zip
```

This command will download a zip file containing several JARs, one per collection type. To unzip and install these JARs to your Terracotta installation use these commands:

```
$ unzip tim-collections-2.0.1-bin.zip
$ cd tim-collections-2.0.1
$ cp *.jar ${TC_INSTALL_DIR}/modules
```

This completes the installation of the autolocked collections TIM. They can now be used separately or together in any Terracotta installation.

Using Autolocked Collections

To install the autolocked collections TIM in your own project, add it to the modules section as shown in Listing 5-3.

Listing 5-3. *Loading Synchronized Collections in the Terracotta Configuration*

```
<tc:tc-config xmlns:tc="http://www.terracotta.org/config">
  <clients>
    <modules>
      <module name="tim-synchronizedcollection" version="2.0.1" />
    </modules>
  </clients>
</tc:tc-config>
```

While autolocked collections are an easy way to get proper clustered locking for access to a synchronized collection, you may wish to provide your own locking at the application level so that composite operations such as making multiple related calls to get() against a collection (synchronized or not) can be locked appropriately. In that case, you should not use the autolocked collection modules and should instead specify the locking explicitly in your Terracotta configuration.

Bulk Loading a Map

One special case for using shared maps is bulk loading, where a large number of items need to be added to a map at once, for instance, when priming a cache. Normally, each put() method to a Map would define an independent transaction, but generally, it is desirable to use a much wider transaction scope when performing a bulk load. This makes better use of bandwidth and minimizes locking.

To handle a scenario like this, it is advisable to wrap the Map implementation in your own class and provide locking on that class at a coarser granularity. Generally, you will find that using very fine-granularity loading (calling put() for every cache item) will yield poor performance due to the large number of transactions. At the other end of the scale, doing a single synchronized block around a single putAll() call is likely to give much better performance at the risk of causing out of memory errors from having one very large transaction. Generally, the optimal performance is seen when batching put() calls, giving a combination of coarser granularity with memory safety.

■**Tip** Terracotta can batch and change the order of transactions without violating the expected behavior of the JVM. As a result, some applications will find that Terracotta is fast at managing fine-grained updates and object changes without manually batching put() calls.

Another interesting aspect to consider is concurrency. Using putAll() or batching put() calls will reduce overall I/O and improve performance but will also reduce concurrency by using a coarser-grained lock scope. Understanding the best trade-off point will depend on your application and should be determined based on experimentation.

Listing 5-4 shows a Cache class that wraps a Map and provides a method to bulk load in batches (batch size can be specified). Note the synchronized block in this method that creates a lock just around each batch of put operations. By varying the batch size, you can vary the size and number of transactions that occur.

Listing 5-4. *Loading a Map in Batches*

```
package org.terracotta.book.caching.batch;

import java.util.ArrayList;
import java.util.HashMap;
import java.util.List;
import java.util.Map;

public class Cache<K, V> {
```

```
private final Map<K, V> data = new HashMap<K, V>();

// ... other methods like get and put

public void putAllBatched(Map<K, V> entries, int batchSize) {
  List<Map.Entry<K, V>> entryList = new ArrayList<Map.Entry<K, V>>(
            entries.entrySet());
  int itemCount = entries.size();
  int batchStart = 0; // first index of current batch
  while (batchStart < itemCount) {
    int batchEnd = batchStart + batchSize;
    if (batchEnd > itemCount) {
      batchEnd = itemCount;
    }

    synchronized (this) {
      for (int i = batchStart; i < batchEnd; i++) {
        Map.Entry<K, V> entry = entryList.get(i);
        data.put(entry.getKey(), entry.getValue());
      }
    }

    batchStart = batchEnd;
  }
}
}
```

We can build a driver program for testing this batched load, as shown in Listing 5-5. This program takes two arguments: the number of items to load into the cache and the number of repetitions to run for each batch size. This test will then load a clustered cache starting with a batch size of one and multiplying the batch size by ten for each subsequent test. For each batch size, a number of repetitions are run, and the best time is output.

Listing 5-5. *Test Program for Batching*

```
package org.terracotta.book.caching.batch;

import java.util.HashMap;
import java.util.Map;

public class CacheMain {
  public static void main(String arg[]) {
    int itemCount = Integer.parseInt(arg[0]);   // to bulk load
    int reps = Integer.parseInt(arg[1]);        // repetitions in test
```

```
    for(int batchSize=1; batchSize<=itemCount; batchSize=batchSize*10) {
      long bestElapsed = Long.MAX_VALUE;
      CacheMain main = new CacheMain(itemCount, batchSize);
      for(int rep=0; rep<reps; rep++) {
        long start = System.currentTimeMillis();
        main.primeCache();
        long elapsed = System.currentTimeMillis() - start;
        if(elapsed < bestElapsed) {
          bestElapsed = elapsed;
        }
      }

      System.out.println("Loaded " + itemCount +
                            " items with batch size = " + batchSize +
                            " best time = " + bestElapsed + " ms");
    }
  }

  private final int batchSize;
  private final Map<String,String> data;
  private final Cache<String,String> cache = new Cache<String,String>();  // Root

  public CacheMain(int itemCount, int batchSize) {
    this.batchSize = batchSize;
    data = generateData(itemCount);
  }

  private Map<String,String> generateData(int count) {
    Map<String,String> data = new HashMap<String,String>();
    for(int i=0; i<count; i++) {
      String key = "key" + i;
      String value = "value" + i;
      data.put(key, value);
    }
    return data;
  }

  public void primeCache() {
    cache.putAllBatched(data, batchSize);
  }
}
```

We can configure Terracotta by specifying the necessary instrumentation, roots, and locking, as shown in Listing 5-6. This application has a single class to instrument, and the cache itself as the single root. Additionally, there is one method that adds a batch to the cache that must be write locked.

Listing 5-6. *Configuration for Batching Test*

```
<?xml version="1.0" encoding="UTF-8"?>
<con:tc-config xmlns:con="http://www.terracotta.org/config">
  <servers>
    <server host="%i" name="localhost">
      <dso-port>9510</dso-port>
      <jmx-port>9520</jmx-port>
      <data>terracotta/server-data</data>
      <logs>terracotta/server-logs</logs>
    </server>
  </servers>
  <clients>
    <logs>terracotta/client-logs</logs>
  </clients>
  <application>
    <dso>
      <instrumented-classes>
        <include>
          <class-expression>org.terracotta.book.caching.batch.Cache
          </class-expression>
        </include>
      </instrumented-classes>
      <roots>
        <root>
          <field-name>org.terracotta.book.caching.batch.CacheMain.cache</field-name>
        </root>
      </roots>
      <locks>
        <autolock>
          <method-expression>
void org.terracotta.book.caching.batch.Cache.putAllBatched(java.util.Map, int)
          </method-expression>
          <lock-level>write</lock-level>
        </autolock>
      </locks>
    </dso>
  </application>
</con:tc-config>
```

When this program is run with Terracotta, you will see output like the following:

```
dso-java.sh -Dtc.config=tc-config.xml -Xms512m -Xmx512m \
org.terracotta.book.caching.batch.CacheMain 100000 10
```

```
Loaded 100000 items with batch size = 1 best time = 1063 ms
Loaded 100000 items with batch size = 10 best time = 226 ms
Loaded 100000 items with batch size = 100 best time = 134 ms
Loaded 100000 items with batch size = 1000 best time = 130 ms
Loaded 100000 items with batch size = 10000 best time = 116 ms
Loaded 100000 items with batch size = 100000 best time = 125 ms
```

First, we see what happens in the most fine-grained case, where a batch has a size of just one. In this case, the number of transactions will be equal to the size of the cache (100,000 items here). The fine-grained batching use case shows the worst time and indicates that the I/O involved has a significant impact.

After that, the size of each batch multiplies by ten. The output indicates that increasing the batch size improves performance to a point, but then performance starts to decrease, probably as the memory overhead and garbage collection start to have an impact. As stated before, using very coarse-grained transactions (such as a single transaction encompassing the entire load) is more likely to yield an OutOfMemoryError scenario.

Terracotta is working to render this batching optimization unnecessary. In the future, Terracotta will automatically adjust transaction boundaries and optimize I/O in the case of a series of many fine-grained transactions.

Locking and Maps

Listing 5-4 and its associated configuration in Listing 5-6 showed how to wrap a Map into a custom Cache class and specify locking at the Cache level using automatically clustered synchronization. The Cache class in Listing 5-4 omits all other methods, but if it had read-oriented methods like get(), we would recommend that the lock-level for that method be specified as *read*, not *write*. This will allow multiple readers in the cluster to concurrently access the HashMap. The write lock level will perform similarly to a synchronized block in Java.

As previously mentioned, the autolocked collection TIMs provide automatic locking for methods in various synchronized collections and will properly specify read and write locks as necessary.

Maps of Maps

One of the benefits of using Terracotta instrumented versions of the Map implementations is that values in the Map can be flushed out of the JVM, since they are stored in the virtual heap. Terracotta will automatically fault the object back into the JVM when it is needed, for example on a get().

■**Note** The java.util.TreeMap implementation uses logical instrumentation to maintain the sorted nature of the internal tree structure across the cluster. Logical instrumentation records calls against the TreeMap and replays them on other JVMs in the cluster. Thus, each JVM maintains its own sorted tree structure. One side effect of this technique is that value objects are never faulted out of the TreeMap structure, in contrast to HashMap and ConcurrentHashMap.

However, the key values in a `HashMap` or `ConcurrentHashMap` are not faulted out of the JVM, so all keys in a `Map` must fit in memory. In the case of a very large `Map`, the size of the key set must not exceed the JVM heap size. If, for example, your key objects include a 100-byte `String` field and two integer fields, the object would be approximately 108 bytes. If the `Map` contains one million keys, the total memory taken by the set of keys is 108MB. Always make sure the set of keys can fit in Java heap.

One strategy that can be used to address this problem is to create a `Map` of `Map`s. This will allow the submap, which is a value of the top-level `Map`, to be faulted out entirely if not in use by a particular node. If a partitioning strategy is used where each node handles a subset of the data, the top-level `Map` should be keyed based on the same partitioning strategy (by ID space, geography, or whatever other means is used). Terracotta will then naturally fault out submaps that are not in use by the partition on a particular node.

A Deeper Look at Caching

Now that you've seen some examples of using simple `Map` implementations for caching, it's time to examine caching in greater depth and see how we can fully leverage the power of Terracotta to handle a broader range of shared data use cases.

Eviction and Expiration

In the simple example at the beginning of this chapter, we checked our cache for the presence of a user and, if necessary, loaded and cached that user. You may have noticed that no code ever removed users from the cache. This means that, over time, the cache will grow without bound and could ultimately contain all users if every user has been accessed.

In some limited cache applications, this may be acceptable. For example, if the maximum number of items in the cache is fixed, the cache will not grow without bound. However, in most use cases, we must consider how items will be evicted (removed) from the cache. Cache eviction can be based on a number of factors such as size (evict when too many items exist), time (periodically evict expired elements), or demand from some external event.

Element eviction generally follows a policy based on either usage or age. The most common usage eviction strategies follow:

- *LRU* (least recently used) will remove the item with the oldest last-accessed timestamp.

- *LFU* (least frequently used) will remove the item that has been used the fewest number of times.

- *FIFO* (first in, first out) works like a queue to remove the oldest item, regardless of use.

Other strategies may also be applicable based on application-specific needs. For example, sometimes, allowing items to expire based on a combination of absolute age and use is helpful.

The policy used in your application will typically depend on the application. If you are using a `Map`-based application, you generally have full control over how and when to evict, and any of the preceding strategies may be employed. If you are using a caching library, the library will often provide one or more eviction algorithms or let you plug in your own.

As one example, we'll discuss later how Terracotta supports eviction and expiration when used with Ehcache.

Persistence

In many cases, it is faster to pull a cached item from disk than it is to retrieve it from the database or other system of record. In those cases, building caches that use disk to grow past the constraints of available JVM heap is worthwhile. Many cache systems provide the ability to spill the cache to disk when it becomes too large. In general, Java-based cache frameworks rely on serialization to persist to disk.

Persistence can also be used to avoid reloading the cache on startup by flushing the cache to disk on shutdown (or periodically) and starting from that backup on restart. This can greatly reduce the time to warm up the cache in a restarted process. The disk cache is usually a risky architecture if cache eviction, cache sorting, and searching are requirements. The disk is slow, and when these operations move from traversing RAM to disk, the application slows down. All these concerns imply that spill to disk is good for managing data when the database cannot respond as fast as the cache's disk but spill to disk does not improve throughput or latency unless the database is significantly slower than the local disk.

Distributed Caching

As you scale your application across multiple nodes, you will also want to scale your application caches. For read-only caches, you can get away with having separate independent caches in each application node. This is somewhat wasteful, as you are typically lazily fetching data from the database on multiple nodes for any hot item but can still provide some benefit.

For read-write caches, it is not acceptable to use independent caches, as they will be out of date, and users will experience inconsistent results when they hit a node that has out-of-date data. The typical approach in this case is to coordinate the state of the cache among the nodes. When one node modifies an item in the cache, it sends an invalidation event to all other nodes in the cache. To maintain cache coherency across the cluster, this invalidation broadcast must either wait for acknowledgement or implement some other complicated versioning scheme. Invalidation is also based on the assumption that there is some more permanent backing store.

There are some major problems with broadcast and acknowledgement. The most obvious problem is that broadcasting introduces a significant performance hit to the caching system, which will necessarily reduce the efficiency of the cache. It is still likely to be faster than going back to the database for the data, but it is adding significant network overhead. Additionally, broadcast messaging introduces coupling between all the nodes in the system, so a bad node can infect other nodes in the cluster as the other nodes wait for acknowledgments from the bad node. In the worst case, a single bad node can actually bring down a cluster, which eliminates the whole benefit of having a cluster in the first place.

Partitioned Data

One important strategy for distributed caching is the concept of data partitioning. Partitioning involves breaking up the data set across nodes such that each node in a cluster handles a subset of the data, and some component (such as a load balancer) directs traffic appropriately in front of the cluster. Partitioning can be used to reduce the need for broadcast and cluster communication. However, it also makes high availability more challenging, as the partitioned cache state lives at only one place in the cluster.

As we discussed in Chapter 2, you can divide the data in the database based on some key, as Figure 5-3 demonstrates.

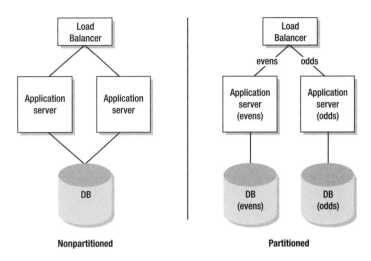

Figure 5-3. *Partitioning with Terracotta (This figure is same as Figure 2-4.)*

We will see in the following section how Terracotta is an excellent companion service to partitioned data.

Leveraging Terracotta

Terracotta provides a scalable, highly available technology for building distributed shared data stores. It addresses the critical issues with distributed caching: persistence, coherency, and performance.

Terracotta provides a virtual, clustered, persistent Java heap and thus provides persistence as an intrinsic part of its architecture. It is not necessary to implement or use a caching technology that spills cache to disk and makes it persistent, because Terracotta can do this automatically by using a persistent L2 server. Also, because that state is persistent, it is available on node start-up and will be faulted into the JVM as necessary without any additional setup.

Terracotta also provides a truly coherent cache without trading off scalability or performance. Changes in the cache can occur at a fine-grained field level and are propagated to the Terracotta server cluster, not directly to all other application nodes. As a cached data value is needed, it will be dynamically faulted into each node that needs it. This avoids the dependence on broadcast and the coupling between nodes in the application cluster.

Performance is a key concern in any distributed system, and Terracotta optimizes performance through a number of techniques. One of the most important differentiators for Terracotta is that Java serialization is not used when transmitting updates through the cluster. Because changes are trapped at the field level, whole object graphs do not need to be transmitted—just the particular changed value. Avoiding serialization alone accounts for a significant performance improvement over many other clustered data solutions, virtually all of which rely on some form of Java serialization. The performance improvement in this case comes from the fact that the CPU and the heap are not burned on allocating and deallocating byte arrays for serialized object data. Additionally, the need to send updates only to the Terracotta server, instead of broadcasting them to the every node in the cluster, yields a significant performance improvement. The biggest performance benefit comes from the fact that the Terracotta server computes the patch updates that each JVM needs, and delivers a custom update payload for each JVM's memory. The JVM then patches its own memory.

Terracotta will automatically fault objects in and out of memory dynamically based on use and is thus a perfect partner in a partitioning strategy. If your cache is distributed across a cluster and access to your data is partitioned, each node will handle a specific subset of the data. For example, each node might handle user names based on their starting letter. Terracotta will naturally only fault the necessary data into the JVM at each node that is needed for that partition. So, each node needs only a portion of the data in memory that perfectly matches the data it is using. This strategy can be used to achieve high performance and scalability.

However, Terracotta also addresses the high availability aspect of scaling out an application across hardware nodes as every node has access to all of the distributed cache if necessary. If a particular node goes down and a load balancer directs new traffic to another node, that node can fault in objects for another partition in addition to its original partition. All of this happens automatically as a consequence of Terracotta's transparent shared virtual heap without any explicit command from the application. See Chapter 11 for a discussion of how to use Terracotta to detect JVM failure and automatically restart JVMs. The server sends JMX events to members of the cluster about nodes coming and going using the capability called cluster membership events.

Caching with Ehcache

In previous sections, we looked at how you can use the standard Java collection APIs to build shared data structures with Terracotta. Using a shared Map is easy and takes care of the ability to save and retrieve cached values but does not address the need to handle eviction and expiration of elements within the cache. Building a custom solution around a Map is certainly possible, but for many uses, you will find it simpler to use a cache framework that provides support for eviction and expiration out of the box.

There are a number of open source caching frameworks available in the market, and Terracotta integrates with several of the most popular. In this section, we'll look at Terracotta integration with Ehcache, an excellent and popular caching solution. Ehcache provides a rich set of caching capabilities, including pluggable expiration and eviction policies, persistent storage, delivery of change events to your own methods, and even support for distributed caches. You can find more information about Ehcache at its web site http://ehcache.sourceforge.net.

Rewriting the Cache Example

To get started with Ehcache, we'll rework the simple example from Listing 5-1. Only a few changes are necessary.

In Listing 5-7, we must import the Ehcache classes and declare a CacheManager. Each CacheManager has its own configuration, which can be obtained in a variety of ways. For this example, we will use the default method of finding an ehcache.xml file in the classpath. For more information on the Ehcache API, see the Ehcache documentation on its web site.

Additionally, the cacheGet() and cachePut() methods have been reimplemented to look up the cache by name and use it appropriately.

Listing 5-7. *Rewritten Cache Example Using Ehcache*

```
package org.terracotta.book.caching.ehcache;

import net.sf.ehcache.Cache;
import net.sf.ehcache.CacheManager;
import net.sf.ehcache.Element;

public class UserEhcacheExample {

  private CacheManager manager = new CacheManager();

  public String findUser(Integer id) {
    String user = cacheGet(id);
    if (user == null) {
      user = fetch(id);
      cachePut(id, user);
      System.out.println("\t- MISS");
    } else {
      System.out.println("\t- HIT");
    }
    return user;
  }

  private String cacheGet(Integer id) {
    Cache userCache = manager.getCache("userCache");
    Element element = userCache.get(id);
    if (element != null) {
      return (String) element.getObjectValue();
    } else {
      return null;
    }
  }

  private void cachePut(Integer id, String user) {
    Cache userCache = manager.getCache("userCache");
    userCache.put(new Element(id, fetch(id)));
  }

  private String fetch(Integer id) {
    switch (id.intValue()) {
      case 0: return "Ari Zilka";
      case 1: return "Alex Miller";
      case 2: return "Geert Bevin";
```

```
    case 3: return "Taylor Gautier";
    case 4: return "Jonas Boner";
    default:
      throw new RuntimeException("Unknown id: " + id.intValue());
  }
}

public static void main(String arg[]) throws InterruptedException {
  UserEhcacheExample userCache = new UserEhcacheExample();
  for (int i = 0; i < 10; i++) {
    helpFind(i % 5, userCache);
  }
}

public static void helpFind(int id, UserEhcacheExample userCache) {
  System.out.print("Find " + id);
  userCache.findUser(id);
}
}
```

The ehcache.xml configuration file (Listing 5-8) defines named cache configurations, in this case, for a cache named userCache. This file is being loaded from the classpath for our example.

Listing 5-8. *ehcache.xml Configuration File*

```
<ehcache xmlns:xsi="http://www.w3.org/2001/XMLSchema-instance"
         xsi:noNamespaceSchemaLocation="ehcache.xsd">

  <cache name="userCache"
      maxElementsInMemory="10000"
      memoryStoreEvictionPolicy="LFU"
      eternal="false"
      timeToIdleSeconds="300"
      timeToLiveSeconds="600"
      overflowToDisk="false"
      diskExpiryThreadIntervalSeconds="120"
       />

  <defaultCache
      maxElementsInMemory="10000"
      memoryStoreEvictionPolicy="LRU"
      eternal="false"
      timeToIdleSeconds="120"
      timeToLiveSeconds="120"
      overflowToDisk="true"
      diskSpoolBufferSizeMB="30"
      maxElementsOnDisk="10000000"
```

```
      diskPersistent="false"
      diskExpiryThreadIntervalSeconds="120"
      />
```

```
</ehcache>
```

Let's look briefly at the ehcache.xml configuration file. This file contains two blocks. The first defines the configuration for a cache named userCache (the one we used in our code). The second block contains a default configuration for unnamed caches created dynamically from the CacheManager. The defaultCache definition is required in the ehcache.xml file.

Let's examine the attributes set on the named userCache in detail:

- maxElementsInMemory: This property sets the maximum size of the cache in memory.

- memoryStoreEvictionPolicy: Setting this property to LFU indicates a least frequently used eviction policy when the memory store is too large.

- eternal: This property can be set to indicate that elements should live forever in the cache, in which case, the later expiration settings have no effect.

- timeToIdleSeconds: This property sets the maximum time an item can live in the cache without being used before it expires.

- timeToLiveSeconds: This property sets the maximum total time an item can live in the cache regardless of use.

- overflowToDisk: This property determines whether caches larger than the in-memory maximum should overflow to disk.

- diskExpiryThreadIntervalSeconds: This property sets the number of seconds between runs of the background disk expiry thread, which will clean up expired elements on disk.

We will reexamine some of these properties in the context of Terracotta integration in the following section.

To run the Ehcache program, we will need the Ehcache JAR file and some dependencies. You can obtain ehcache.jar from the Ehcache web site. You will also need to download the Apache Commons Logging library from http://commons.apache.org/logging/.

You can then run the program with the following command line:

```
java -cp .:ehcache-1.3.0.jar:commons-logging-1.0.4.jar \
  org.terracotta.book.caching.ehcache.UserEhcacheExample
```

The results we will see are identical to the output that we saw when running the Map-based version. The major difference with the Ehcache version is that expiration and eviction policies are enabled, so when the cache gets big or contains items that have been there for a while, items will be automatically removed from it.

Using Ehcache with Terracotta

Ehcache has support for distributed caching in a number of configurations. Terracotta provides a drop-in solution that provides an alternate implementation of distributed caching that yields significant performance and scalability benefits over the built-in Ehcache options.

Enhancements and Configuration

The Terracotta Ehcache integration provides a number of important enhancements for distributed caching, including fine-grained read/write locking, an optimized distributed eviction policy, increased scalability, and clusterwide cache coherency.

When using Terracotta with Ehcache, the standard memory eviction policies (LRU, LFU, and FIFO) are replaced by a new time-based eviction policy. The eviction is designed to minimize the faulting of objects across the network by handling evictions close to the point of use. If your application works on a set of nodes with access to data partitioned on a per-application basis, Terracotta will perform eviction locally for each partition as much as possible. A global evictor will also take care of evictions for cache entries no longer used in any node. When eviction occurs, the entry is removed from the cache in every node in the cluster.

To configure the Terracotta eviction policy, the following Ehcache properties are used; some have altered meanings:

- `maxElementsInCache`: This property is ignored by Terracotta integration. The number of objects that can be stored in the distributed Terracotta cache is unbounded, and the cache is managed instead by the distributed eviction policy.

- `timeToIdleSeconds`: This property has the same meaning as in normal memory eviction.

- `timeToLiveSeconds`: This property has the same meaning as in normal memory eviction.

- `eternal`: This property is ignored by Terracotta eviction policy. To simulate, you can set the `timeToIdleSeconds` and `timeToLiveSeconds` to zero.

- `diskExpiryThreadIntervalSeconds`: This property has the same memory as in normal disk eviction but applies instead to the Terracotta distributed eviction policy, specifying the frequency with which expiration and eviction will occur.

Additionally, due to the nature of the Terracotta integration, some standard Ehcache features are unsupported, specifically notifications (which are traditionally used for the built-in distributed cache support and are not needed with Terracotta) and disk storage. Terracotta persists the cache in shared virtual heap and to disk on the server if configured in that manner, so there is no need for disk-based storage.

Downloading and Installing Ehcache Integration

To use the Ehcache TIM, you will first need to download and install it from the Terracotta Forge at http://forge.terracotta.org. To download the binary distribution for tim-ehcache, version 1.0.2, issue this command:

```
$ curl \
-o tim-ehcache-1.0.2-bin.zip \
http://forge.terracotta.org/projects/tim-ehcache/downloads/tim-ehcache-1.0.2-bin.zip
```

This command will download a zip file containing several JARs. The Ehcache support is actually broken into multiple TIMs: ehcache-commons, ehcache-1.2.4, and ehcache-1.3. To unzip and install these JARs to your Terracotta installation, run these commands:

```
$ unzip tim-ehcache-1.0.2-bin.zip
$ cd tim-ehcache-1.0.2
$ cp *.jar ${TC_INSTALL_DIR}/modules
```

Now that we have installed the Ehcache TIMs, we can use this module from any application using this Terracotta installation.

Using Ehcache with Terracotta

To enable support for distributed Ehcache, you will need to declare a dependency on the Terracotta Ehcache integration module in the tc-config.xml configuration, as shown in Listing 5-9. To include the Ehcache module, we add a module dependency in the <clients> block.

Listing 5-9. *Terracotta Configuration tc-config.xml*

```
<?xml version="1.0" encoding="UTF-8"?>
<tc:tc-config xmlns:tc="http://www.terracotta.org/config"
  xmlns:xsi="http://www.w3.org/2001/XMLSchema-instance"
  xsi:schemaLocation="http://www.terracotta.org/schema/terracotta-4.xsd">

  <servers>
    <server host="%i" name="book.ehcache-hostname"/>
    <update-check>
      <enabled>true</enabled>
    </update-check>
  </servers>

  <system>
    <configuration-model>development</configuration-model>
  </system>

  <clients>
    <modules>
```

```
      <module name="tim-ehcache-1.3" version="1.0.2"/>
    </modules>
    <logs>%(user.home)/terracotta/client-logs/book.ehcache/%D</logs>
  </clients>

  <application>
    <dso>
      <instrumented-classes>
        <include>
          <class-expression>
org.terracotta.book.caching.ehcache.UserEhcacheExample
          </class-expression>
        </include>
      </instrumented-classes>
</dso>
  </application>
</tc:tc-config>
```

Currently, the Ehcache TIM also provides integration for the JSR 107 JCache API to Ehcache and thus requires the inclusion of the JSR 107 JAR from http://sourceforge.net/projects/jsr107cache/.

Next, you will need to run your application as a Terracotta application using dso-java.sh:

```
dso-java.sh \
–cp .:ehcache-1.3.0.jar:commons-logging-1.0.4.jar:jsr107cache-1.0.jar \
–Dtc.config=tc-config.xml org.terracotta.book.caching.ehcache.UserEhcacheExample
```

When you do so, you will see results similar to running the Terracotta-enabled Map application. The cache is clustered and all nodes will see changes made on any particular node.

Summary

Caching is a necessary part of almost any application architecture. It is common to start with a simple caching system only to find later that it is insufficient for the real needs of your data size, freshness, and scalability requirements. Scaling a system like this after the fact can be a difficult undertaking.

With Terracotta, you can start simple but use Terracotta's clustered, persistent virtual heap to mitigate many of the pains related to scaling an application cache. And the best part is that you can achieve this scale with your original simple code.

In this chapter, you saw how you can build simple but powerful distributed caches using built-in JDK collections and how you can leverage existing open source caching libraries to get more sophisticated features and behavior, while still leveraging the benefits of Terracotta.

In the next chapter, we take a look at caching at work inside Hibernate, a popular object-relational mapping framework. We'll explore in detail how Terracotta can scale Hibernate-backed data access in your application to achieve scalability that's orders of magnitude greater than using just Hibernate by itself.

CHAPTER 6

Hibernate with Terracotta
Using Terracotta to Offload the Database

Hibernate provides a powerful tool to access databases. It is a mature technology, widely used in many types of applications, including stand-alone Java, web, J2EE, and Spring-based applications. By providing a simple model for translating data to and from a database, Hibernate eases the burden of working with the database. Hibernate helps eliminate the need to write SQL and perform the mundane chores of instantiating objects, filling them with data from the database, and mapping objects in memory into tables in the database

While the focus of this book is not Hibernate, most Terracotta applications talk to a database, and our treatment of clustering and scaling applications across machines would be incomplete without addressing Hibernate. With Terracotta, we can improve the performance of Hibernate in a clustered environment using many of the tools and techniques you have already learned regarding POJO clustering.

When scaling out a cluster of Hibernate-enabled applications, the database commonly becomes a bottleneck. In this chapter, we will see how Terracotta can be used to eliminate these common Hibernate bottlenecks working with either Hibernate's caching interface or POJOs outside of Hibernate.

To understand how Terracotta works with Hibernate, we will cover the basic concepts around which Hibernate is built first. The first is object-relational mapping (ORM).

Object-Relational Mapping

Object-relational mapping (ORM) simply means translating the data from the database's relational model to the Java heap's object-oriented (OO) model. At its core, ORM means translating the tables, columns, and rows of a database into the object instances, fields, and reference pointers of the Java heap, and vice versa.

While many techniques are employed to perform this job, all ORM tools, such as Hibernate, iBatis, and TopLink, must solve fundamentally the same problem. Because this chapter is about Hibernate, we will focus on how Hibernate performs the ORM job.

How Does Hibernate Work?

The Hibernate architecture presents a very good abstraction, on which the Hibernate technology is built. At its core, Hibernate allows a Java developer to interact with objects and the database to interact with data by providing a well defined set of translation points between the two. Three pieces make up the core set of abstractions that comprise the Hibernate architecture; let's look at each in detail:

- *First-level cache*: Oftentimes thought of as the session, the first-level cache is a place to store our objects in memory as POJOs. Because we deal with only objects in our code, the first-level cache is largely invisible to us as users of Hibernate. One must be aware of it, however, because objects copied outside of Hibernate—into the application heap space—must typically be treated with care.

- *Transaction boundaries*: These are the beginning and ending edges of the unit of work. Within a single unit of work, all data is read or written transactionally, meaning it has read-isolation semantics and is committed atomically. Transaction boundaries are quite visible to us as users of Hibernate, since they usually translate into beginTransaction() and commit() API calls, although they may also be hidden inside frameworks or other abstractions that obviate the need for making these calls by hand, such as inside of a servlet filter.

- *Second-level cache*: This is a place to store a copy of our database data in memory as raw data. Hibernate provides a pluggable model, so many implementations exist that provide second-level caching. Except for configuration and performance considerations, the second-level cache is largely invisible to us as users of Hibernate.

Figure 6-1 shows how these components work together.

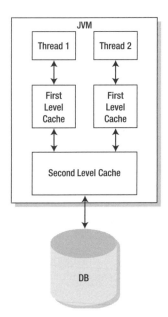

Figure 6-1. *Simplified CaptionHibernate architecture*

Typical Hibernate Invocation

A typical interaction with Hibernate is illustrated by the following pseudo code:

```
session.beginTransaction();
Object foo = { Hibernate HQL }
foo.getSomething();
foo.setSomethingElse(somethingElse);
session.getTransaction().commit();
```

First, we tell Hibernate to begin a new transaction or, in other words, begin a new unit of work. In the second line, we retrieve a POJO from the session (first-level cache). If the object does not exist already in the session, Hibernate will perform a query against the database to retrieve it and store it in the session. It's important to note that all subsequent requests to Hibernate that match this object will return the *same* physical object located in the session on the Java heap.

In the third and fourth lines, we perform some operation(s) on the object, whether it is to read some fields or update some fields. Finally, in the last line, we commit the transaction, or the entire unit of work, which will flush all of the changes made to all of the objects held in the session back to the database.

Using Terracotta to Improve Hibernate

There are two places where it makes sense to plug in Terracotta to the Hibernate model. Which one you choose to use depends on your application's requirements.

- The first place you can use Terracotta is to cluster the second-level cache used by Hibernate. This option is the easiest option to choose, because it requires only a simple configuration change. No changes will have to be made to your application to choose this option. However, due to the design of the second-level cache, clustering the second-level cache cannot take full advantage of all of the benefits that the Terracotta solution can provide.

- The second place you can use Terracotta is to provide clustering of the session objects (don't get confused with HTTP sessions). This option, because it clusters Hibernate POJOs, can take full advantage of the Terracotta solution, and thus can provide performance improvements over the second-level cache option. However, unlike the second-level cache option, this option may, depending on your application, require some small changes to your application logic.

How Terracotta Improves Hibernate Performance

To help you understand where to integrate Terracotta with your Hibernate application, we'll look at the array of options already available to improve Hibernate performance without Terracotta. After that, we'll evaluate how Terracotta can be added to further improve the scalability and availability of our solution.

First, though, you need to understand the basic steps for improving performance with a Hibernate enabled application.

Basic Steps for Improving Performance of a Hibernate Application

The following sections show the basic steps that any Hibernate developer must follow to improve performance:

1. Determine your application's baseline performance.

2. Add Hibernate.

3. Enable the second-level cache.

4. Cluster the session objects (the detached instances).

5. Benchmark the enhancements.

To provide a baseline, we start with a typical conversational application. This conversational application will make three requests to complete the conversation. Within each request, the example will execute one read operation and two write operations. Of course, a real-world application would vary much more, by varying the number of overall conversational requests as well as the number of data operations per request; this example serves merely to provide a clear understanding of the impact of each decision along the Hibernate performance curve.

Baseline Performance

As Figure 6-2 shows, a baseline JDBC application with no Hibernate framework calls will communicate directly with the database for each request. This results in three conversational requests, each with three operations, for a total of nine operations.

This example can be implemented by simply programming directly to the JDBC API. Of course, this approach is simple but fails to give us good performance, especially for applications that make many fine-grained changes during each conversational request. For complex applications, managing JDBC by hand often is not as simple as this trivial example might otherwise suggest.

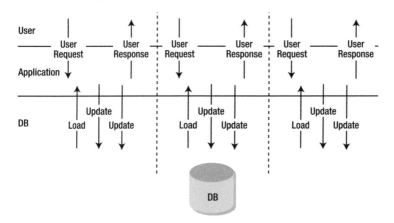

Figure 6-2. *The baseline JDBC application makes nine SQL calls.*

Let's sum up this approach: This application performs a total of nine operations. Its advantage is simplicity, but it scales poorly. The trade-off for the simplicity of this application, then, is in its performance. JDBC is easy to use, but we very quickly find out it does not scale, both in terms of application complexity and performance.

There are no clustering concerns for this application. Multiple systems can use JDBC directly with little to no consideration from the developer other than handling exceptions on commit.

Also, Terracotta won't really be of help in this baseline application (although, of course, the objects could be cached directly using any of the POJO techniques already discussed in other chapters of this book). This application is designed to use the database for high availability and scalability, but a scalable highly available database instance can cost millions of dollars per year to run—so we need to look toward a better solution.

Add Hibernate to Save Three DB Calls

As shown in Figure 6-3, simply adding Hibernate reduces the overall number of database operations, because instead of making a database operation for each update, Hibernate stores those updates in the first-level cache and pushes them all in a single *unit of work* when the transaction commits. This savings takes our previous example down from nine operations to six.

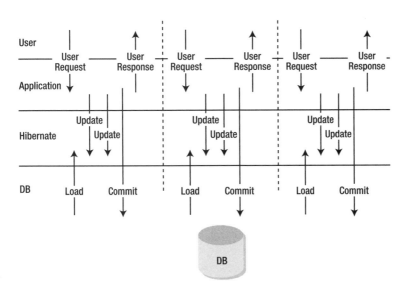

Figure 6-3. *The Hibernate application makes only six SQL calls.*

Adding Hibernate to our previously trivial JDBC application eliminates the interim updates to the database before each commit operation. Notice in Figure 6-3 that the updates in the application go only to Hibernate without passing through to the underlying database. Hibernate's ability to skip updating the database until the developer calls commit() helps make the application run faster. This performance advantage comes in addition to the fact that Hibernate can abstract most of the database interface from your code base.

While straight JDBC is the more easily understood implementation, many would argue that Hibernate simultaneously makes the application perform better and makes it easier to maintain, due to the fact that it eliminates redundant SQL calls to the database and eliminates the need to write custom SQL code. There is also nothing about this architecture that makes it harder to cluster than its JDBC-based counterpart.

Interestingly enough, the fictitious application depicted in Figures 6-2 and 6-3 has yet to be able take advantage of Terracotta in any significant fashion. Terracotta is designed to give high availability and scalability to most applications, but this architecture, like the JDBC example, already implicitly uses the database to do so. Again, to get true availability and scalability, we must look at more expensive solutions to augment the basic database server such as SAN storage for availability and database clustering for scalability.

Enable the Second-Level Cache to Save Five SQL Calls

As shown in Figure 6-4, once you enable second-level caching, the application remembers the data that was queried during previous conversational requests, thus eliminating the redundant queries to the database and delivering a reduction in the overall number of operations from nine to six, and now down to four.

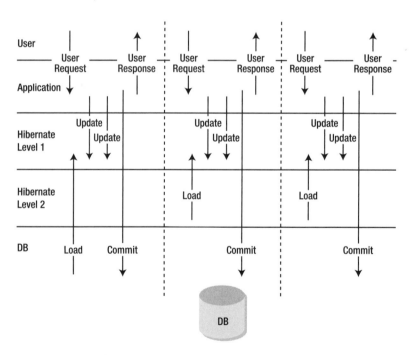

Figure 6-4. *The second-level cache application makes only four SQL calls.*

This time, there is a cache in place inside Hibernate. The cache makes sure that redundant SELECT operations that would fetch already retrieved objects are eliminated. The cache also provides a mechanism for batching UPDATE operations. The cache reduces the total SQL operations in the example to four.

While Hibernate has managed to make the application go significantly faster with almost no code changes thus far, risks are beginning to emerge. When second-level caching is enabled, Hibernate no longer queries the database every time the application uses a database entity. If two copies of the application are running at once, they cannot see the changes each other is making to the database. The data in cache can easily become stale on either node, depending on how application requests are routed or balanced between servers.

Unlike in the previous steps, the tradeoffs we have to make now are significantly more difficult. Previously, we concerned ourselves only with simplicity and implementation issues, but any optimizations we made did not have an impact on the behavior or correctness of the application. Now, we must consider the effects that adding the second-level cache will have on our application. In particular, the second-level cache can now become out of sync with the database. The generally accepted solution here is to set some explicit expiration time that will force Hibernate to refresh the entry based on some sort of expiry time, or time to live (TTL). In some cases, you may have already found a TTL is unacceptable, and you might have been forced to turn off caching altogether.

■**Note** We have one more risk—if our application is the only consumer of the data, we can assume with relative safety that the data will only ever be modified by us, and therefore, we do not have to worry about it being modified out of our control. If, however, other applications update the database at the same time this application does, second-level caching with or without Terracotta cannot be turned on. The only option here is POJO caching and database triggers notifying the POJOs of changes made by other applications.

Without a clustering strategy, data written to the second-level cache in one JVM may not be reflected in another JVM in the cluster. Even if our application is the only consumer of the data, we now have to consider that our application is separated into many pieces, which must be synchronized to provide a coherent view of the data. With data stored at the application tier, we must now consider what happens when there is a cache miss: Do we want to load the data from the database in every node, resulting in a clusterwide cache miss? Or can we cluster the data, thereby eliminating the clusterwide miss?

Terracotta can be used to cluster the second-level cache, ensuring that the data written in one node is consistent on all nodes, and eliminating the stale data problem. Simultaneously, Terracotta eliminates the clusterwide cache misses. Finally, due to its virtual memory ability, Terracotta can maintain a cache that is much larger than the physical memory available to any one node. This is important if the hot data set for your application does not fit into the physical memory space of any one node. See Chapter 5 on distributed caching for more details.

Clustering the Session Objects

Clustering the session objects, or what Hibernate refers to as detached instances, is the fastest mode of integration with Terracotta, as shown in Figure 6-5. Detaching POJO instances of database-mapped objects from Hibernate eliminates all unnecessary database operations, and stores everything in memory. Objects can be read at zero latency from RAM. Objects can also be written at low in-memory latency as well. The database simply becomes the system of record and gets updated only when you want it to be updated. The database is essentially divorced entirely from managing the intermediary state. This approach reduces the original nine operations in our simple JDBC application down to just two—one load operation and one store operation.

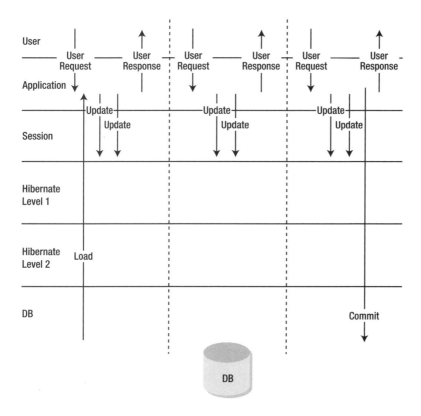

Figure 6-5. *The detached instances application makes only two SQL calls.*

The detached mode architecture proves to be the fastest performing option for integrating Terracotta and Hibernate. Not only is the database invoked only two times versus the original JDBC application's nine database calls, but the objects the application interacts with are now pure POJOs in memory. While Hibernate second-level cache objects are, in fact, byte arrays that need to be marshaled back and forth from POJO to cache entry, detached mode entities are purely heap-based objects and thus can be accessed at literally zero latency.

You must make sure to store detached POJOs in Terracotta; otherwise, those POJOs will be lost on system failure or workload failover across JVMs.

Terracotta can counteract the concerns with detached mode. The concerns are—as stated—loss of JVM memory as well as side effects of serialization on POJOs when those POJOs are clustered such as the violation of object identity discussed in Chapter 2. While most clustering solutions cannot safely help cluster detached POJOs, Terracotta does not have serialization and availability limitations.

In Chapters 1 and 2, you learned that Terracotta provides the same level of data integrity and availability that a database can provide. When using Terracotta in conjunction with Hibernate, we can leverage this availability guarantee to eliminate the risk of losing our intermediary state while working with that state as detached (POJO) instances. Terracotta is not limited to small serializable object graphs—it can be used with arbitrarily large object graphs regardless of whether or not those objects implement certain interfaces.

Benchmarking the Enhancements

Table 6-1 shows results we get using a simple benchmarking program to measure the time it takes to perform a fixed number of updates or reads, using Terracotta with the techniques presented in the preceding sections.

Table 6-1. *Relative Performance of Combinations of Hibernate and Terracotta*

Operation	Type	Results
Update		
	Hibernate	1,000 operations / second
	Hibernate with a second-level cache	1,800 operations / second
	Hibernate with detached instances clustered with Terracotta	7,000 operations / second
Read		
	Hibernate	1,000 operations / second
	Hibernate with a second-level cache	1,800 operations / second
	Hibernate with detached instances clustered with Terracotta	500,000 operations / second

As you can see, we gain some benefit by opting to use a second-level cache, but we gain the most by using detached instances. These findings are, of course, not too surprising, because detached instances are really just POJOs, and Terracotta is designed as a plain Java, or POJO, clustering solution.

■**Note** These results were obtained using a MacBook Pro and the HSQLDB database and are meant only to enable direct comparison between using Hibernate with Terracotta and using Hibernate without it. Explicit testing underneath a specific use case is recommended to measure the benefit for a particular application or in a specific hardware environment.

Configuring Hibernate to Work with Terracotta

We've talked about the benefits you will get by using Hibernate and Terracotta together. This section will give you practical information on how to configure Terracotta to work with your Hibernate-based application.

First, as outlined previously, you must decide where you will integrate Terracotta: as a second-level cache, for detached instances, or both.

Configuring a Second-Level Cache

Configuring Hibernate to use Ehcache as a second-level cache with Terracotta consists of a few simple steps:

1. Configure Ehcache.

2. Enable Ehcache second-level caching in Hibernate.

3. Configure Terracotta.

Configuring Ehcache

Note that the Ehcache configuration in this section is a suggested configuration and will likely need to be adjusted to your particular environment. Typically, your Ehcache configuration will live at the root of the classpath in a file named ehcache.xml. It would contain settings such as these:

```
<ehcache>
    <diskStore path="java.io.tmpdir"/>
    <defaultCache
        maxElementsInMemory="10000"
        eternal="false"
        overflowToDisk="false"
        timeToIdleSeconds="300"
        timeToLiveSeconds="300"
        diskPersistent="false"
        diskExpiryThreadIntervalSeconds="120"
        memoryStoreEvictionPolicy="LRU"/>

    <cache name="..." ... />
</ehcache>
```

Enabling Ehcache Second-Level Caching in Hibernate

You must enable Ehcache as your second-level cache in your Hibernate configuration as follows:

```
<property name="hibernate.cache.use_second_level_cache">true</property>
<property name="hibernate.cache.use_query_cache">true</property>
<property name="cache.provider_class">
  net.sf.ehcache.hibernate.EhCacheProvider
</property>
```

Configuring Terracotta

Also, you must tell Terracotta that you will be using both Hibernate and Ehcache. A few modules are required to get all of the proper configuration. Note that the versions of these modules may change (please check http://www.terracotta.org for the latest information):

```
<clients>
  <modules>
    <module name="clustered-cglib-2.1.3" version="1.0.0" />
    <module name="clustered-hibernate-3.1.2" version="1.0.0" />
    <module name="clustered-ehcache-commons-1.0" version="1.0.0" />
    <module name="clustered-ehcache-1.3" version="1.0.0" />
  </modules>
</clients>
```

Configuring Terracotta for Use with Detached Instances

Configuring Terracotta with detached instances likewise requires a few simple steps:

1. Configure Terracotta to use the Hibernate integration module.

2. Store the detached instances.

3. Reattach the detached instances.

Refactoring Your Application

Now that we are using a detached instance strategy, we must change the strategy we use to get objects for use by our business logic, and we must delay committing these objects until we are completely finished with them. Hibernate calls this strategy an application transaction that spans a long-running unit of work (see the Hibernate documentation for more information: http://www.hibernate.org/hib_docs/reference/en/html/objectstate.html).

Depending on your application, you may need to refactor your use of the session.beginTransaction() and session.getTransaction().commit() calls.

For example, some applications use a strategy that automatically calls the session.beginTransaction() and session.getTransaction().commit() calls using a servlet filter. By inserting the servlet filter in front of the regular servlet, you are freed from the tedious task of having to remember to call session.beginTransaction() and session.getTransaction().commit().

Configuring Terracotta to Use the Hibernate Integration Module

For all applications using clustered detached instances, the first step is to configure Terracotta for use with Hibernate. To do so, place the following in tc-config.xml:

```
<clients>
  <modules>
    <module name="clustered-cglib-2.1.3" version="1.0.0" />
    <module name="clustered-hibernate-3.1.2" version="1.0.0" />
  </modules>
</clients>
```

Storing the Detached Instances

To use detached instances in your application, you must store them somewhere and retrieve them when your application needs them. How you do this is up to you and depends on the requirements of your application, but application developers typically employ one of three common strategies.

Store the Detached Instances in the HTTP Session Context

If you are working in a web application and have access to the HTTP session context, and the Hibernate objects you are storing pertain to the current user, you might opt to store the POJOs (detached instances) in the HTTP session context.

To store the detached instances in the HTTP session context, simply use the setAttrribute() method in the HTTP session, just as you would with any other object you would like to be cached in the session:

```
//~ retrieve the foo object
session.beginTransaction();
Object foo = { Hibernate HQL }
session.getTransaction().commit();
//~ store in the session
request.setAttribute("fooObject", foo);
```

Store the Detached Objects in a HashMap

In other contexts, where you do not have access to an HTTP session context or you have data that pertains to more than one user, storing the detached instances in the HTTP session context may not make sense. Another option is to store them in a HashMap.

To store the detached objects in a HashMap, simply use the get() and put() methods of the HashMap, as shown in the following code snippet. The most appropriate key might be the primary key used to fetch the row from a table in the database. To ensure that the objects are available in the Terracotta cluster, this HashMap must be marked as a clustered object using the techniques outlined in Chapter 4 (it must be a part of a clustered graph of objects or marked as a Terracotta root).

```
//~ retrieve the foo object
session.beginTransaction();
Object foo = { Hibernate HQL }
session.getTransaction().commit();
//~ store in the map
myClusteredeMap.put("fooObject", foo);
```

Store the Detached Objects in a Clustered Cache

Storing the detached instances in a clustered cache may work better than a HashMap for your application. A clustered cache implementation often has more features, such expiry times for items, and is a good choice when more sophisticated features are needed than the Map interface has to offer.

To store the detached instances in a clustered cache, simply configure a clustered cache using the techniques outlined in Chapter 5 and store the objects in the cache:

```
//~  retrieve the foo object
session.beginTransaction();
Object foo = { Hibernate HQL }
session.getTransaction.commit();
//~  store in the cache (ehcache)
myCache.put(new Element("fooObject", foo));
```

Reattaching the Detached Instances

At some point in your application business logic, you must write the detached instances back to the database. This point in your application marks the end of the long-running unit of work. These points vary from application to application, but typical examples are the business logic that executes as the result of selecting the Buy option in a standard shopping cart application or the finish stage of a multiscreen web flow. To reattach detached objects, simply use the Hibernate saveOrUpdate() API:

```
//~  get the object from the HTTP session
Object foo = request.getAttribute("fooObject");
//~  flush the object to the database
session.saveOrUpdate(foo);
session.getTransaction().commit();
//~
```

Suggestions for Further Reading

For more information on working with detached instances, you should refer to the Hibernate documentation, Section 10.6, located at http://www.hibernate.org/hib_docs/reference/en/html/objectstate.html.

Debugging, Testing, and Tuning Concerns

In general, debugging and tuning Hibernate and Terracotta are separate exercises. You should tune your Hibernate settings according to the best practices described in Chapter 19 of the Hibernate documentation: http://www.hibernate.org/hib_docs/reference/en/html/performance.html. Even when using detached mode, unit test on a single JVM first, and make sure the application calls saveorUpdate() at the correct points. Confirm that data reaches the database and that there are no race conditions. Then add Terracotta to the mix, both for second-level clustered caching as well as clustering and making durable detached objects.

When using these two technologies together, there are some basic things you will want to know. These considerations are covered in the following sections.

Verifying Ehcache Configuration Clustering

You can identify if your Ehcache is clustered in one of three ways:

- Use the Terracotta administration console to inspect the data in the Ehcache store. In the console, open the roots tab from the panel on the left, and look for a root named net.sf.ehcache.CacheManager.singleton. This automatic root is created by the Terracotta Ehcache TIM for the Ehcache singleton, and it holds all Ehcache CacheManager instances. If you see this entry, your Terracotta configuration is configured correctly to cluster Ehcache.

- Enable the Hibernate SQL debug property in your hibernate.xml, to ensure that cache hits do not output SQL:

```
<!-- Echo all executed SQL to stdout -->
<property name="show_sql">true</property>
```

- Use the Statistics object in Hibernate to query, at run time, the hit and miss counts of your second-level cache:

```
Statistics stats = HibernateUtil.getSessionFactory().getStatistics();
stats.setStatisticsEnabled(true);
QueryStatistics queryStats = stats.getQueryStatistics("from Event");
queryStats.getCacheHitCount();
```

Tuning the Second-Level Cache

In general, the tuning strategies you use should be the same as those outlined in Section 19.2 of the Hibernate documentation. When used with Terracotta, you should entertain a few special considerations.

You should make sure that your cache entries are configured with an appropriate TTL to prevent your cache from growing too large over time. With Terracotta Network Attached Memory, your application can use significantly more virtual space than can be allocated in the local JVM. This can often be an advantageous and desired benefit, but you want to make sure that you don't abuse this feature and store more data than you intend in the second-level cache. Ehcache can specify TTL settings when the CacheManager is constructed or can be controlled using the Ehcache configuration file. Refer to the Ehcache documentation for more details on the maximum idle time to live and maximum idle time settings.

All caches perform best when there is high locality of reference. For now, we will quickly remind you of the motherboard analogy. The locality of reference is the state where the data needed for a particular set of CPU instructions is available in that CPU's data cache: no disk or network I/O is required in order to access data. For more information on locality of reference as it pertains to Terracotta and JVM-level clustering, see Chapter 12. If your application has low locality of reference or is performing primarily writes instead of reads (i.e., is write heavy), you should consider whether using a cache is helping the performance of your application or if that cache is just wasting memory and CPU in unneeded garbage collection.

Tuning Detached Instances

Since detached instances are just POJOs, tuning these is no different than tuning POJO or distributed cache instances with Terracotta. For more information, see Chapter 12 for general tuning information or Chapter 5 for specific information about tuning distributed cache performance.

Summary

This chapter has shown the challenges we face when moving a Hibernate application from a single node to a clustered environment. Terracotta is able to not only alleviate these challenges but to boost overall application performance across the cluster.

Two main strategies exist for integrating Terracotta with a Hibernate enabled application:

- Using a clustered Ehcache implementation as a second-level cache

- Clustering Hibernate created POJOs outside of the session, also known as detached instances

In Chapter 5, you learned about distributed caching, and now you have a better understanding of how caching paradigms and Terracotta can help Hibernate applications to detach from the database. In Chapter 7, we will explore clustering for web applications using Terracotta. We will learn how HTTP session information can be shared in a transparent, highly available fashion. For Hibernate-based applications, the HTTP session proves to be one location where we can store detached POJOs. Furthermore, HTTP session clustering that is scalable and highly available can help us keep certain data around web conversations out of the database altogether.

Clustered the HTTP sessions provide us another way to share state without resorting to the database. Across these various integration points, we can start to see Terracotta providing us much more than a distributed caching library—Terracotta provides us a general-purpose solution that we can use when battling any and all challenges our existing applications present in the process of scaling out across Java processes.

■ ■ ■

CHAPTER 7

Extending HTTP Sessions with Terracotta

HTTP sessions are traditionally used for web applications where the state is stored on the server side. While this approach is convenient on a single server, as soon as your application grows and multiple servers are needed to fulfill the load, sessions can become both a performance bottleneck and a development burden.

In this chapter, we will explore how Terracotta makes working with HTTP sessions as convenient in a cluster as on a single machine. You'll see how each shortcoming is addressed and how extremely easily you can integrate Terracotta with standard Java web applications.

What Are HTTP Sessions?

Web sites have long since outgrown their initial static nature and are now highly interactive and sometimes even full-fledged applications. For these applications to work, each user needs to be able to have a state that is maintained during interaction with the web site. The HTTP specification that made the World Wide Web so prevalent never evolved to provide a solution for this state management. Some of its characteristics, like query string parameters and cookies combined with hidden HTML form parameters, did allow for certain application state management needs to be fulfilled. These were, however, quite limited, and when application state became bigger and needed to be secured, technologies such as servlet containers came up with a solution to store user data on the server. Figure 7-1 depicts the difference between HTTP session state maintained on the application server and cookie state maintained by the web browser.

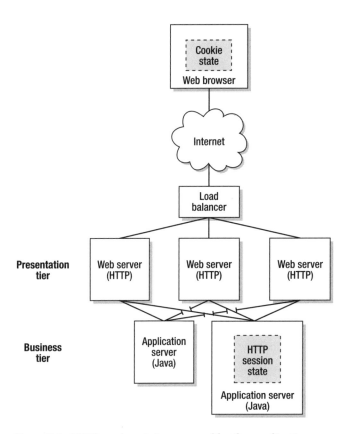

Figure 7-1. *HTTP session state managed by the application server on behalf of the web browser*

Server-Side State Management

Each user that interacts with a web site is by definition anonymous until he has identified himself. This is a fundamental difference with desktop applications, where the interacting user is trusted as long as the operating system authenticates the user at login time and grants him access to his documents. A web application relies on a server that is accessed by many users, from many computers and devices, from anywhere. This makes it more difficult to know who actually has access to which data. The HTTP specification doesn't facilitate this, causing people to resort to custom solutions for this problem. The solution that has historically gained the most traction is to give users a cookie with a unique identifier as soon as they start using the application. The web browser presents this unique identifier each time the user interacts with the web application. The logic on the server is then able to look up the data that corresponds to the ticket and use it to tailor the application's functionalities for that particular user.

Through the Java EE servlet specification, the HTTP session interface provides developers with a standard API that allows them to do exactly what has been described in the previous paragraph. They don't need to be bothered with the implementation details of how to give out cookies and how to tie those to data. They can simply start a user session and easily store and retrieve the data in an isolated fashion. All that data remains in memory on the server and, depending on the implementation of the API, can be stored in a variety of locations like on the file system or in a database.

The API is very simple; to create a new session or retrieve an existing one, you simply call the getSession() method on the HTTP request instance that is provided to your servlet by the container. Optionally, an argument can be provided to explicitly create a new session or retrieve one that already exists. Listing 7-1 shows the methods of the HttpServletRequest interface that are relevant.

Listing 7-1. *Methods of HttpServletRequest That Are Relevant to HTTP Sessions*

```
public interface HttpServletRequest{
  HttpSession getSession();
  HttpSession getSession(boolean create);
}
```

Afterward, to store data into the session and retrieve data from the session, a simple map-like API is provided by the HttpSession interface. Listing 7-2 shows the methods that are relevant.

Listing 7-2. *Methods of HttpSession to Work with Session Attributes*

```
public interface HttpSession{
  Object getAttribute(String name);
  Enumeration getAttributeNames();
  void removeAttribute(String name);
  void setAttribute(String name, Object value);
}
```

There's nothing complicated here. Details about the entire API can be found online at the Java Servlet Technology web site (http://java.sun.com/products/servlet/), which can be a useful resource for topics, like the general usage of HTTP sessions, that are outside the scope of this book. We're going to focus on the features that are the most important and how they tie into a distributed usage of HTTP sessions through Terracotta.

Automatic Time-Out of Stale Data

Another fundamental difference between web and desktop applications is that web applications cannot tell that a user stopped using the application. On the desktop, the application is quit, or the computer is turned off, causing all the live memory to be cleared. With a web application, however, the user can stop using the application without ever notifying the server by, for example, visiting another URL, quitting the browser, or just stepping away from a public terminal. Since web servers are visited by many users, maintaining sessions for every user that might return could quickly eat up all available memory.

To solve this, sessions have an automated expiration time that is measured from the request in which they were last used. This expiration event is called eviction. If a session has expired, it will automatically be invalidated, and all the associated data will be cleared. The expiration time can be set up through a web application's web.xml configuration file in the <session-config> section or programmatically for each individual session instance. Listing 7-3 shows the HttpSession interface methods that are relevant.

Listing 7-3. *Methods of HttpSession That Are Related to the Expiration Time*

```
public interface HttpSession{
  long getLastAccessedTime();
  int getMaxInactiveInterval();
  void setMaxInactiveInterval(int interval);
}
```

The last accessed time is expressed in milliseconds since midnight January 1, 1970, GMT, and the interval is expressed in seconds. All servlet containers have a default value for the maximum inactive interval; on Tomcat, this is 30 minutes.

Manual Invalidation to Clear Out Data

Even though sessions are cleared automatically to preserve the server's resources, there are many situations where manual invalidation is also useful. The most logical way to use this is to preserve even more server resources when users do explicitly log out of an application. This prevents the session data from lingering around until it has expired, even though it will never be used again.

Another useful technique is to invalidate a session when a user has finished performing a long transactional process, and the temporary data is no longer needed. Invalidating sessions at the end of a many-page business transaction or workflow ensures that no data lingers longer than it needs to—problems can be created if critical session attributes aren't cleared at the right time. Invalidating the entire session ensures that a user starts with a clean slate, after, for example, having placed an order. Starting fresh becomes even more important when sensitive data is stored in a session, like credit card numbers.

The HttpSession interface provides a simple invalidation method for this, as shown in Listing 7-4.

Listing 7-4. *Method of HttpSession to Manually Invalidate a Session*

```
public interface HttpSession{
  void invalidate();
}
```

Events to Coordinate State Modification

Complex frameworks often associate data elements like global application state with a session by setting them as session attributes. This can then be used by each component in the application to quickly access global data and coordinate how all the components should interact. Such state is usually tied into the entire life cycle of the application and needs to be notified when users are or aren't working with it. If you implement the HttpSessionBindingListener, such notifications are sent automatically by the servlet container. Listing 7-5 documents the methods of the interface.

Listing 7-5. *Complete HttpSessionBindingListerner Interface*

```
public interface HttpSessionBindingListerner {
  void valueBound(HttpSessionBindingEvent event);
  void valueUnbound(HttpSessionBindingEvent event);
}
```

There is no need to do anything special to enable these notifications. The servlet container will simply detect if a session attribute value implements the HttpSessionBindingListener interface. When the attribute is added to the session, the valueBound method is called, and when this value is removed, the valueUnbound method is called.

Note that we do not recommend relying on these events to clean up system resources, like JDBC connections, in your applications. These resources should be managed independently by, for example, using an IoC framework like Spring. In general, it's a good guideline to keep sessions purely focused on data and not let resources bleed into them.

Session State Persistence

Web sites are generally expected to be available all the time. Users become quickly frustrated if the information a site provided disappears for no obvious reason, and this frustration usually translates into reduced repeat visits. This expectation translates to the requirement for high stability and predictable latency of the underlying application, which, in turn, requires total availability of its data. Sadly, the infrastructure that is used to run applications is rarely problem-free. Both software and hardware failure can happen unexpectedly. In failure situations, important data should be protected and automatically become available again when a failed server is brought back to life.

Session state persistence provides the ability to failover from one JVM to another, and while it's not part of the standard specification, most servlet containers provide a solution that allows you to turn on this feature with a configuration parameter. Apache Tomcat even ships with this feature enabled by default. Usually, these persistence implementations will serialize all the session attributes to disk and deserialize from disk to reconstitute a session across server restarts. Persisting the session's state like this has shortcomings, though, such as a higher demand for processing power, higher disk utilization, and the requirement for all value classes containing session attributes to implement the Serializable interface. However, in most cases, being able to persist a session is the basis for replicating sessions across different servers. Terracotta takes a totally different approach for distributing HTTP sessions that avoids most these pitfalls of session persistence.

Distributed HTTP Sessions

As the popularity of a web site increases, so does the load on their servers. The ability to respond to this increasing demand for resources is called scalability. When servers go down, the ability to migrate those users seamlessly to another server represents much of the availability challenge. As discussed in Chapters 1 and 2, Terracotta makes it easier to spread applications across machines. For web applications, using Terracotta means that a load balancer, session distribution through DSO, and a web application server are sufficient for scalability and availability. With Terracotta, servers running in a cluster will act like one huge web application server, and users will not notice individual server performance or availability issues. Using distributed HTTP sessions is an easy way to share the state of web applications across such a Terracotta-enabled cluster.

Motivation for Using HTTP Sessions

When a cluster is created for a web application, users should not have to worry which server is available when they're connecting to the application. Users would become frustrated if they had to check which machine is the least active and connect to that one—they should be able to just connect to an application and let the back-end automatically select the most appropriate server. Also, since users can take a long time when working with a web application, selecting the right server should be possible at any moment and not only at the start of an application. To be able to achieve this, the state of the web application must be transferable from one server to another.

Accessing Sessions State from Other Nodes

Usually, when an arbitrary application is turned into a clustered one, developers are forced to search for the classes that contain state that has to be shared across the different cluster nodes. Web applications with sessions are easier to cluster than arbitrary applications, since all the server-side application state is stored in those sessions. HTTP sessions can thus be extended to become an API for transparently handling state across a web application cluster. Developers then only need to be concerned with ensuring that all conditions are present for sessions to become distributed. Since this is not standardized, each servlet container and application server vendor has its own implementation of distributed HTTP sessions. We will not cover these in detail.

Web containers tend to either store session data in a database or replicate sessions across a network of application servers. Let's focus on network replication as the containers that scale best do not use the database for session storage. Network replication means that session data is copied to the other servers in the cluster. This allows the data to be available in case a user is redirected to any of the other servers. Some vendors provide optimizations here, for example, to lazily pull in sessions on other servers instead of constantly pushing all the data out. A common approach, though, is to serialize the entire session and transfer it to the other nodes in the cluster each time the session changes, even for a single value. As you can imagine, this process can create quite some network chatter and impose large CPU requirements once replication is enabled in a cluster. Developers should also be careful to not add objects that can't be serialized by Java to a session; all the classes that participate in the application state thus have to implement the Serializable interface. You'll see how Terracotta addresses all these issues in the next section.

Dynamic Horizontal Scale-Out to Handle Traffic Spikes

Apart from allowing a server infrastructure to grow over time by adding new nodes to a cluster as the number of users of an application increases, distributed HTTP sessions are also very handy for reacting dynamically to traffic spikes. It's not uncommon nowadays for web applications to become hugely popular in a short period of time as communities of users discover them. This word-of-mouth popularity over the web can be scary, as can what's commonly referred to as the "Slashdot effect"—this refers to a sudden and dramatic increase of users on a web site about which a news announcement is posted to the front page of a very popular web site, such as Slashdot.org. Investing in hardware and cluster reconfiguration each time a news announcement is about to be posted would not be financially viable. Worse even, since other people can unexpectedly write such articles, web sites can be swarmed without any warning and instantly become unresponsive.

Server virtualization solutions come to the rescue here. Services like Amazon's Elastic Compute Cloud (EC2) allow disk images of servers to be prepared beforehand (see `http://aws.amazon.com/ec2`). A cluster can be set up to monitor the load of each participating server. Whenever the load exceeds a certain amount, new virtual servers can be launched to join the cluster in a matter of seconds, assuming a precreated standard disk image exists. Also, when the monitoring software detects that servers in the cluster are often idle, nodes can be shut down to reduce the cost of running the cluster. If distributed HTTP sessions are used for shared state across a web application cluster, all state will be available on the new nodes and transferred from the removed nodes. This is a typical example of where vertical scalability is inappropriate, and horizontal scalability provides rapid dynamic adaptation to changing usage patterns for an appropriate cost factor.

Terracotta batches shared state operations lazily from a central server, allowing dynamic changes to the topology of a cluster to be highly optimized. Only the previously existing sessions that are used in new nodes will have to be transferred. This is depicted in Figure 7-2. Notice how only sessions d, e, and f from the second, failed application server instance migrate to the newly added server.

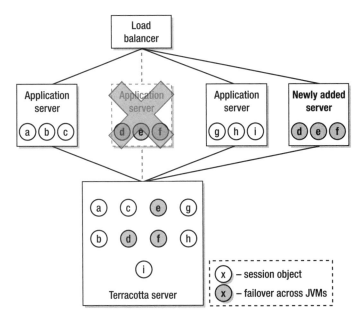

Figure 7-2. *Session failover with Terracotta where only impacted sessions migrate*

In general, only a very small percentage of user sessions will be moving between application servers. New users can easily be directed to the latest nodes that have joined the cluster, as those servers should report to any Layer 7 load balancer, such as F5's Big IP or Cisco's Content Director switch, as faster and less burdened than all other server nodes. What we are implying is that existing users stay on the nodes they started working with, new users get the newly added servers, and at any time, any server failure will result in a small number of user sessions rebalanced evenly across the entire server cluster. Similarly, since the central server is aware of the state of all the nodes, just shutting down some of them is also easy. If a user has to gain access to a session on another node, that session will be provided by Terracotta on the fly. See Chapters 3 and 4 if you want to understand more about how this works.

High Availability in Case of Server Failure

Software and hardware can and will fail sooner or later; you can be sure of that. If your application must be highly available, you need to decide how to react to these failures. For many years, people have been buying redundant power supplies, RAID discs, hot backup systems, and other solutions for each server of an important application to prevent failure and to reduce the downtime in case failure does happen. Recently, commodity hardware has become good enough to be used in place of enterprise-class servers, even while lacking the expensive systems' stability guarantees, such as CPUs placed on daughter boards (so that individual CPUs can fail without crashing the server) and dual redundant power supplies. A new and popular trend is to simply expect that everything will fail and to plan for it. With application servers and hardware, the plan tends to involve something like lots of simple, small servers running Intel-type technology with a few gigabytes of RAM and small local disks with two network cards in the machine. This approach makes an entire machine modular and low impact when it crashes. Failure becomes a part of the design of your application, not an exception.

When the application state is stored in sessions that are distributed over the cluster, each server node is disposable and can be replaced by any other machine that is able to handle the same application logic. The state will be provided through the distributed session's mechanism, as long as the infrastructure responsible for dispatching the state is also designed to be fault tolerant. Terracotta assumes that you will run the Terracotta server on roughly the same class of machine as you run your application. Thus, the Terracotta server is designed to fail over automatically on any issue. The central Terracotta server can be configured to have another machine available on standby as a passive server. If the active server goes down, the passive one will automatically take over to continue distributing the sessions. Chapter 4 gives you more detail about how to configure this; other scenarios like multiple active servers are also possible, if you want another machine to take over instantly without having to start up first.

Alternatives to HTTP Sessions

HTTP sessions are not always an appropriate mechanism for maintaining application state. Also, sometimes, applications have been created to externalize the state to another tier and aim for statelessness in web servers. These approaches are largely driven by application requirements, use cases, and design decisions. The two most important approaches that are used instead of distributed HTTP sessions are distributed caches and central database stores. Interestingly enough, applications that rely heavily on distributed caches or a central database might rely less on those stores if the applications had a reliable and scalable clustered session implementation. Consider this as you read the rest of the chapter: is there state that you can migrate from your database to the HTTP session now that a scalable replication service exists? We're not covering the alternatives in detail but will give you enough information to allow you to decide when to use distributed HTTP sessions.

Distributed Caches

When the application state is not tied to individual users, distributed caches might be more appropriate. They function in a similar fashion as sessions but are globally available from the entire application, meaning caches can be easily accessed outside the scope of a request and can safely store objects shared by more than one session. This global availability can also make them useful when state is shared among different tiers, for example, a web server and a desktop application. Terracotta integrates with many of the standard open source caching solutions, and its support for regular JDK maps is advanced enough to consider them caches also. More information about distributed caches can be found in Chapter 5.

A Database As a Central Store

If an application is not very interactive and mostly reads user-independent data, it could be sufficient to make every web server stateless and to always go back to a central database server. This makes every web server totally disposable, and running a cluster is as simple as adding new machines without having to coordinate the state. Retrieving data from the database at every request limits the performance of the cluster, however, to the capacity of the database. Adding a local cache to each web server can easily solve this by allowing copies of the most frequently accessed elements to be maintained locally, which dramatically reduces the load on the database. Many LAMP (Linux, Apache, MySQL, Perl/PHP) and Ruby on Rails applications are created in such a fashion.

In the Java world, the local cache in front of the database could be replaced with a distributed cache that uses Terracotta, which makes the central database approach even more useful when data is regularly updated. The appropriate entries merely have to be removed from the distributed cache when they are modified. Up-to-date entries will be faulted into the cache when they are accessed later. This approach forms the basis of object-relational mapping solutions where Terracotta plugs in as the second-level cache. You can read more about this in Chapter 6.

Distributed HTTP Sessions with Terracotta

In the previous section, we talked about the general principles of distributed HTTP sessions and briefly mentioned where Terracotta can improve on the usual replication-based approach. In this section, we'll delve deeper into the features that Terracotta provides, and you'll see how they are implemented behind the scenes.

How Terracotta Sessions Work

Distributed HTTP sessions with Terracotta are based entirely on the virtual heap principles that we discussed in Chapters 2 through 4. A central data root, in this case, a session map inside a container's session manager, is distributed across the cluster and instrumented so that any session operations are made available to the Terracotta server as well as the application cluster. When a session is created, it is also sent to Terracotta. When a session is read or accessed, its contents can be paged in from Terracotta just in time. When a session is updated or deleted, Terracotta is made aware of the changes. Terracotta always keeps the sessions in sync across the application cluster. From a developer's point of view, nothing changes and the application is automatically clustered.

Transparently Plugs into Web Containers

As you saw in the first section of this chapter, the HTTP session API is standardized by the servlet specification. This allows Terracotta to create its own implementation that is highly optimized for our distributed virtual heap. Even though Terracotta is able to take any regular Java class and make it distributed, a lot of optimizations can be done to improve the performance in a cluster. By using its own session implementation, Terracotta is, for example, able to avoid faulting attributes into nodes when the session eviction logic is running or to prevent the transfer of all attributes when only a single one is used in a session.

The good news is that you don't have to worry about the custom implementation at all. When Terracotta is activated for a supported servlet container or application server, Terracotta transparently instruments the supported product's internals to work better in a Terracotta-based world. The Terracotta-specific version of the servlet session hooks in underneath both your application as well as the container without any specific configuration necessary. You merely have to indicate the names of the web applications that should become clustered in the Terracotta configuration file, and all the rest is automatically taken care of. The next section will show you how this is done.

Note The intrepid reader who skips ahead to Chapter 9 will notice that HTTP session clustering for web applications does not follow the notion of Terracotta Integration Modules. Session distribution with Terracotta predates Integration Modules. Terracotta may decide to move some or all container-specific session behavior to modules. For now, session distribution with Terracotta is a special case in that Terracotta's implementation is exposed to the user and must be installed into the container before distribution will occur. More information on various containers is available at `http://www.terracotta.org/confluence/display/integrations/Home`.

Appropriate Lock Granularity and Isolation

Two aspects to locking have a profound impact on the performance and concurrency of a cluster: granularity and isolation. In generic terms, lock granularity refers to the relationship between the object being locked and the object being changed. Think of two objects in a graph, a root object with five child objects underneath the root. Locking the root to edit the child is a coarse-grained locking, while locking the child to edit itself is fine-grained. Update isolation, following the example, exists or is maintained as long as two children of the root, locking separately of each other, do not block each other, commingle field updates, or otherwise corrupt each other's state.

In the context of HTTP sessions, each session should be able to update its internals independently from other sessions but still ensure that the data can't be corrupted during simultaneous access. This includes updating the timestamp when the session was last used.

Similarly, when the eviction logic is executed to remove expired sessions, the entire cluster shouldn't need to wait for the operation to be finished.

Also, the retrieval of sessions should be executed in perfect concurrency. However, when a session is stored, exclusive access to the session store should be ensured. The retrieval should thus use read lock isolation, while the storage uses write lock isolation.

Concurrency can be optimized in many other ways. Terracotta's session implementation properly locks shared data elements across a cluster to strive for optimal performance.

Benefits

Earlier in this chapter, we touched on some of the benefits of using Terracotta for distributing HTTP sessions. This section will cover some additional important features.

No Serialization

As we discussed in the section about session state persistence, serialization is usually used to transfer the session state to another node in a cluster. Terracotta doesn't rely on this. In Chapter 4, you learned that Terracotta plugs in at the byte code level and is able to break down every Java class into basic types that can be shared with other nodes without having to rely on serialization. This makes the developer's life a lot easier because it eliminates the worry of bringing a single-server web application to a cluster. Often, in the early stages of an application's life, a lot of attention is brought to ensuring that it's bug-free and works as intended. Testing often occurs on a small or unit scale, and scalability testing is conducted near the end of the development effort when the entire application can be assembled in one place. Terracotta's HTTP session support allows the clustering to simply be activated on either the developer's workstation or when the application is deployed in the performance lab or production environment, without having to ensure that all the classes in the session implement the `Serializable` interface. Developers using Terracotta for session replication can write units of application functionality, test them with JUnit or whatever they like, and test them again on two JVMs running on the same desktop.

Ensuring that data structures are properly serialized and deserialized is also very error-prone, particularly when data structures evolve over time and older persisted state needs to be compatible with newer classes. Not having to worry about this reduces the development effort and makes your application more resilient to changes over time.

Rolling Upgrades

Terracotta stores the shared state in a logical structure that is dissociated from the actual class structure of the objects in your shared state. Each class field gets a dedicated logical key that is associated with the field's value. When the session state is retrieved by another node, these logical keys are looked up when an object in the session is instantiated by Terracotta. If fields have been added to a newer version the class, these will simply use their default values if no appropriate logical keys can be found. Once these new fields are part of the session state, their values will be stored in the same fashion as the other fields. If fields are removed, their logical keys will simply not be looked up, and the values will not be applied. In other words, the class object in each JVM drives which fields are accessible to your application code and which version of each field to access. A class that changes over time does not break the instances stored in the Terracotta server.

Figure 7-3 illustrates the behavior of a web application that changes over time. The first change introduces a new field, and the second change removes a field. In the figure, versions 2 and 3 of the session logic can see the age object in session whereas version 1 cannot. Version 1 never requests the age object and thus everything works. Further, version 3 is the only version that cannot see the order history object and will therefore not act on that object while the two previous versions can still see the order history object even though servers with version 3 of the application logic are present in the cluster.

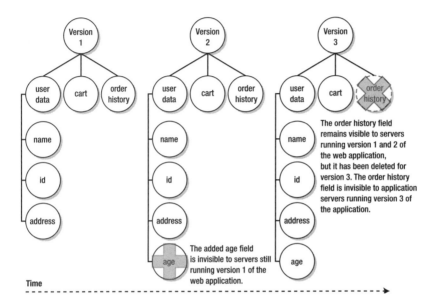

Figure 7-3. *Terracotta's transparent object versioning works well when rolling web application changes into production.*

The approach illustrated in Figure 7-3 allows data classes to evolve over time without backwards compatibility problems with existing state. You're thus free to properly use rich object-oriented data structures with class hierarchies that are appropriate for your application logic.

Fine-Grained Changes

Chapter 4 explains how Terracotta's virtual heap is able to detect the tiniest change to a large object graph and to expose only that change to the cluster. For distributed HTTP sessions, the same benefits exist. Instead of having to serialize the entire session state over and over again, only the real changes to your state will be pulled in by other nodes that use modified sessions.

Simultaneous Linear Scalability and High Availability

Balancing scalability and availability is traditionally a hard problem. Linear scalability requires throughput to remain constant as more resources are brought to bear to meet application load; this scalability is typically achieved by sharing no information or objects across application server instances. High availability requires that application state be available on every application server instance and conflicts with linear scalability as a result. Nevertheless, in the web application world, you must find a way to add application servers as your web traffic increases without introducing replication overhead while doing so. High availability demands that you should also be able to serve any request from any application server, so the user experience is uninterrupted in the event of one or more of the application servers being taken offline.

Without Terracotta, scalability and availability are at odds. Because the Terracotta virtual heap is optimized for fine-grained changes and pushes those changes only where needed in the cluster, the throughput of an attached JVM can be made constant, regardless of how many nodes are attached. At the same time, because the objects on the Terracotta virtual heap are durable and can be faulted in as needed from any member of the cluster, user and application state can be made highly available. Because the mechanism of the virtual heap is transparent, this balance between linear scale and high availability comes without increasing the complexity of your application code.

To achieve linear scale, you must deploy a load balancer capable of sticky session routing. Load balancers such as F5's Big IP or Cisco's local, content, and global directors employ various strategies for routing the same user to the same machine for processing all HTTP requests. Some devices use the IP address of the end user's browser. This is not a good strategy at scale, because networks such as AOL use web proxies and caching for their end users; all AOL users appear to come from one of only a handful of IP addresses.

Sticky load balancers that are aware of session cookies (JSESSIONID in many popular web containers) will work very well with Terracotta underneath them. In such environments, the user will remain sticky to a single application server instance, thus helping you to avoid the cost of session replication altogether. Sessions will be stored on the server that needs them as well as in Terracotta in case of application server instance failure. On failover, the end user gets rerouted by the load balancer, because the balancer detects that the original application server is down or slow. When the session access is attempted by the new application server instance, the user's session dynamically faults in through Terracotta to the new node. The user will be none the wiser with regard to node failure, and your cluster will scale linearly at the same time.

No Need to Set Attributes After Each Change

Since Terracotta ensures that object identity is preserved and all the fine-grained changes are automatically propagated for shared object instances, actually storing attributes into a session is not necessary for the clusterwide state to be updated.

Other distributed session implementations can't detect changes to attribute values without being notified through the setAttribute() method. In these situations, developers actually have to change their code when they move an application from a single server to a cluster. Some containers and application servers allow you to configure them so that every session is automatically replicated on every HTTP request, even if no changes were made. This takes away the development burden but imposes a very high and needless load on the systems and network.

Terracotta again behaves exactly like what you're familiar with when working on a single node.

Easy to Set Up

We'll be covering integration modules in detail in Chapter 9. They allow Terracotta configuration and instrumentation to be packaged into self-contained JAR files that can be included into your own `tc-config.xml` file with a single line of XML. Most of the supported servlet containers are shipped inside the core Terracotta download. To use them, you need to follow the installation instructions available at `http://www.terracotta.org/` for your specific application server type. The installation includes making sure the Terracotta libraries are installed into the JVM and that Terracotta is added as a boot class loader (as discussed in Chapters 3 and 4). A few containers are supported via integration modules that simply need to be included in your configuration file to be enabled. When other application servers or servlet containers are supported later on, Terracotta will use integration modules to bundle them. In the next section, we will demonstrate the changes required to a typical Tomcat instance when introducing Terracotta.

Using Terracotta and HTTP Sessions

It's time to leave the theory behind and look at some practical examples. We'll look at several ways of using HTTP sessions and how to distribute sessions with Terracotta.

Shared Session State

This first example is very simple and merely illustrates that session state can be distributed. We maintain a simple counter that increases every time the Refresh button is clicked in the web browser. When the counter reaches ten, the active session is invalidated, and the counter starts over again. We implement this functionality using a Java servlet. The source code of the example follows in Listing 7-6.

Listing 7-6. *Source Code of SessionExample1.java Servlet*

```java
import java.io.PrintWriter;
import java.io.IOException;

import javax.servlet.ServletException;

import javax.servlet.http.HttpServlet;
import javax.servlet.http.HttpServletRequest;
import javax.servlet.http.HttpServletResponse;
import javax.servlet.http.HttpSession;
public class SessionExample1 extends HttpServlet {
  protected void service(HttpServletRequest req, HttpServletResponse res)
      throws ServletException, IOException {
    res.setContentType("text/html;charset=UTF-8");
    PrintWriter out = res.getWriter();
    HttpSession session = req.getSession();
    Integer count = (Integer)session.getAttribute("count");
    if (null == count) {
      count = 0;
```

```
    }
    count = count + 1;
    session.setAttribute("count", count);
    try {
      out.println("<html>");
      out.println("<head><title>Session Example 1</title></head>");
      out.println("<body>");
      out.println("<p>Current count "+count+"</p>");
      out.println("</body>");
      out.println("</html>");
    } finally {
      out.close();
    }
    if (count >= 10) {
      session.invalidate();
    }
  }
}
```

The web.xml file for the example servlet is shown in Listing 7-7.

Listing 7-7. *Source Code of the web.xml File to Deploy the Example Servlet*

```
<?xml version="1.0" encoding="UTF-8"?>
<!DOCTYPE web-app
    PUBLIC "-//Sun Microsystems, Inc.//DTD Web Application 2.3//EN"
    "http://java.sun.com/dtd/web-app_2_3.dtd">
<web-app>
  <servlet>
    <servlet-name>SessionExample1</servlet-name>
    <servlet-class>SessionExample1</servlet-class>
  </servlet>
  <servlet-mapping>
    <servlet-name>SessionExample1</servlet-name>
    <url-pattern>/sessionexample1</url-pattern>
  </servlet-mapping>
</web-app>
```

Package and Configure the Web Application

To try out this example, you first have to create the directory structure for a Java web application. Execute the following commands to create this structure and place the example files in it:

```
> cd %HOMEPATH%
> md example1\WEB-INF\classes
> move SessionExample1.java example1\WEB-INF\classes
> move web.xml example1\WEB-INF
```

Now, you need to compile the servlet to be able to run it:

```
> cd %HOMEPATH%\example1\WEB-INF\classes
> javac -cp <TC_HOME>\lib\servlet-api-2.4.jar SessionExample1.java
```

Finally, you should create a WAR file that can be deployed in a servlet container:

```
> cd %HOMEPATH%\example1
> jar cvf example1.war .
```

You will end up with an example1.war archive that is ready to be deployed.

Install and Run the Application with the Terracotta Sessions Configurator

Terracotta ships with a handy graphical user interface that allows you to configure web applications. It also allows you to deploy them into servlet containers with HTTP-enabled distributed sessions. Launching this tool is easy:

```
> <TC_HOME>\tools\sessions\sessions-configurator.bat
```

After executing this command, you will see a window appear that looks similar to Figure 7-4.

Figure 7-4. *Terracotta Sessions Configurator startup window*

By default, the Sessions Configurator uses the Apache Tomcat version that is shipped with Terracotta. Other servlet containers can also be used, and we'll show you how in the last section of this chapter. For now, let's just settle on Tomcat and import your web application into it. This is simply done by selecting "Import webapp" from the File menu, as shown in Figure 7-5.

Figure 7-5. *Sessions Configurator menu to import a new web application*

You will be presented with a file selector, and you should select the example1.war archive you just created. A dialog will tell you when the import task is complete. Afterward, a new item will appear in the left pane of the Sessions Configurator, named example1. This is your web application deployed to the servlet container.

Let's run the example now by starting the two Tomcat instances that are set up by default in the right pane. Go ahead and click the "Start all" button. The Tomcat servers first go into a wait state while the Terracotta server starts; afterward, they'll become ready, and the Sessions Configurator will look like Figure 7-6.

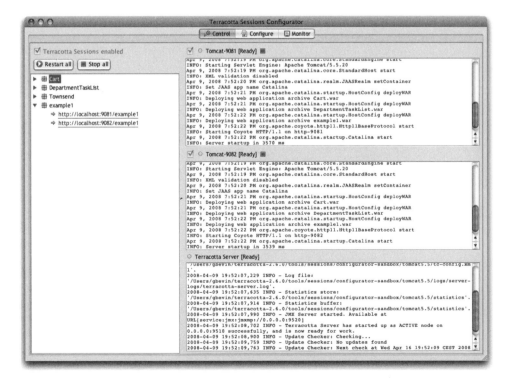

Figure 7-6. *Sessions Configurator after starting all the Tomcat instances*

Trying the Example

Now, launch a web browser to visit the application that is running on the first web server on port 9081. The full URL is http://localhost:9081/example1/sessionexample1. Reload the page a few times to see the counter increase. You'll see something similar to Figure 7-7.

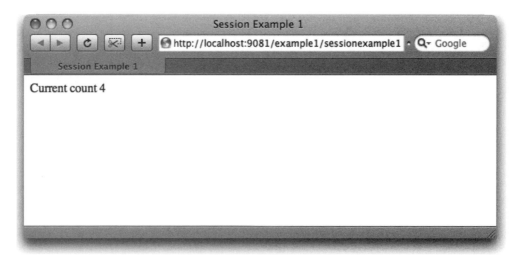

Figure 7-7. *Basic session example after reloading the browser a few times*

Next, you should open a second browser window and visit the application that is running on the second web server on port 9082; the full URL this time is http://localhost:9082/example1/sessionexample1 (only the port number changed). You'll notice that the counter continued with the value that it had on the first server, and the value was increased on the second server. This clearly shows that the state is shared among different servers, as shown in Figure 7-8.

Figure 7-8. *Basic session example after visiting the second Tomcat instance in the cluster*

Now, for more fun, try to open the same page in another browser or from a browser on another machine (substitute localhost with the IP address of the machine that runs the servers). You'll see that the state is really stored on the server. Also, try reloading until the counter reaches the value 10. Since the session will be invalidated, the next time you visit the application, the counter will have the value 1.

Finally, notice that there are two red rectangles to the right of the Tomcat server instances. Feel free to click these to stop the Tomcat servers. If you stop a server, you'll see a green arrow appear that allows you to start it up again. At the bottom of the right pane, the Terracotta server continues to run, which means when you've restarted a Tomcat instance, the shared session state will be provided so that everything can continue as if nothing happened.

■**Caution** The Terracotta server runs automatically inside the configurator. If you have other servers running from previous chapters' experiments, kill them before running the configurator. Also note that the server is not configured in persistent mode, which means stopping and restarting the Terracotta server will result in lost sessions. We will discuss this issue more after the examples.

HTTP Sessions with Structured Session Attributes

In the first example, you couldn't see much difference with how session clustering works with Terracotta and how clustering would work with traditional HTTP session replication. In this example, we're going to create a shopping cart with very basic functionality that contains a set of sorted items. At the top of the page, you see the current state of your cart. Below, you're able to add a name with the amount that you want to order. If you provide a new amount for an item already present in the cart, the item is not replaced; the new amount is simply added to the existing cart item. When you provide zero as the amount or press the remove button, the corresponding item will be removed from the cart. We will go over the source code of this example later in this section. Figure 7-9 shows what it all looks like.

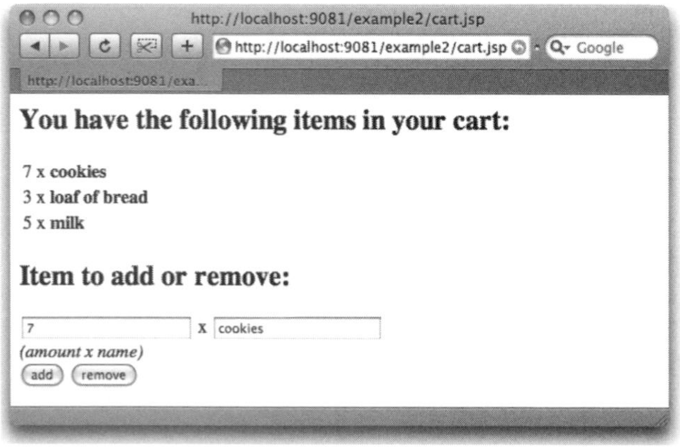

Figure 7-9. *Screenshot of second session example, a basic shopping cart*

This example is a little bit larger than the previous one. It consists of a cart.jsp file that handles HTTP requests (shown in Listing 7-8) and provides a user interface to inspect and modify the shopping cart. This shopping cart is implemented in the example/Cart.java class. The items in the cart are modeled through the example/Item.java class.

Listing 7-8. *Source Code of cart.jsp for the Structured Session Attributes Example*

```
<%@page import="java.util.Iterator,example.Item"%>
<html>
    <jsp:useBean id="cart" scope="session" class="example.Cart"/>
    <body><%
        String operation = request.getParameter("operation");
        String name = request.getParameter("name");
        String amount = request.getParameter("amount");
        if (operation != null && name != null) {
            if (operation.equals("add")) {
                cart.addItem(new Item(name, Integer.parseInt(amount)));
            } else if (operation.equals("remove")) {
                cart.removeItem(name);
            }
        }
        if (null == name) name = "";
        if (null == amount) amount = "";%>
        <h2>You have the following items in your cart:</h2>
        <table><%
        for (Item i : cart.getItems()) {%>
            <tr>
                <td align="right"><%=i.getAmount()%></td>
                <td>x</td>
                <td><b><%=i.getName()%></b></td>
            </tr><%
        }%>
        </table>
        <form method="post" action="<%=request.getContextPath()%>/cart.jsp">
            <h2>Item to add or remove:</h2>
            <div>
                <input type="text" name="amount" value="<%=amount%>"/> x
                <input type="text" name="name" value="<%=name%>"/>
            </div>
            <div><em>(amount x name)</em></div>
            <div>
                <input type="submit" name="operation" value="add"/>
                <input type="submit" name="operation" value="remove"/>
            </div>
        </form>
    </body>
</html>
```

Here, an HTML form is constructed at the bottom of the JSP file. This sets up two text fields for the item name and amount and two submission buttons for the operation that has to be performed. When the JSP is initialized, an instance of the cart is retrieved from the session. If no cart is in the session yet, a new one will be created. Afterward, the parameters that were sent through the HTML form are retrieved and evaluated. If the operation parameter is add, a new item is added to the cart. Similarly, if the operation is remove, the submitted item name will be removed. The middle section of the JSP obtains the items that are already in the cart and iterates over them to display the item names and amounts in a table.

It's worth noting that session-specific code only happens through the <jsp:useBean> tag. As soon as the cart object has been retrieved from the session, all the operations on the cart are done as regular Java method calls without storing anything back into the session. This is one of the situations where using Terracotta provides a lot of benefit. Other distributed sessions solutions will require you to set the cart object back as a session attribute when all the operations on it have been performed. Terracotta doesn't need this and continues to work in a cluster according to the same rules that you already know from a nonclustered application.

Listing 7-9 shows the Cart.java file used as the shopping cart.

Listing 7-9. *Source Code of Cart.java for the Structured Session Attributes Example*

```
package example;

import java.util.Collection;
import java.util.Collections;
import java.util.Iterator;
import java.util.TreeSet;
public class Cart {
  private Collection<Item> items = new TreeSet<Item>();

  public Collection<Item> getItems() {
    return Collections.unmodifiableCollection(items);
  }

  public void addItem(Item item) {
    Iterator<Item> it = items.iterator();
    while (it.hasNext()) {
      Item i = it.next();
      if (i.equals(item)) {
        if (item.getAmount() <= 0) {
          it.remove();
        } else {
          i.setAmount(item.getAmount());
        }
        return;
      }
    }
    if (item.getAmount() > 0) {
      items.add(item);
    }
```

```
  }

  public void removeItem(String name) {
    addItem(new Item(name, 0));
  }
}
```

The addItem() method provides the core of the cart functionality. It looks for an existing cart item, and if the item is found, it is removed or updated with the new amount. This is another operation where Terracotta will show its usefulness. When the item amount is updated, only that value is propagated to the other nodes in the cluster. You will learn later in this section how you can see that this is actually happening.

Listing 7-10 shows the Item.java class.

Listing 7-10. *Source Code of Item.java for the Structured Session Attributes Example*

```
package example;

public class Item implements Comparable {
  private String name;
  private int amount;

  public Item(String name, int amount) {
    setName(name);
    setAmount(amount);
  }

  public String getName() {
    return name;
  }

  public void setName(String name) {
    if (null == name) throw new IllegalArgumentException();
    this.name = name;
  }

  public int getAmount() {
    return amount;
  }

  public void setAmount(int amount) {
    this.amount = amount;
  }

  @Override
  public boolean equals(Object o) {
    return name.equalsIgnoreCase(((Item)o).name);
  }
```

```
  @Override
  public int hashCode() {
    return name.toLowerCase().hashCode();
  }

  public int compareTo(Object o) {
    return name.compareToIgnoreCase(((Item)o).name);
  }
}
```

The Item class is a regular Java bean where the equals(), hashCode(), and compareTo() methods have been implemented to disregard the amount as a significant data element for the item. This means that items with the same name will be considered equal, even when the name differs in case.

Note that neither the Cart class nor the Item class implements the Serializable interface. However, when you try out the example with several Tomcat instances, as explained in the next section, you'll see that the session state is properly shared.

Listing 7-11 shows the web.xml file for the application.

Listing 7-11. *Source Code of web.xml for the Structured Session Attributes Example*

```
<?xml version="1.0" encoding="UTF-8"?>
<!DOCTYPE web-app
    PUBLIC "-//Sun Microsystems, Inc.//DTD Web Application 2.3//EN"
    "http://java.sun.com/dtd/web-app_2_3.dtd">
<web-app>
</web-app>
```

This web.xml file is empty, because nothing has to be set up in the servlet container. The cart.jsp file will be deployed automatically by the servlet container, and you can access it directly.

Packaging and Configuring the Web Application

To try out this example, you have to create the directory structure for a Java web application. Execute the following commands (in Microsoft Windows format) to create this structure and place the example files in it:

```
> cd %HOMEPATH
> md example2\WEB-INF\classes\example
> move Cart.java Item.java example2\WEB-INF\classes\example
> move cart.jsp example2
> move web.xml example2\WEB-INF
```

Now, you need to compile the back-end classes:

```
> cd %HOMEPATH%\example2\WEB-INF\classes
> javac example\*.java
```

Finally, you should create a WAR file that can be deployed in a servlet container:

```
> cd %HOMEPATH%\example2
> jar cvf example2.war .
```

You will end up with an example2.war archive that is ready to be deployed. Deploy it now.

Manually Configuring and Installing the Example into Tomcat

As you learned in Chapter 3, Terracotta has a configuration file that is used by the server and the clients to perform the application clustering. Listing 7-12 shows the minimal tc-config.xml file that you need to set up a Terracotta server and a Tomcat server without the Sessions Configurator.

Listing 7-12. *The tc-config.xml File for the Structured Session Attributes Example*

```xml
<?xml version="1.0" encoding="UTF-8"?>
<tc:tc-config xmlns:tc="http://www.terracotta.org/config">
  <servers>
    <server host="%i" name="sample">
      <data>data/server-data</data>
      <logs>logs/server-logs</logs>
    </server>
  </servers>
  <clients>
    <logs>logs/client-logs/%(webserver.log.name)</logs>
  </clients>
  <application>
    <dso>
      <instrumented-classes>
        <include>
          <class-expression>example.Cart</class-expression>
        </include>
        <include>
          <class-expression>example.Item</class-expression>
        </include>
      </instrumented-classes>
      <web-applications>
        <web-application>example2</web-application>
      </web-applications>
    </dso>
  </application>
</tc:tc-config>
```

You've already seen why classes need to be included in the <instrumented-classes> section. For this example, we included the two back-end classes. We don't need to do anything special for instrumenting session-related classes. This is done automatically through the <web-applications> section of the configuration file. You just have to list all the web application names that should use distributed HTTP sessions. In this example, that's the example2 web application.

Now, locate the root directory of your Tomcat installation; we'll refer to it from now on as `<TOMCAT_HOME>`. You should replace every occurrence of `<TOMCAT_HOME>` with the appropriate directory on your file system. To make things easier later on, let's move the `tc-config.xml` file to the Tomcat home directory as follows:

```
> move tc-config.xml <TOMCAT_HOME>
```

You now have to make Tomcat aware of Terracotta by adding a file to the `bin` directory that will properly configure the environment. This file is called `setenv.bat`, and it should contain what you see in Listing 7-13. Make sure to put it in the `<TOMCAT_HOME>/bin` directory; otherwise, it will not be picked up when Tomcat is started. Also, don't forget to properly replace `<TC_HOME>` with the root directory of your Terracotta installation.

Listing 7-13. *Contents of the Tomcat bin/setenv.bat File*

```
set TC_INSTALL_DIR=<TC_HOME>
set TC_CONFIG_PATH="localhost:9510"
call %TC_INSTALL_DIR%\bin\dso-env.bat -q
set JAVA_OPTS=%TC_JAVA_OPTS% %JAVA_OPTS%
```

Go ahead and see if the example application is working as expected. Start up the Terracotta server with your `tc-config.xml` file:

```
> <TC_HOME>\bin\start-tc-server.bat -f <TOMCAT_HOME>\tc-config.xml
```

You can now start Tomcat in another terminal with its standard script:

```
> cd <TOMCAT_HOME>
> bin\startup.bat
```

The example application is available at the URL `http://localhost:8080/example2/cart.jsp`; visit it in your web browser to see that it works.

Also, feel free to install a second Tomcat instance elsewhere on your hard disk. If you modify its `conf/server.xml` configuration file to change the TCP/IP ports, you can run it alongside the first Tomcat instance. You need to start the Terracotta server only once, so don't do that again. However, don't forget to put the `setenv.bat` file in the `bin` directory of your second Tomcat server; otherwise, that server will not use Terracotta. After you start up your second Tomcat instance and access it in your web browser, you should see that the sessions are automatically shared between the instances. You can even try to install Tomcat on another machine and change the `TC_CONFIG_PATH` variable in the `setenv.bat` file so that it points to the IP address of the machine where the Terracotta server runs.

Verifying Fine-Grain Change Detection

It's one thing to take our word for the fact that Terracotta supports fine-grained changes, but nothing beats seeing it working with your own eyes. Terracotta supports a whole collection of debug settings, and two of them come in handy for demonstrating fine-grained changes. Open the `tc-config.xml` file of this example; locate the `<clients>` section; and add the contents of Listing 7-14 before the terminating tag.

Listing 7-14. *Debug Settings for tc-config.xml to See Fine-Grained Changes*

```
<dso>
  <debugging>
    <runtime-logging>
      <field-change-debug>true</field-change-debug>
      <new-object-debug>true</new-object-debug>
    </runtime-logging>
  </debugging>
</dso>
```

Make sure you shut down the Terracotta server and your Tomcat instances, and start them all again. Visit the example URL at `http://localhost:8080/example2/cart.jsp`, and create a couple of items in the cart. Then, modify the amount of an existing item by entering another number in the first form field and the name of an existing item in the second form field. Submit the form, and open the file `<TOMCAT_HOME>/logs/client-logs/terracotta-client.log`. You'll see something similar to Listing 7-15 at the end of the file.

Listing 7-15. *Excerpt of terracotta-client.log with Debug Statements That Show Fine-Grained Changes*

```
<<snip>> com.terracottatech.dso.runtime - New DSO Object instance created
  instance: example.Item@2ade54
  object ID: ObjectID=[1009]
<<snip>> com.terracottatech.dso.runtime - DSO object field changed
  class: com.terracotta.session.SessionData,
  field: com.terracotta.session.SessionData.lastAccessedTime
  newValue type: java.lang.Long, identityHashCode: 0xb5b633
<<snip>> com.terracottatech.dso.runtime - DSO object field changed
  class: example.Item,
  field: example.Item.amount
  newValue type: java.lang.Integer, identityHashCode: 0xd40b9d
<<snip>> com.terracottatech.dso.runtime - DSO object field changed
  class: com.terracotta.session.SessionData,
  field: com.terracotta.session.SessionData.lastAccessedTime
  newValue type: java.lang.Long, identityHashCode: 0xe9ee3f
```

You can clearly see that a new item was created when it was first added to the session; afterward, the `amount` field of that entry was changed when a new value was submitted. Also, each time the session is used, the `lastAccessedTime` field of the session data is updated.

Understanding HTTP Sessions with Terracotta

Now that you've learned about the theory and the practice behind HTTP session clustering, we're going to cover some areas that are specific to Terracotta.

Supported Platforms

We explained in the beginning of this chapter that Terracotta provides its own implementation of HTTP sessions that is optimized for clustered usage. To make this implementation as easy to use as possible, it's integrated with various application servers, servlet containers, and frameworks, so you can add just the appropriate parameters and integration modules to the configuration file and be able to use clustered HTTP sessions without any additional effort.

Terracotta has worked closely with the development teams of a number of web application technologies to provide seamless integration. At the time of this writing, Terracotta version 2.6 currently supports the following products:

- Apache Tomcat

- BEA WebLogic

- IBM WebSphere Application Server and Community Edition

- Jetty

- Apache Geronimo

- JBoss

- Apache Struts 1.1

- RIFE

- Wicket

Support for containers and frameworks continually evolves, so be sure to check `http://www.terracotta.org/` for a complete and up-to-date list.

Architecture Considerations

Terracotta does its best to keep data where it's used. If a session is used on a particular server, Terracotta will keep it instantiated on the heap, assuming there isn't too much data to fit in RAM. The typical scale-out architecture for web applications includes an array of application servers fronted by a load balancer. The user agent connects to the load balancer, which then decides how to route the requests to the application servers. If a user's request traffic should be routed to a different server by the load balancer, Terracotta will automatically fault that session into heap on the new server. That being said, there are some deployment architecture decisions that you can make to greatly improve the performance of your cluster.

The Effects of a Round-Robin Load Balancer

How the load balancer decides to route requests is of great importance to achieving scalability with Terracotta. A naive load balancing approach is to cycle through the application servers, irrespective of the properties of the incoming request—this approach is typically referred to as a round-robin load distribution mechanism. It evenly distributes the request load across the available application servers, but it will have a negative impact on Terracotta scalability.

In the event that all of the session data will fit on the physical heap of the application servers, a round-robin load balancer will tend to pin all of the active session data into the local heap of all of the application servers. This happens because requests for any given session will tend to be evenly distributed across the active servers. During the processing of those requests, the session data will be automatically faulted into whichever server is handling the request until, eventually, every server will have served a request for every session. Therefore, every session will reside on each server's heap, which will cause every change to every session to be propagated to every application server. The amount of network traffic, processing, and overhead to keep session state in sync across the cluster multiplies with the number of application servers. Because this architecture doesn't scale linearly, at some point, adding new servers to meet increasing demand will result in diminishing returns and a hard limit on the scalability of the application.

This situation gets remarkably worse when not all of the active session data will fit into available physical heap on the application servers. In this case, not only is there the extra overhead of keeping all of the session data in sync, but the Terracotta object cache in each application server will start to thrash. This happens because, as the amount of heap taken up by session data increases beyond what will fit into the Terracotta object cache, the Terracotta client will take steps to evict objects from the cache. However, since a round-robin load balancer distributes all sessions to all application servers evenly, there will be no active sessions that are used less than others; to conserve memory, the Terracotta virtual memory subsystem will be evicting active session data, which will soon need to be faulted in again.

This cache churn will seriously affect the performance of the Terracotta virtual heap, further degrading scalability. You may have experienced a situation very much like this on your own computer if your active memory usage has ever exceeded the available physical RAM. As the programs on your computer compete for access to memory that doesn't all fit into RAM, your memory I/O degrades from RAM speed to disk speed causing your computer to become sluggish and unusable.

Using a Sticky Load Balancer

Given the negative impact of a round-robin load balancer on Terracotta scalability, we strongly caution against using one. Instead, a much friendlier load-balancing scheme is one that maintains session affinity between users and the servers hosting their session. This kind of sticky load balancer tends to keep data for a particular session on only one application server, greatly increasing locality of reference. Since data for any given session is only in the physical heap of one server, changes to it need not be propagated to any other application server, eliminating much of the network and processing overhead of maintaining the virtual heap.

Also, since data for any given session is only in the physical heap of one server, it doesn't take up heap space on any other application server, reducing the overall amount of physical heap required and minimizing cache churn. Accurately provisioning your cluster is also easier, since you know how many active sessions will fit into the physical heap of an application server. When the number of active sessions grows beyond what will fit in physical heap, you can provision more application servers, keeping the number of sessions per server constant and ensuring that all of the active objects will fit in the local Terracotta cache. As an example, assume your application session objects take 1KB each, and you have 1MB of memory per server. A server can therefore handle 1000 sessions. If your web site will be visited by 10,000 users at any one time—sometimes referred to as concurrent users—you would need approximately ten servers to handle all the session objects without experiencing Terracotta cache eviction.

Running a Terracotta Cluster

As we cautioned earlier, stopping the Terracotta server implies freezing the application cluster. Specifically, any session that needs to be created or updated will need the Terracotta server to complete the session operations. Conversely, any session resident in an application server node's memory that is only being read from does not need the Terracotta server. Since it is impossible to predict when end users will read or write their session data and when specific application nodes will go down or otherwise invoke a session failover in the load balancer, Terracotta must always be up and running to ensure no delays or pauses for end users.

To achieve 100 percent uptime, a Terracotta-based application cluster includes built-in high-availability replication services. You can run Terracotta in a highly available manner in two ways. The first is called networked active passive (NAP) mode. This mode needs only TCP/IP support and a second instance of Terracotta to ensure consistent service to the application cluster. In the second mode, Terracotta works with shared disk storage (SAN is preferred) to make its data available to multiple Terracotta server instances. NAP is preferred because it is easy to set up and requires no additional hardware to operate.

Summary

Scale-out architectures have made simple HTTP session usage difficult. As a result, the use of HTTP sessions for storing user state has been largely discouraged in favor of stateless architectures where that data is kept off-server. However, from the application developer's point of view, using the session for user state is often the best answer. In fact, some popular web application frameworks make heavy use of the HTTP session. Using the Terracotta virtual heap to store session data in conjunction with a sticky load balancer that yields high locality of reference can transparently provide very high scalability with high availability to your web application.

In Chapters 1 and 2, you were first introduced to the idea of stateful programming with a stateless runtime environment. For HTTP session replication—where Terracotta was first applied—the push toward stateless programming has complicated the container and the architecture. Terracotta has simplified or removed most of the trade-offs of session replication by not replicating session at all and instead distributing the session objects efficiently in the application cluster.

A real application must have both domain objects stored in the database and conversational state stored in the session. Let's move on to Chapter 8, where we'll discuss Terracotta for Spring. We'll cluster a combination of domain objects and session objects, and introduce you to dependency injection in a Terracotta-based application.

CHAPTER 8

■ ■ ■

Clustering Spring

The Spring framework has recently become one of the primary choices for POJO-based web and enterprise development. Spring is, among other things, a dependency injection container that allows the developer to write business logic in POJOs and declaratively configure and inject dependencies, infrastructure services that are needed, and so on.

Spring's main goal has been to bring back simplicity to Java enterprise development by returning to POJOs that can be tested and deployed without a specific execution environment. Spring effectively helps you separate the enterprise qualities from the functional parts of your application: You write your application using an object model that best expresses its meaning. Spring then injects into your applications the gory enterprise details of how data is accessed, how the life cycles of objects are managed, and other such aspects of enterprise applications. This way, you can write code that is about your application, not about talking to a database, participating in transactions, or preparing messages to be shipped to other JVMs as messages.

Handily, Terracotta shares Spring's philosophy, making Terracotta and Spring a well-matched pair. Terracotta was designed specifically to let you write code about your application, avoiding manual development of code that makes your application highly available or scalable. As such, Terracotta's dedicated support for the Spring Framework allows developers to create regular nonclustered Spring applications, test them as usual, and when needed, declaratively define which Spring beans (in which application contexts) they want to have clustered. Terracotta will then ensure that these Spring beans are clustered as effectively as possible while retaining exactly the same semantics across the cluster as on the single node.

You can think of Terracotta as allowing you to cluster a Spring application context across multiple JVMs as if they were all on the same JVM. The singleton beans, session scoped beans, and custom scoped beans in a particular application context that have been declared as clustered in Terracotta will be shared among all instances of that application context in every JVM attached to the Terracotta cluster. Additionally, application events for that application context can be configured to be automatically sent to all listeners of that application's events in all JVMs.

In this chapter, we will take a tour through the process of turning a non-Spring clustered application into a Spring-enabled clustered application, showing you how you can integrate Terracotta and Spring in a simple, effective, and natural fashion.

A Sample: Spring Beans Without a Database

The application we'll be working with is similar in spirit to the inventory sample that comes with the Terracotta kit and that you'll see elsewhere in this book (we will performance-tune and visualize the inventory application in Chapter 12). However, it has been rewritten to adhere more closely to the DI paradigm.

The application represents a simple retail store with an inventory of products that can be viewed and modified. The store entities are modeled with five components:

- Product: A Product object contains the SKU, name, price, and inventory level of a particular product in the store.

- Department: Department objects group products into like sets. For example, there might be a Shoes department with all of the shoes products in it. The same product might be a member of more than one department.

- Departments: This controls access to all Department objects.

- Inventory: This represents all of the products in the entire store, irrespective of their departments. It provides a view onto all of the products in the store.

- Store: The Store is the main component that contains all of the other components. Access to products, departments, and inventory is controlled through the Store.

In addition to the entity components, a number of other supporting classes implement application and display logic. These include a class called CLI that contains the application loop and user-input functions for the command-line interface.

■**Note**   The code for the sample project can be retrieved from http://www.apress.com.

A first look at the store component, shown in Listing 8-1, reveals that all of the other components that the Store object itself interacts with are passed to it via the Store() constructor. This is the essence of DI. The store component is responsible for exactly one thing—providing access to the components of the store. It constructs none of its state by itself; therefore, the actual implementation of the other system components it interacts with is completely independent of the implementation of the store. The store's dependencies are injected into it through constructor arguments.

■**Note**   There are many styles of DI beyond passing in constructor arguments; we won't discuss all of them. There is also much more to Spring than just DI. To explore Spring, DI, and inversion of control more deeply, visit the Spring Framework web site at http://www.springframework.org/.

The Store class contains references to a Departments object and an Inventory object. The Departments object is responsible for the life cycle of the various departments in the store.

Listing 8-1. *The Store Class*

```
package org.terracotta.book.inventory.entity;

import org.terracotta.book.inventory.display.DepartmentDisplay;
import org.terracotta.book.inventory.display.InventoryDisplay;

public class Store {

  private final Departments departments;
  private final Inventory inventory;

  public Store(final Departments departments, final Inventory inventory) {
    this.departments = departments;
    this.inventory = inventory;
  }

  public int getDepartmentCount() {
    return this.departments.getDepartmentCount();
  }

  public Department newDepartment(final String name) {
    return departments.newDepartment(name);
  }

  public void displayInventory(InventoryDisplay inventoryDisplay) {
    inventory.display(inventoryDisplay);
  }

  public void displayDepartments(DepartmentDisplay departmentDisplay) {
    departments.displayDepartments(departmentDisplay);
  }

  public Product getProductBySKU(String sku) {
    return inventory.getProductBySKU(sku);
  }
}
```

Our simple implementation of the Departments class uses a Set to contain all of the Department objects. You can imagine, however, a more sophisticated Departments class that persists the Department data to a permanent store. Because the Store doesn't create the Departments class itself, the actual implementation of the Departments class is completely decoupled. Changing which Departments implementation is used in our Store is as simple as passing a different object into the Store's constructor.

With that said, let's take a look at the Departments class, shown in Listing 8-2.

Listing 8-2. *The Departments Class*

```
package org.terracotta.book.inventory.entity;

import java.util.Set;
import java.util.TreeSet;

import org.terracotta.book.inventory.display.DepartmentDisplay;
import org.terracotta.book.inventory.util.DepartmentByNameComparator;

public class Departments {
  private final Set<Department> departments;
  private final DepartmentFactory departmentFactory;

  public Departments(final DepartmentByNameComparator comparator,
        final DepartmentFactory departmentFactory) {
    this.departmentFactory = departmentFactory;
    departments = new TreeSet<Department>(comparator);
  }

  public Department newDepartment(final String name) {
    Department department = departmentFactory.newDepartment(name);
    synchronized (departments) {
      departments.add(department);
    }
    return department;
  }

  public void displayDepartments(final DepartmentDisplay departmentDisplay) {
    synchronized (departments) {
      for (Department department : departments) {
        department.display(departmentDisplay);
      }
    }
  }

  public int getDepartmentCount() {
    synchronized (departments) {
      return departments.size();
    }
  }
}
```

The Departments class is responsible for controlling the life cycle of Department objects. Its only state is a Set containing all of the extant Department objects and a reference to a factory object that creates new Department objects. It contains methods that display departments, but all of the actual display logic is delegated to display policy classes.

The Department class, shown in Listing 8-3, has a reference to a set that contains all of the Product objects in that department. It also has a field for the department name and a reference to the Inventory object. When a Product object is added to a Department, it is also passed to the Inventory object, so the Inventory object will be made aware of the new Product addition.

Listing 8-3. *The Department Class*

```java
package org.terracotta.book.inventory.entity;

import java.util.Set;
import java.util.TreeSet;

import org.terracotta.book.inventory.display.DepartmentDisplay;
import org.terracotta.book.inventory.util.ProductByNameComparator;

public class Department {

  private final String name;
  private final Set<Product> productsByName;
  private final Inventory inventory;

  public Department(final ProductByNameComparator comparator,
        final Inventory inventory, final String name) {
    this.inventory = inventory;
    this.name = name;
    productsByName = new TreeSet<Product>(comparator);
  }

  public String getName() {
    return this.name;
  }

  public void addProduct(Product product) {
    synchronized (productsByName) {
      productsByName.add(product);
    }
    inventory.addProduct(product);
  }

  public void display(final DepartmentDisplay departmentDisplay) {
    departmentDisplay.displayDepartment(this);
    synchronized (productsByName) {
      departmentDisplay.displayProducts(productsByName);
    }
  }
}
```

The Product class, shown in Listing 8-4, is simply a structure that contains data about a particular product. It provides methods for accessing the fields of the product and for modifying the mutable fields.

Listing 8-4. *The Product Class*

```
package org.terracotta.book.inventory.entity;

public class Product {
  private final String sku;
  private final String name;
  private double price;
  private int inventoryLevel;

  public Product(final String sku, final String name, final double price,
        final int inventoryLevel) {
    this.sku = sku;
    this.name = name;
    this.price = price;
    this.inventoryLevel = inventoryLevel;
  }

  public String getSku() {
    return sku;
  }

  public String getName() {
    return name;
  }

  public synchronized double getPrice() {
    return price;
  }

  public synchronized int getInventoryLevel() {
    return inventoryLevel;
  }

  public int addInventory(int count) {
    return modInventory(count);
  }

  public int subtractInventory(int count) {
    return modInventory(count * -1);
  }

  private synchronized int modInventory(int count) {
    inventoryLevel += count;
```

```
      return inventoryLevel;
  }

  public synchronized void setPrice(double newPrice) {
    price = newPrice;
  }
}
```

The CLI class, shown in Listing 8-5, contains the application logic of the command-line interface for this example. The run() method contains the application loop that requests user input to display and modify the catalog.

Listing 8-5. *The CLI Class*

```
package org.terracotta.book.inventory.cli;

import org.terracotta.book.inventory.display.DepartmentDisplay;
import org.terracotta.book.inventory.display.InventoryDisplay;
import org.terracotta.book.inventory.display.ProductDisplay;
import org.terracotta.book.inventory.entity.Department;
import org.terracotta.book.inventory.entity.Product;
import org.terracotta.book.inventory.entity.Store;

public class CLI implements Runnable {
  private final Store store;
  private final String[] initMenu = { "Use default items", "Enter items by hand" };
  private final String[] viewMenu = { "Exit", "View departments", "View inventory",
                                      "Modify product" };
  private final String[] modifyProductMenu =
    { "Escape", "Change price", "Change inventory" };

  private final DepartmentDisplay departmentDisplay;
  private final InventoryDisplay inventoryDisplay;
  private final CLIHelper helper;
  private final ProductDisplay productDisplay;

  public CLI(final CLIHelper helper, final DepartmentDisplay departmentDisplay,
      final ProductDisplay productDisplay, final InventoryDisplay inventoryDisplay,
      final Store store) {
    this.helper = helper;
    this.departmentDisplay = departmentDisplay;
    this.productDisplay = productDisplay;
    this.inventoryDisplay = inventoryDisplay;
    this.store = store;
  }

  public void run() {
    helper.println("Welcome to the Terracotta inventory demo.");
```

```
      if (store.getDepartmentCount() == 0) {
        helper.println("The store is currently empty.  Let's add some departments ➡
and products...");
        int choice = helper.askMenu(initMenu);
        switch (choice) {
        case (0):
          helper.println("Adding default products");
          Department dept = store.newDepartment("Shoes");
          dept.addProduct(new Product("SAND", "Sandals", 15.96, 29));
          dept.addProduct(new Product("LOAF", "Loafers", 59.99, 45));

          dept = store.newDepartment("Sports");
          dept.addProduct(new Product("BBAL", "Basketball", 12.95, 30));
          dept.addProduct(new Product("SK8Z", "Ice Skates", 61.99, 5));
          break;
        case (1):
          addDepartments();
          break;
        }
      }
      while (true) {
        // brain-dead application loop
        helper.println("");
        helper.printSeparator();
        helper.println("Main Menu");
        helper.printSeparator();
        int choice = helper.askMenu(viewMenu);
        switch (choice) {
        case 0:
          helper.println("Goodbye.");
          return;
        case 1:
          displayDepartments();
          break;
        case 2:
          displayInventory();
          break;
        case 3:
          modifyProduct();
          break;
        }
      }
    }

  private void displayInventory() {
    helper.printSeparator();
    helper.println("Inventory Display");
```

```java
    helper.printSeparator();
    store.displayInventory(inventoryDisplay);
  }

  private void displayDepartments() {
    helper.printSeparator();
    helper.println("Department Display");
    helper.printSeparator();
    store.displayDepartments(departmentDisplay);
  }

  private void addDepartments() {
    String addMore = "y";
    while (!"n".equals(addMore)) {
      addDepartment();
      addMore = helper.ask("Add more departments? [y|n]");
    }
  }

  private void addDepartment() {
    helper.println("Add department.");
    String name = helper.ask("Enter department name: ");
    Department department = store.newDepartment(name);
    String addMore = "y";
    while (!"n".equals(addMore)) {
      addProduct(department);
      addMore = helper.ask("Add more products in this department? [y|n]");
    }
  }

  private void addProduct(Department department) {
    helper.printSeparator();
    helper.println("Add product.");
    String sku = helper.ask("Enter product SKU: ");
    String name = helper.ask("Enter product name: ");
    Double price = (Double) helper.ask("Enter product price: ", Double.class);
    Integer inventoryLevel =
      (Integer) helper.ask("Enter product inventory level: ", Integer.class);
    Product product =
      new Product(sku, name, price.doubleValue(), inventoryLevel.intValue());
    department.addProduct(product);
  }

  private void modifyProduct() {
    helper.printSeparator();
    helper.println("Modify Product");
    helper.printSeparator();
```

```
    Product product = null;
    while (product == null) {
      String sku = helper.ask("Enter sku:");
      product = store.getProductBySKU(sku);
      if (product == null) {
        helper.println("No product found by that sku.");
      }
    }
    productDisplay.display(product);
    int choice = helper.askMenu(modifyProductMenu);
    switch (choice) {
    case 0:
      return;
    case 1:
      double newPrice = (Double) helper.ask("Enter new price: ", Double.class);
      product.setPrice(newPrice);
      break;
    case 2:
      int delta =
        (Integer) helper.ask("Increment/decrement inventory by: ", Integer.class);
      product.addInventory(delta);
      break;
    }
    helper.printSeparator();
    helper.println("Modified Product");
    helper.printSeparator();
    productDisplay.display(product);
  }
}
```

The Main class, shown in Listing 8-6, wires up all of the components and starts the command-line interface (CLI) application. This demonstrates one way of implementing DI without using a framework like Spring. Later, we will look at how you can use Spring to declare the relationships among the components in a configuration file and have Spring magically do the wiring that you see here in the Main class. The IOImpl class is not covered here but is included in the example code available online if you want to compile and run these samples. IOImpl simply sets System.in and System.out as the input and output streams.

Listing 8-6. *The Main Class*

```
package org.terracotta.book.inventory.cli;

import org.terracotta.book.inventory.display.DepartmentDisplay;
import org.terracotta.book.inventory.display.InventoryDisplay;
import org.terracotta.book.inventory.display.ProductDisplay;
import org.terracotta.book.inventory.entity.DepartmentFactory;
import org.terracotta.book.inventory.entity.Departments;
import org.terracotta.book.inventory.entity.Inventory;
```

```
import org.terracotta.book.inventory.entity.Store;
import org.terracotta.book.inventory.util.CurrencyFormatFactory;
import org.terracotta.book.inventory.util.DepartmentByNameComparator;
import org.terracotta.book.inventory.util.ProductByNameComparator;
import org.terracotta.book.inventory.util.StringUtil;

public class Main {

  public static void main(String[] args) {
    IO io = new IOImpl();
    StringUtil util = new StringUtil();
    CurrencyFormatFactory currencyFormatFactory = new CurrencyFormatFactory();
    int skuWidth = 8;
    int nameWidth = 30;
    int priceWidth = 10;
    int inventoryLevelWidth = 10;
    ProductDisplay productDisplay =
      new ProductDisplay(io, util, currencyFormatFactory,
                         skuWidth, nameWidth,  priceWidth, inventoryLevelWidth);
    DepartmentDisplay departmentDisplay = new DepartmentDisplay(io, productDisplay);
    InventoryDisplay inventoryDisplay = new InventoryDisplay(io, productDisplay);
    ProductByNameComparator productByNameComparator = new
        ProductByNameComparator();
    Inventory inventory = new Inventory(productByNameComparator);
    Departments departments = new Departments(new DepartmentByNameComparator(),
        new DepartmentFactory(productByNameComparator, inventory));
    Store store = new Store(departments, inventory);
    new CLI(new CLIHelper(io), departmentDisplay, productDisplay, inventoryDisplay,
        store).run();
  }
}
```

Running the Example on a Single JVM

Now that you've seen the code of the important classes, let's run the example as a stand-alone application without Spring or Terracotta to see how it works.

Once you have acquired the example source code, open a terminal, and change directories to the top-level project directory. From now on, the instructions will assume that you are executing the commands (shown on Linux) from this top-level directory.

The first step is to compile the code like so:

```
%> javac -d bin -sourcepath src/main/java \
  src/main/java/org/terracotta/book/inventory/cli/Main.java
```

The -d flag tells Java to place the compiled classes in the bin directory (this is for compatibility with the Eclipse, which compiles code into the bin directory by default). We need to tell javac to compile only the Main class, because all of the dependencies can be reached from it.

Next, run the Main class, making sure to add the bin directory to the classpath:

```
%> java -cp bin org.terracotta.book.inventory.cli.Main
```

You should see this in your console:

```
Welcome to the Terracotta inventory demo.
The store is currently empty.  Let's add some departments and products...
Choose an action by number:
[ 0 ] Use default items
[ 1 ] Enter items by hand

==>
```

When the application first starts, the store is empty, so you are prompted to add items to the store. You can either let the application fill the store with default items by typing **0**, or you can add items by hand. You should now be taken to the main menu:

```
Welcome to the Terracotta inventory demo.
The store is currently empty.  Let's add some departments and products...
Choose an action by number:
[ 0 ] Use default items
[ 1 ] Enter items by hand

==> 0
Adding default products


====================================================================
Main Menu
====================================================================
Choose an action by number:
[ 0 ] Exit
[ 1 ] View departments
[ 2 ] View inventory
[ 3 ] Modify product

==>
```

To see the contents of the store that were just added, you can choose to look at them grouped by department or just view the entire inventory in alphabetical order. Let's choose "View departments". You will see output like this:

```
Choose an action by number:
[ 0 ] Exit
[ 1 ] View departments
[ 2 ] View inventory
```

```
[ 3 ] Modify product

==> 1
==================================================================
Department Display
==================================================================
------------------------------------------------------------------

Department Shoes
SKU         | Product Name              |     Price |  Inventory
------------------------------------------------------------------

LOAF        | Loafers                   |    $59.99 |         45
SAND        | Sandals                   |    $15.96 |         29
------------------------------------------------------------------

Department Sports
SKU         | Product Name              |     Price |  Inventory
------------------------------------------------------------------

BBAL        | Basketball                |    $12.95 |         30
SK8Z        | Ice Skates                |    $61.99 |          5


==================================================================
Main Menu
==================================================================
Choose an action by number:
[ 0 ] Exit
[ 1 ] View departments
[ 2 ] View inventory
[ 3 ] Modify product

==>
```

Now that you've seen all of the products, let's modify one of the them:

```
==================================================================
Main Menu
==================================================================
Choose an action by number:
[ 0 ] Exit
[ 1 ] View departments
[ 2 ] View inventory
[ 3 ] Modify product

==> 3
==================================================================
Modify Product
==================================================================
```

```
Enter sku:
==>
```

Enter the SKU for the sandals, and you will be given a choice to modify either the price or the inventory level. Let's put the sandals on sale and lower the price to $12.99. The application will print the modified product, so you can see the new price reflected. It will then take you back to the main menu:

```
=====================================================================
Modify Product
=====================================================================
Enter sku:
==> SAND
SAND    | Sandals                    |      $15.96 |          29
Choose an action by number:
[ 0 ] Escape
[ 1 ] Change price
[ 2 ] Change inventory

==> 1
Enter new price:
==> 12.99
=====================================================================
Modified Product
=====================================================================
SAND    | Sandals                    |      $12.99 |          29


=====================================================================
Main Menu
=====================================================================
Choose an action by number:
[ 0 ] Exit
[ 1 ] View departments
[ 2 ] View inventory
[ 3 ] Modify product

==>
```

Feel free to experiment by changing the prices or inventory levels of other products.

Running the Example Clustered with Terracotta

Now that you've seen the application run on a single JVM, let's use Terracotta to cluster the store, so the application can run on multiple JVMs.

The example project comes with two Terracotta configuration files. The one we will use now is designed to work with a non-Spring application and is shown in Listing 8-7. It explicitly declares roots and includes classes for instrumentation.

Listing 8-7. *tc-config-no-spring.xml*

```xml
<?xml version="1.0" encoding="UTF-8"?>
<con:tc-config xmlns:con="http://www.terracotta.org/config">
  <servers>
    <server host="%i" name="localhost">
      <dso-port>9510</dso-port>
      <jmx-port>9520</jmx-port>
      <data>terracotta/server-data</data>
      <logs>terracotta/server-logs</logs>
    </server>
  </servers>
  <clients>
    <logs>terracotta/client-logs</logs>
  </clients>
  <application>
    <dso>
      <instrumented-classes>
        <include>
          <class-expression>
            org.terracotta.book.inventory.entity..*
          </class-expression>
        </include>
        <include>
          <class-expression>
            org.terracotta.book.inventory.cli.CLI
          </class-expression>
        </include>
        <include>
          <class-expression>
            org.terracotta.book.inventory.util.DepartmentByNameComparator
          </class-expression>
        </include>
        <include>
          <class-expression>
            org.terracotta.book.inventory.util.ProductByNameComparator
          </class-expression>
        </include>
      </instrumented-classes>
      <locks>
        <autolock>
          <method-expression>
            * org.terracotta.book.inventory.entity..*(..)
          </method-expression>
```

```
          <lock-level>write</lock-level>
        </autolock>
      </locks>
      <roots>
        <root>
          <field-name>org.terracotta.book.inventory.cli.CLI.store</field-name>
        </root>
      </roots>
    </dso>
  </application>
</con:tc-config>
```

All of the objects in the `org.terracotta.book.inventory.entity` package will be clustered, so we use a class expression to include all classes in that package for instrumentation. The two comparator objects in the `util` package will be clustered also, so we add include expressions for them.

The `store` reference in the `CLI` class is declared as a root field. The `CLI` object never becomes a shared object. However, it manipulates shared objects directly, so it must also be instrumented.

The only methods that modify clustered objects are in the entity classes, so we use a method expression to declare all methods in the `entity` package to be automatically locked.

To run the example clustered with Terracotta, first start the Terracotta server in a separate terminal window. Make sure you specify the correct Terracotta configuration file and remember to replace `<$TC_HOME>` with the directory where you unzipped the Terracotta download:

```
%> <$TC_HOME>/bin/start-tc-server.sh -f tc-config-no-spring.xml
```

Back in your application terminal, use the `dso-env` script to determine the JVM arguments that need to be added to the `java` command. You will see output that looks like this, with slight variations depending on the version of Terracotta you are using and where you installed it:

```
<$TC_HOME>/bin/dso-env.sh localhost:9510
```

```
2008-03-24 14:33:28,124 INFO - Terracotta 26, as of 20080218-120204 (Revision
7031 by cruise@rh4mo0 from 2.6)
2008-03-24 14:33:28,669 INFO - Configuration loaded from the server at
'localhost:9510'.
-Xbootclasspath/p:<$TC_HOME>/lib/dso-boot/dso-boot-
hotspot_osx_150_13.jar  -Dtc.install-root=<$TC_HOME>/bin/..
-Dtc.config=localhost:9510
```

■Note Passing `localhost:9510` as an argument to `dso-env` tells Terracotta that the client JVMs should receive their configuration from the Terracotta server. This is a good practice that will ensure that all of the Terracotta client JVMs operate with the same configuration.

Now that you know what the Terracotta JVM arguments are, you can run Java with Terracotta enabled (the actual values of the Terracotta arguments you pass to Java will probably be slightly different than those shown here):

```
%> java \
  -Xbootclasspath/p<$TC_HOME>/bin/../lib/dso-boot/dso-boot-
hotspot_osx_150_13.jar  \
  -Dtc.install-root=<$TC_HOME>/bin/..  \
  -Dtc.config=localhost:9510 \
  -cp bin \
  org.terracotta.book.inventory.cli.Main
```

The application will operate exactly the same as it did before. The store, however, will be clustered. If you look at the runtime clustered object graph in the Terracotta administration console, you will see the Store, Inventory, Departments, Department, and Product objects on the Terracotta virtual heap.

To see the effect of clustering, go through the steps of adding items to the store and modifying a product or two. Next, start the application again in a different JVM in a new terminal window. Now, instead of prompting you to fill an empty store, the application instance running in the new JVM will find that there are already items in the store and skip straight to the main menu. When you view the inventory or departments lists, you will see all of the modifications to the store that you made in the first JVM reflected automatically in the new JVM.

You can continue to make modifications to the store in either JVM and view those modifications in the other JVM. Of course, you can shut down both application JVMs and start new ones to prove that the store data is durable.

A Note on DI and Terracotta

Before we move on to use Spring with this example, a few observations should be reiterated. The most important thing to notice is that the DI coding style has encouraged the code to have a very good separation of concerns. It is no accident that all of the clustered objects live in the same package. Lots of other classes help perform various display activities, and the CLI object contains all of the application logic, but none of those objects ever join the cluster.

The fact that only entity objects ever need to be clustered reinforces the second important point about Terracotta and the separation of concerns. Terracotta was never intended to cluster the *entire* Java heap. It is designed to cluster just those parts of the heap that ought to be shared across all instances of your application.

The Terracotta team occasionally receives feedback that the framework is not "perfectly drop-in." This is done on purpose. Clustering every byte of a Java heap would be not only wildly inefficient, but in many cases nonsensical. What would you do, for instance, with a clustered AWT Graphics context? By giving you declarative control of what parts of the Java heap ought to be clustered (in the form of what you pick as your roots and what objects join clustered object graphs), Terracotta lets you keep important application state data clustered, while leaving data that doesn't need to be clustered alone.

In your experiments with Terracotta, if you find that you need to make a lot of things transient because objects with no business being in the cluster are being sucked into clustered object graphs, your code may be commingling concerns that ought to be separated. Coding in a DI style reinforces the separation of concerns that will make Terracotta integration very natural.

Growing Spring Beans

So far, you have seen the example running as a stand-alone application and as a Terracotta clustered application. Now, let's look at how it might work as a Spring application and as a clustered Spring application.

Luckily, the example was coded with inversion of control in mind, so adapting it for Spring is trivial. We need only two new things to get the application to function with Spring. The first is the Spring application context configuration file, shown in Listing 8-8. In this Spring configuration, we tell Spring about Spring beans. Spring beans are components that Spring knows are part of an application and that need to be wired together in a particular way.

Listing 8-8. *The Spring Application Context Configuration File (applicationContext.xml)*

```xml
<?xml version="1.0" encoding="UTF-8"?>
<!DOCTYPE beans PUBLIC "-//SPRING//DTD BEAN//EN"
  "http://www.springframework.org/dtd/spring-beans.dtd">

<beans default-lazy-init="false">
  <bean id="stringUtil" class="org.terracotta.book.inventory.util.StringUtil"
      singleton="true"/>

  <bean id="productByNameComparator"
      class="org.terracotta.book.inventory.util.ProductByNameComparator"
      singleton="true"/>
  <bean id="departmentByNameComparator"
      class="org.terracotta.book.inventory.util.DepartmentByNameComparator"
      singleton="true"/>


  <bean id="inventory" class="org.terracotta.book.inventory.entity.Inventory"
      singleton="true">
    <constructor-arg><ref bean="productByNameComparator"/></constructor-arg>
  </bean>

  <bean id="departmentFactory"
      class="org.terracotta.book.inventory.entity.DepartmentFactory"
      singleton="true">
    <constructor-arg><ref bean="productByNameComparator"/></constructor-arg>
    <constructor-arg><ref bean="inventory"/></constructor-arg>
  </bean>

  <bean id="departments" class="org.terracotta.book.inventory.entity.Departments"
      singleton="true">
    <constructor-arg><ref bean="departmentByNameComparator"/></constructor-arg>
    <constructor-arg><ref bean="departmentFactory"/></constructor-arg>
  </bean>
```

```xml
<bean id="store" class="org.terracotta.book.inventory.entity.Store"
      singleton="true">
  <constructor-arg><ref bean="departments"/></constructor-arg>
  <constructor-arg><ref bean="inventory"/></constructor-arg>
</bean>

<bean id="io" class="org.terracotta.book.inventory.cli.IOImpl"
      singleton="true"/>
<bean id="currencyFormatFactory"
      class="org.terracotta.book.inventory.util.CurrencyFormatFactory"
      singleton="true"/>

<bean id="productDisplay"
      class="org.terracotta.book.inventory.display.ProductDisplay"
      singleton="true">
  <constructor-arg><ref bean="io"/></constructor-arg>
  <constructor-arg><ref bean="stringUtil"/></constructor-arg>
  <constructor-arg><ref bean="currencyFormatFactory"/></constructor-arg>
  <!-- SKU width -->
  <constructor-arg type="int"><value>8</value></constructor-arg>
  <!-- name width -->
  <constructor-arg type="int"><value>30</value></constructor-arg>
  <!-- price width -->
  <constructor-arg type="int"><value>10</value></constructor-arg>
  <!-- inventory level width -->
  <constructor-arg type="int"><value>10</value></constructor-arg>
</bean>

<bean id="departmentDisplay"
      class="org.terracotta.book.inventory.display.DepartmentDisplay"
      singleton="true">
  <constructor-arg><ref bean="io"/></constructor-arg>
  <constructor-arg><ref bean="productDisplay"/></constructor-arg>
</bean>

<bean id="inventoryDisplay"
      class="org.terracotta.book.inventory.display.InventoryDisplay"
      singleton="true">
  <constructor-arg><ref bean="io"/></constructor-arg>
  <constructor-arg><ref bean="productDisplay"/></constructor-arg>
</bean>

<bean id="cliHelper" class="org.terracotta.book.inventory.cli.CLIHelper"
      singleton="true">
  <constructor-arg><ref bean="io"/></constructor-arg>
</bean>
```

```
<bean id="cli" class="org.terracotta.book.inventory.cli.CLI" singleton="true">
  <constructor-arg><ref bean="cliHelper"/></constructor-arg>
  <constructor-arg><ref bean="departmentDisplay"/></constructor-arg>
  <constructor-arg><ref bean="productDisplay"/></constructor-arg>
  <constructor-arg><ref bean="inventoryDisplay"/></constructor-arg>
  <constructor-arg><ref bean="store"/></constructor-arg>
</bean>

</beans>
```

In our application context configuration, we have configured a number of beans, each corresponding to the components of our application, culminating in the declaration of the cli bean. Spring will use this configuration to construct instances of these beans and wire them together. If you look carefully, you will notice that this configuration file looks very similar to the Main class earlier in the chapter, except that the relationships among the components are declared in XML instead of Java.

Every bean in this example is declared as a singleton, which means that there will be only one instance of each bean per application context.

The final step to converting this application to make use of Spring is to add a main() method that sets in motion the creation of the application context, wires the beans, and starts the run() loop in the CLI object. For that, we create an analog to the Main class from earlier that we'll call SpringMain; it's shown in Listing 8-9.

Listing 8-9. *The SpringMain Class*

```
package org.terracotta.book.inventory.cli;

import org.springframework.beans.factory.BeanFactory;
import org.springframework.context.support.ClassPathXmlApplicationContext;

public class SpringMain {
  public static void main(String[] args) {
    BeanFactory factory = new ClassPathXmlApplicationContext(new String[] {
        "applicationContext.xml" });
    CLI cli = (CLI) factory.getBean("cli");
    cli.run();
  }
}
```

SpringMain creates a new BeanFactory (an application context) based on the applicationContext.xml configuration. Spring does all of the rest of the work of instantiating the beans and passing to them all of the right arguments based on what the bean relationships are declared to be in the configuration file. Once the application context is created, we get the cli bean out of the application context and start the application loop in the run() method.

Before we can run the Spring-enabled application, we need to compile SpringMain like so:

```
%> javac -cp lib/spring-2.0.8.jar -d bin -sourcepath src/main/java \
    src/main/java/org/terracotta/book/inventory/cli/SpringMain.java
```

Now, to run the Spring-enabled application, we need to add the Spring libraries and dependencies to the command line and tell Java to start the SpringMain class:

```
%> java -cp .:bin:lib/spring-2.0.8.jar:lib/commons-logging.jar \
    org.terracotta.book.inventory.cli.SpringMain
```

Now, you should see output that looks something like this:

```
Mar 24, 2008 4:32:34 PM org.springframework.context.support.
AbstractApplicationContext prepareRefresh
INFO: Refreshing org.springframework.context.support.
ClassPathXmlApplicationContext@34a7d8: display name ➡
[org.springframework.context.support.ClassPathXmlApplicationContext@34a7d8];
startup date [Mon Mar 24 16:32:34 PDT 2008]; root of context hierarchy
Mar 24, 2008 4:32:34 PM ➡
org.springframework.beans.factory.xml.XmlBeanDefinitionReader ➡
 loadBeanDefinitions
INFO: Loading XML bean definitions from class path resource [applicationContext.xml]
Mar 24, 2008 4:32:34 PM org.springframework.context.support.
AbstractApplicationContext obtainFreshBeanFactory
INFO: Bean factory for application context [org.springframework.context.support.
ClassPathXmlApplicationContext@34a7d8]:
org.springframework.beans.factory.support.DefaultListableBeanFactory@45f939
Mar 24, 2008 4:32:34 PM org.springframework.beans.factory.support.
DefaultListableBeanFactory preInstantiateSingletons
INFO: Pre-instantiating singletons in org.springframework.beans.factory.support.
DefaultListableBeanFactory@45f939: defining beans [stringUtil,
productByNameComparator,departmentByNameComparator,inventory,departmentFactory,
departments,store,io,currencyFormatFactory,productDisplay,departmentDisplay,
inventoryDisplay,cliHelper,cli]; root of factory hierarchy
Welcome to the Terracotta inventory demo.
The store is currently empty.  Let's add some departments and products...
Choose an action by number:
[ 0 ] Use default items
[ 1 ] Enter items by hand

==>
```

The application should work exactly the same as the non-Spring version. The only difference is in how the objects are wired together. As you can see, since the code was written with DI in mind, we have made no changes to our existing code to convert it to a Spring application.

Clustering Spring Beans

Nearly everything is in place to use Terracotta to cluster the Spring beans we have configured. The only thing we need now is a Terracotta configuration that is Spring-aware. Since Terracotta has explicit support for Spring, the configuration will be even simpler for this Spring-enabled version of our example application than it was for the plain Java version.

Terracotta provides a Spring-specific set of configuration tags in the configuration file; these tags help to raise the abstraction level from working with fields, classes, and methods to working with services (beans). This means that Spring users do not have to leave their domain to configure the distribution of their beans; instead, they can refer to their beans using the same names as in the Spring configuration file. Listing 8-10 shows our example file.

Listing 8-10. *The Terracotta Spring Configuration File (tc-config-spring.xml)*

```xml
<con:tc-config xmlns:con="http://www.terracotta.org/config">
  <servers>
    <server host="%i" name="localhost">
      <dso-port>9510</dso-port>
      <jmx-port>9520</jmx-port>
      <data>terracotta/server-data</data>
      <logs>terracotta/server-logs</logs>
    </server>
  </servers>
  <clients>
    <logs>terracotta/client-logs</logs>
  </clients>
  <application>
    <spring>
      <jee-application name="*">
        <application-contexts>
          <application-context>
            <paths>
              <path>applicationContext.xml</path>
            </paths>
            <beans>
              <bean name="store" />
            </beans>
          </application-context>
        </application-contexts>
        <instrumented-classes>
          <include>
            <class-expression>
              org.terracotta.book.inventory.util.DepartmentByNameComparator
            </class-expression>
          </include>
          <include>
            <class-expression>
              org.terracotta.book.inventory.util.ProductByNameComparator
            </class-expression>
          </include>
        </instrumented-classes>
      </jee-application>
```

```
    </spring>
  </application>
</con:tc-config>
```

Notice that not all beans are declared as clustered. In fact, the only bean we declared as clustered is the `store` bean. This is because Terracotta analyzes the dependency graph of clustered Spring beans and determines the appropriate configuration for them. From that dependency graph, Terracotta is able to determine which classes need to be instrumented and which methods must be automatically locked.

Apart from defining which beans should be clustered, we need to define three more things:

- We have to define the path to the Spring bean definition file. In this example, it is `applicationContext.xml`.

- There are two classes that aren't recognized by Terracotta in the `store` bean dependency graph, `DepartmentByNameComparator` and `ProductByNameComparator`, so we must explicitly configure them for instrumentation.

- We have to define the name of the JEE application associated with this application context. If the Spring application is deployed as a web application, the JEE application name is usually the name of the WAR file the web application is deployed in. This means that the configuration is local to this specific web application. Because this example is a stand-alone Spring application, we use the wildcard character (*) as the application name.

NONDISTRIBUTED BEAN FIELDS

By default, all of a clustered bean's references (fields) are also clustered (i.e., the whole object graph that is referenced from the clustered bean is clustered). But you are allowed to define certain fields as nondistributable, which means that they will not be clustered and will maintain a local value. This ability allows you to effectively limit the graph. Avoiding DSO-based replication is very important in certain cases since the bean might have references to objects that are holding on to operating-system–specific resources, such as files and sockets, that are by nature not clusterable. The fields are referred to by their names in the Java code. Here is an example:

```
<beans>
  <bean name="beanName">
    <non-distributed-field>myFieldOne</non-distributed-field>
    <non-distributed-field>myFieldTwo</non-distributed-field>
  </bean>
</beans>
```

Running with Clustered Spring Beans

Now, all of the pieces are in place to run the application with clustered Spring beans. This time, start the Terracotta server with the `tc-config-spring.xml` as the configuration file argument:

```
%> <$TC_HOME>/bin/start-tc-server.sh -f tc-config-spring.xml
```

Once the server starts, run one instance of the application in a terminal window like so:

```
%> java \
  -Xbootclasspath/p:\
<$TC_HOME>/bin/../lib/dso-boot/dso-boot-hotspot_osx_150_13.jar  \
  -Dtc.install-root=<$TC_HOME>/bin/.. \
  -Dtc.config=localhost:9510 \
  -cp .:bin:lib/spring-2.0.8.jar:lib/commons-logging.jar \
  org.terracotta.book.inventory.cli.SpringMain
```

Go through the same process of adding products to the store and modifying them; then, start another instance. Not surprisingly, the clustered Spring application works just like the clustered application without Spring.

There is one difference between the two application versions, however. In the clustered application without Spring, we declared the store field of `CLI` to be a Terracotta root field. Since Terracotta clusters Spring beans for you, you don't have to specify a root. If you start the Terracotta administration console, you will see that Terracotta has created a root for you that contains the clustered beans in the Spring context (see Figure 8-1).

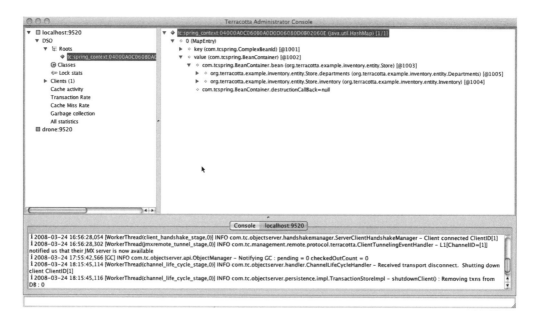

Figure 8-1. *Automatically created root for Spring application contexts*

Terracotta Session Clustering for Spring

Terracotta has support for clustering of Spring Web Flow and session scoped beans. To turn on this feature, you have to set `session-support` to `true`.

```
<!-- Under c:config/application/spring/jee-application -->
<session-support>true</session-support>
```

This also turns on regular HTTP session clustering for the web application defined in the enclosing `<jee-application>` element.

Summary

In this chapter, we have gone through the process of creating a plain Java application, clustering it, and augmenting it to work as a Spring application and, finally, as a clustered Spring application.

As you've seen, an application that is designed using the inversion of control pattern, which Spring reinforces, works very well with Terracotta, even if you aren't using it with Spring. The separation of concerns that DI promotes tends to make very clear what objects belong on the virtual heap when you cluster your application. Furthermore, the Spring integration that Terracotta provides makes configuring your Spring application to work with Terracotta easy. But, what about applications that work with other technologies? Is there a way to provide tight integration between Terracotta and third-party technologies other than Spring?

In the next chapter, we explore how to use and build Terracotta Integration Modules (TIMs). TIMs provide a convenient and portable way to encapsulate all of the configuration and supporting code required to work with a particular library or application. Terracotta provides a number of TIMs that make using Terracotta with other existing technologies as easy as with Spring. And you can build and publish your own TIMs to work with your own code or libraries or with technologies that don't already have explicit Terracotta support.

■■■

CHAPTER 9

Integration Modules

This chapter discusses the Terracotta Integration Module (TIM) framework, which allows you to specify sets of clustering configurations as components, and include those components in your own configuration. We will investigate how to use TIMs and how to build them from scratch, which you might do to cluster an external library or framework where you need clustering or when modularizing the clustering configuration of your own application.

Clustering by Configuration

Terracotta's approach to clustering is founded on the idea of transparency. The best abstraction to use when writing scalable distributed software is the same abstraction you use when writing scalable concurrent single-JVM software. Thus, clustering occurs via external configuration rather than by the use of an API and new libraries in your code.

A key consequence of this approach is that external configuration can be applied to existing libraries even when they were not originally designed for that purpose. Configuration-driven clustering allows you to take advantage of the many great open source libraries available today in your distributed system.

Terracotta supports the concept of external configuration for a library or component with the Terracotta Integration Module (TIM). A TIM consists of configuration information and occasionally code that specifies how the component should be clustered and instrumented, how locking is performed, and so on.

A TIM itself is contained in a JAR file. The TIM has within it a manifest, some Terracotta configuration defined in an XML file, and possibly some code that can be applied to modify the original library if necessary.

Using TIMs

We will begin our exploration of TIMs by looking at an example of when they are useful and at how you can use modules created by Terracotta or someone else.

Clustering a Synchronized Map

By default, most collection classes are unsynchronized. A class like `HashMap` has no synchronization and can only be used safely in a single thread at a time. However, the Java Collections

API contains a utility class named Collections with a synchronizedMap() method that will wrap any Map passed to it with another class that synchronizes on the Map for every method call (similar to Hashtable).

If you then cluster that synchronized Map, you will need to specify clustered locks for access to every method on the Map object. Typically, you will need to specify write-level autolocks on all methods that modify the state of the Map and read-level autolocks on all other methods. You would do this in your tc-config.xml file by adding a <locks> section as shown in Listing 9-1.

Listing 9-1. *The Locks Stanza in tc-config.xml*

```
<locks>
  <autolock>
    <method-expression>
      void java.util.Collections$SynchronizedMap.clear()
    </method-expression>
    <lock-level>write</lock-level>
  </autolock>
  <autolock>
    <method-expression>
      Object java.util.Collections$SynchronizedMap.clone()
    </method-expression>
    <lock-level>read</lock-level>
  </autolock>

  ...for every method in Set...

</locks>
```

This locking code will work fine, but you will need to use this in every application that uses a synchronized Map. An alternative is to bundle up this lock configuration into a TIM, which can then be included in any application that needs it.

Importing a TIM

As it turns out, Terracotta provides the synchronized Map autolock configuration in the Autolocked Collections Terracotta Integration Module called tim-synchronizedmap.

To include a TIM, you simply include it in the <clients> section of your Terracotta configuration. Listing 9-2 shows an example fragment of how to include the tim-synchronizedmap module in your configuration's <clients> section of your application's Terracotta configuration file (usually tc-config.xml).

Listing 9-2. *Requiring a Module in tc-config.xml*

```
<clients>
  <modules>
    <module name="tim-synchronizedmap" version="2.0.0" />
  </modules>
</clients>
```

Each module declaration consists of three attributes:

- `name`: The module name, which is required.

- `version`: The module version, which is required.

- `group-id`: The module group identifier, which is optional. If not specified, it is assumed to be `org.terracotta.modules`.

At run time, Terracotta will read your configuration and the included modules and include the configuration from each module in your application's configuration. An integration module's configuration may itself include other configuration modules, which will be included as well. This allows you to, in effect, create modules that are bundles of other modules.

In this example, the previous autolock configuration no longer needs to be included, as the module will pull it in as a chunk of additional configuration.

Module Repositories

The next question is how does your application know where to find the JAR files that define the modules included in your application? Terracotta looks for modules in a module repository, which is nothing but a directory that serves as a collection of JAR files.

Modules do not need to be in a single repository; multiple repositories may be specified and will be searched in order. Terracotta always first searches an implicit repository defined as follows:

```
file://<terracotta-install-dir>/modules
```

The module repository structure is compatible with the Maven repository structure, although it requires only the actual JAR files to be present.

■**Note** See `http://maven.apache.org/guides/introduction/introduction-to-repositories.html` for more information on Maven repositories.

The directory path is based on the `group-id` and TIM name. The JAR file in that directory is named based on the TIM name and version. For example, the module specified in Listing 9-2 translates to the following repository path:

```
org/terracotta/modules/tim-synchronizedmap/2.0.0/tim-synchronizedmap-2.0.0.jar
```

You can specify additional repository locations in the `<clients>` configuration element using the `<repository>` element. For example, Listing 9-3 shows multiple repositories that will be searched. The Terracotta installation `modules` subdirectory will be searched first, so there is no need to specify it. Further, the `<repository>` elements will be searched in the order specified, so as Listing 9-3 illustrates, you can use shared repositories on file servers on the network yet override shared ones by searching a local repository first. Currently, only repositories defined via a `file://` URL are supported.

Listing 9-3. *Specifying Repositories in tc-config.xml*

```
<clients>
  <modules>
    <repository>file:///usr/local/share/terracotta/modules</repository>
    <repository>file://share/mygroup/terracotta/modules</repository>
    <repository>file://othershare/mycompany/terracotta/modules</repository>
    <module name="tim-synchronizedmap" version="2.0.0 " />
  </modules>
</clients>
```

Generally, you will want to list the repositories in order from the most volatile directories on your local machine, such as those where you are currently developing modules, to the most stable or frozen modules shared on your network. In Listing 9-3, the Terracotta installation directory is searched first, then the user's local repository, followed by the user's group repository, and finally the company repository.

You can obtain TIMs in several places: from the Terracotta download kit, from the Terracotta Forge, or by making one yourself. The Terracotta kit contains a `modules` subdirectory, as previously discussed, that can serve as a module repository.

The Terracotta Forge

The Terracotta Forge provides an open repository for the development of code and projects related to Terracotta. Most importantly, the Forge provides a place where both Terracotta and community members can develop and share TIMs. The Forge can be accessed at `http://forge.terracotta.org` and has an associated module repository.

Each project hosted on the Terracotta Forge has access to the following resources:

- Subversion source code repository

- Wiki space

- Web forum

- Project-specific web site generation and hosting

- Automated build

- Automated testing

- Automated project artifact creation and deployment

The Forge also provides a set of resources shared among all projects:

- Mailing lists

- A Maven 2 artifact repository

- Issue tracking with JIRA

- Maven Archetypes for creating typical project types

Many of these capabilities are based on Maven, which will be discussed in detail later in this chapter. The automated build, test, artifact deployment, and web site generation are done through Maven using a continuous integration server.

Terracotta provides many TIMs on the Terracotta Forge. Over time, it is expected that all TIMs will be available on the Forge and that the preferred mechanism for obtaining TIMs will be from the Forge artifact repository.

To host your own project on the Forge, visit the web site, and follow the instructions there to register and propose a project.

Creating a TIM

In this section, you will learn how you can make your own TIM, either for an external library or for a component within your own application.

TIM Anatomy

The three major parts of a TIM JAR file are the manifest, the Terracotta configuration fragment, and optionally, code that will be discussed later.

The Terracotta module system is based on the OSGi (the Open Services Gateway initiative) platform, a popular standard for modular plug-in–based Java systems. For example, the Eclipse ecosystem is also based on OSGi and assembly via plug-ins.

■Note The OSGi Alliance is a board of participating members and directors who work together and vote on specifications regarding, essentially, dynamic dependency resolution and library loading capabilities for Java applications. The specification is available at `http://www.osgi.org/Specifications/HomePage`.

Creating a Manifest

In OSGi, code is distributed in the form of plug-ins, which may be contained in JAR files called bundles. A bundle is nothing more than a JAR file with special properties defined in the JAR file manifest. The JAR specification defines the manifest as existing at the location `META-INF/MANIFEST.MF`. This file is simply a text file with a well-defined format for specifying properties, line wrapping, and so on.

Listing 9-4 shows an example of a TIM manifest following the JAR manifest and OSGi conventions. In this case, this is the manifest for the automatically locked synchronized `Map` seen in prior sections and available on the Terracotta Forge.

Listing 9-4. *Manifest from the Synchronized Map Integration Module*

```
Manifest-Version: 1.0
Bundle-Name: Terracotta Synchronized Map
Bundle-Description: Terracotta Autolock SynchronizedMap Configuration
Import-Package: org.terracotta.modules.configuration
```

```
Bundle-RequiredExecutionEnvironment: J2SE-1.5
Bundle-Vendor: Terracotta, Inc.
Bundle-ManifestVersion: 2
Bundle-SymbolicName: org.terracotta.modules.tim-synchronizedmap
Require-Bundle: org.terracotta.modules.modules-common;bundle-version:=
 2.5.0
Bundle-Category: Terracotta Integration Module
Bundle-Version: 2.0.0
Bundle-Copyright: Copyright (c) 2007 Terracotta, Inc.
```

Many of the properties in this manifest will be automatically inserted for you when using popular tools to create JARs such as Ant or Maven. For example, the manifest in this listing was built using Maven in the Terracotta Forge. For more information on the most common and important bundle properties, see Table 9-1. Because a TIM is an OSGi bundle, it is actually possible to use any valid OSGi bundle manifest property.

Table 9-1. *Manifest Properties Supported by OSGi and Terracotta*

Manifest Property	Description	Importance
Manifest-Version	The JAR manifest version; should always be 1.0.	Recommended
Archiver-Version	The purely informational software building the JAR.	Optional
Created-By	The purely informational company or software creating the JAR.	Optional
Built-By	The purely informational name of the user building the JAR.	Optional
Bundle-Name	Descriptive name for this bundle.	Recommended
Bundle-Description	The bundle's description.	Recommended
Import-Package	Import packages needed for use from dependencies.	Optional
Export-Package	Export packages needed by modules using this one.	Optional
Bundle-RequiredExecutionEnvironment	The required minimum execution environment. The most likely constants you will need are J2SE-1.4, J2SE-1.5, and JavaSE-1.6.	Recommended
Bundle-Vendor	The vendor name providing the bundle.	Optional
Bundle-ManifestVersion	The OSGI bundle manifest version.	Recommended
Bundle-SymbolicName	The symbol name of the bundle, which is important for declaring dependencies from other bundles.	Required

Manifest Property	Description	Importance
Require-Bundle	The bundles required by this bundle (a comma-separated list), sorted by symbolic name and optionally by version in the form `<bundle-symbolicname>; bundle-version:=<bundle-version>.`[1]	Optional
Bundle-Category	The purely informational bundle category.	Recommended
Bundle-Version	The bundle version, which is used for dependency checking.	Recommended
Bundle-Copyright	Copyright for bundle.	Optional
Bundle-Activator	Specifies the class within the JAR that starts up with the bundle. Use this only if you need to contribute code with your bundle.	Optional
Bundle-DocURL	A URL for documentation on this bundle.	Optional

1. *OSGi supports a number of dependency versioning styles, but Terracotta only supports exact versions.*

Terracotta Configuration

After the manifest, the Terracotta configuration fragment is the next most important file in the TIM. It specifies a fragment of configuration XML that will be logically inserted into the Terracotta configuration referencing this TIM.

■Tip If a user includes your TIM, which includes another TIM, the logical runtime configuration will be the combination of the configuration defined in the user's project and *both* TIMs. This is a useful feature that allows you to modularize your own TIM or even your own application by hiding common configuration in another TIM.

The configuration fragment is an XML fragment that honors the logical structure of the XML within a full Terracotta configuration file yet eliminates certain stanzas. Listing 9-5 shows how you would go about embedding the autolock configuration from Listing 9-1. You should notice that there are no `<clients>`, `<servers>`, `<dso>`, or `<application>` stanzas. These stanzas should not be present in a TIM fragment.

The fragment must be contained in a file named `terracotta.xml`. That file is treated as a subtree of the `application/dso` element in a Terracotta configuration file, meaning that you should view the fragment as logically inserted in a configuration file at a point in the file starting with the `dso` element. The entire contents of a valid `dso` configuration section are wrapped in the `terracotta.xml` file via an XML tag called `<xml-fragment>`, which is just a container.

Listing 9-5. *Autolocks Stanza from Listing 9-1 Represented in an Integration Module*

```
<xml-fragment>
  <locks>
    <autolock>
      <method-expression>
        void java.util.Collections$SynchronizedMap.clear()
      </method-expression>
      <lock-level>write</lock-level>
    </autolock>
    <autolock>
      <method-expression>
        Object java.util.Collections$SynchronizedMap.clone()
      </method-expression>
      <lock-level>read</lock-level>
    </autolock>

  ...for every method in Set...

  </locks>
</xml-fragment>
```

The example in Listing 9-5 has only a `<locks>` section, but you can also include any child of the `<dso>` configuration element, such as `<instrumented-classes>`, `<roots>`, and so on.

Creating a Simple TIM

Creating a TIM that requires no code is easy. Follow these steps:

1. At your project root, create a subdirectory called `META-INF`.

2. In the `META-INF` directory, create a `MANIFEST.MF` text file using the information in the prior section.

3. Create a `terracotta.xml` text file at the root using the information in the prior section.

4. Issue the following command to build the module:

   `jar cvfm tim-bar-1.0.jar META-INF/MANIFEST.MF terracotta.xml`

You can then follow these steps to use this TIM in another project:

1. Place the module in a module repository at the appropriate location. The `Bundle-SymbolicName` should map to a path in the repository with the `.` character replaced with the correct path separator. For example, if the `Bundle-SymbolicName` was `com.foo.tim-bar`; the module repository path would be `com/foo`; and the JAR should be named `tim-bar-1.0.jar`.

2. In a new project, create a `tc-config.xml` that contains the following module:

   `<module name="tim-bar" version="1.0" group-id="com.foo"/>`

3. If necessary, include the module repository containing your module JAR in the
`tc-config.xml`:

```
<repository>file:///usr/local/share/terracotta/modules</repository>
```

That's all there is to it. Bundling external configuration into a TIM is an easy way to let
others cluster a library or application just like you do.

Creating TIMs with Maven

The prior section provided instructions on creating your own TIM. Terracotta also provides
full Maven integration if you wish to manage your TIM project with Maven and build the TIM
through the Terracotta Maven plug-in, which makes it even easier.

■**Note** This section assumes that you have downloaded and installed Maven by adding it to your path.
See the Maven documentation located at `http://maven.apache.org/download.html` for instructions on
downloading and installing it.

Maven provides a standardized project object model, build life cycle, and a broad set of
built-in goals for performing common tasks. One concept in Maven is that of an archetype
that can be used to create a new project that is typical for some particular context. Maven provides built-in archetypes for common project types. Terracotta provides several archetypes
specific to Terracotta.

To create your own TIM Maven project, you can use the `tim-archetype` provided by
Terracotta with the following command:

```
mvn org.apache.maven.plugins:maven-archetype-plugin:1.0-alpha-7:create \
 -DarchetypeGroupId=org.terracotta.maven.archetypes \
 -DarchetypeArtifactId=tim-archetype \
 -DarchetypeVersion=1.0.5 \
 -DgroupId=org.myfavoriteframework \
 -DartifactId=tim-mymodulename \
 -Dversion=1.0.0 \
 -DremoteRepositories=http://www.terracotta.org/download/reflector/maven2
```

■**Caution** The names, versions, and URLs in this command are subject to change. Check the Terracotta
Forge web site for current details.

This command first specifies the identification information for the archetype plug-in
itself and specifies the `groupId`, `artifactId`, and version for the TIM project you wish to create.

When executed, this command will retrieve the TIM archetype from the Terracotta repository and create a new project for you in a subdirectory named after the artifactId (in this case, tim-mymodulename).

You will see the package structure in your newly created Maven project area in Figure 9-1.

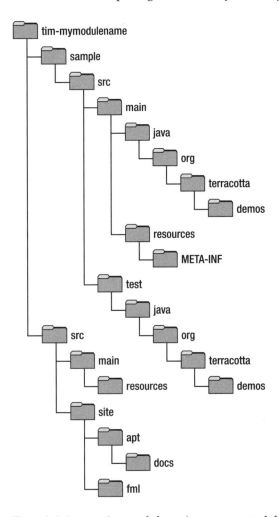

Figure 9-1. *Integration module project area created through a Maven archetype*

At the root of the project, you will find a pom.xml file and two subdirectories—sample and src. pom.xml is the Maven configuration file (POM stands for project object model). It will be preconfigured with reasonable defaults. It also references a parent project (tim-parent) that defines important configuration details that are inherited. You should edit and update the Maven file based on the instructions in the file.

The src directory is where code and resources for the project will live. Most simple TIMs do not have code, and thus the only file created in the src directory will be the terracotta.xml file in src/main/resources. You will need to edit this file to specify the configuration for your TIM.

The `src/site` directory contains default files used to build a web site pertaining to this project. These files will likely be useful to you only if you plan to publish a site around this project or host this project on the Terracotta Forge.

The `sample` directory contains a sample application that demonstrates how to use the TIM produced by this project in another application. Most likely, the item of most interest will be the Terracotta configuration file at `sample/src/main/resources/tc-config.xml`. This file will contain a reference to the module you created.

To actually build your project and produce a TIM, go to the project root and type the following:

```
mvn install
```

This command will create a new subdirectory called `target` and produce a JAR file in the `target` directory (along with some other files) called `tim-bar-1.0.0.jar` in this case. This JAR file is the TIM module. You'll notice that there was no need to define the bundle manifest; Maven created it automatically as a result of the default `pom.xml` and the parent POM configuration.

The Maven `install` command also installs the TIM into your local Maven repository, which can serve as a Terracotta module repository. You can then refer to it in your application's Terracotta configuration and load it from there, if you wish.

Module Versioning

The examples given in this chapter show version numbers in the context of both OSGi bundles and Maven projects. The versioning schemes in these two contexts are similar but not identical.

Often when working with an unreleased version of a project in Maven, you will call the release a snapshot release. These are typically done nightly or even more frequently with a continuous integration system and are not expected to be stable.

There is an important difference between the snapshot version identifiers used in Maven versus those used in the OSGi bundle manifest. In Maven, `SNAPSHOT` versions use a hyphen as in `2.5.0-SNAPSHOT`. In OSGi, that would be an invalid version, and we must instead use a period, as in `2.5.0.SNAPSHOT`. In the module section of your `tc-config.xml` file, either form can be used; the Terracotta module resolver will find the module, but the hyphenated `-SNAPSHOT` Maven form is preferred.

In the Maven POM, dependencies are supplied with a version, and in this case, Maven is resolving the dependency, so the Maven form (`-SNAPSHOT`) must be used. Similarly, in the Maven project version, the `-SNAPSHOT` form must be used.

For a TIM project built by Maven, the Terracotta manifest plug-in included with the Terracotta Maven plug-in will automatically build bundles with the proper `.SNAPSHOT` form from a Maven `-SNAPSHOT` version.

In summary, you should use the `-SNAPSHOT` form in all Maven files and Terracotta configuration files. The only place you must use the `.SNAPSHOT` form is in a bundle manifest if you are building the TIM without Maven.

Including Code in a TIM

Earlier in this chapter, we mentioned that it was possible to include not just configuration but code in a TIM. Let's now consider why you might do this and how you can do it. Terracotta's philosophy is to transparently distribute an application's or library's state by applying external configuration. In the majority of cases, properly concurrent and even many nonconcurrent applications can be configured externally to work in a clustered environment.

You can include code in a TIM that achieves the equivalent of anything and everything that can be done in the `terracotta.xml` file fragment. It's unlikely that coding your configuration like this is useful unless you need to reflectively or dynamically instrument a large number of classes, locks, and so on, where it may be more efficient or maintainable to instrument in code.

You can also include code that will actually modify an existing library or application at run time by replacing or modifying classes provided by someone else. If you need to do this, including or contributing code to the application through a TIM is the only solution, as this cannot be done in XML configuration.

The remainder of this chapter will examine in detail how to contribute code with both of these goals and create bundles that use it.

Defining a Bundle Activator

To provide any code in a TIM, you need to specify the `Bundle-Activator` property in the bundle manifest with the fully qualified name of a class that implements `org.osgi.framework.BundleActivator`. Terracotta provides a base class with many helpful methods that implements this interface, and we highly recommend that you subclass your activator from `org.terracotta.modules.configuration.TerracottaConfiguratorModule`. You can then override or use the many methods provided by that class.

So the shell of your class will look like Listing 9-6 and should be referenced in your bundle manifest with `Bundle-Activator=org.myfavoriteframework.MyConfiguratorModule`.

Listing 9-6. *The Structure of a Bundle Activator Class Used in Contributed Code*

```
package org.myfavoriteframework;

import org.terracotta.modules.configuration.TerracottaConfiguratorModule;

public class MyConfiguratorModule extends TerracottaConfiguratorModule {

}
```

To compile this class, you will need to include the following JARs in your classpath:

- `terracotta-api.jar`: This public subset of Terracotta code forms the API for the TIM code, available in `$TC_HOME/lib`.

- `osgi_r4_core-1.0.jar`: This core OSGi bundle API is available, among other locations, at `http://mirrors.ibiblio.org/`.

The sections following this one provide more detail on how to fill in your activator code to perform code-based configuration or class replacement.

Configuration with Code

To contribute configuration with code instead of in a `terracotta.xml` file, you should override the following protected method:

`TerracottaConfiguratorModule.addInstrumentation(BundleContext context)`

The `addInstrumentation()` method is called when the bundle is started and can be used to apply all typical Terracotta configuration, as specified in the Terracotta configuration file. The `TerracottaConfiguratorModule` will instantiate a protected field of type `com.tc.object.config.StandardDSOClientConfigHelper`. See Table 9-2 for a list of methods provided by `StandardDSOClientConfigHelper` for modifying the configuration.

Table 9-2. *Helper Methods for Configuring Terracotta Via Code*

StandardDSOClientConfigHelper Method	Description
`addIncludePattern(String classPattern)`	Add instrumented classes based on a pattern.
`addIncludePattern(String classPattern, boolean honorTransient)`	Add instrumented classes based on a pattern, and specify whether to honor the transient keyword (by not clustering those fields).
`addExcludePattern(String classPattern)`	Exclude specified classes from instrumentation.
`addPermanentExcludePattern(String classPattern)`	Specify classes that can never be instrumented.
`addRoot(String rootName, String rootFieldName)`	Add a root field to the configuration.
`addWriteAutoLock(String methodPattern)`	Add a write autolock to a specified method pattern.
`addReadAutoLock(String methodPattern)`	Add a read autolock to a specified method pattern.
`addAutoLock(String methodPattern, ConfigLockLevel lockType)`	Add an autolock to a method pattern of a specified type.
`addAutoLockExcludePattern(String methodPattern)`	Exclude a set of methods from automatic locking.

These methods allow your bundle activator class to modify the instrumented classes, roots, and locks as in the Terracotta configuration file. Many TIM bundle activators available on the Terracotta Forge consist primarily of calls to these methods to define configuration.

Class Replacement and Modification

So far, we have talked about writing code to duplicate things we can do with a `terracotta.xml` file in the bundle. Now, we will examine some things that can't be done any other way. The two primary capabilities we will discuss are class replacement and class modification.

Sometimes, classes in a library cannot efficiently be clustered. One example of this is a cache evictor. A cache evictor is usually implemented via a thread that iterates across the cache looking for objects that have timed out in some way. Eviction in a clustered environment cannot be implemented via a simple `iterator`, because every object in the cache will be forced into the JVM doing the work of iterating through the collection underlying the cache. The evictor in the example would significantly impact application performance while running. Another example might be clustering a class that is not thread-safe.

In such cases, it may be necessary to entirely replace one or more classes with alternate versions that provide data structures and synchronization that can more readily be clustered. Due to the maintenance issues this creates regarding adhering to the library's own interfaces and internal structure, this technique should be considered carefully.

The methods involved in class replacement and modification are defined in Tables 9-3 (methods on the StandardDSOClientConfigHelper class) and 9-4 (helper methods on the TerracottaConfiguratorModule class itself).

Table 9-3. *Available Methods on the StandardDSOClientConfigHelper Class*

StandardDSOClientConfigHelper Method	Description
getOrCreateSpec(String className) : TransparencyClassSpec	This method gets the Terracotta specification for a particular class. This specification defines whether the class can be instrumented, whether it is portable (clustered), whether it is physically or logically instrumented, and so on. It also provides hooks for additional bytecode instrumentation.
getOrCreateSpec(String className, String applicatorName) : TransparencyClassSpec	This method is similar to the previous one, but it adds a change applicator to the class specification, which will modify the bytecode of the class.
addCustomAdapter(String className, ClassAdapterFactory adapterFactory)	Add a custom class adapter (an ASM bytecode manipulation adapter) to a particular class with this method.

Table 9-4. *Available Helper Methods on the TerracottaConfiguratorModule Class*

TerracottaConfiguratorModule Method	Description
getExportedBundle(BundleContext context, String targetBundleName) : Bundle	This helper method finds the bundle with the given name.
addClassReplacement(Bundle bundle, String originalClassName, String newClassName)	For the given bundle, replace a class with another alternate class.
getOrCreateSpec(String className, boolean markAsPreInstrumented) : TransparencyClassSpec	This helper method retrieves the TransparencyClassSpec and optionally marks the class as preinstrumented (modified in the boot JAR).
getOrCreateSpec(String className) : TransparencyClassSpec	This helper method retrieves the TransparencyClassSpec and marks the class as preinstrumented (modified in the boot JAR).
addExportedTcJarClass(String className)	Export a class that normally lives in the tc.jar to *all* classloaders in the system, making it available to any calling class or method.

TerracottaConfiguratorModule Method	Description
`addExportedBundleClass(Bundle bundle, String className)`	Load the class in the specified bundle, and add it to the classpath of *all* classloaders in the system, making it available to classes regardless of classloader context.
`registerModuleSpec(BundleContext context)`	This abstract method is intended to be over-ridden by bundle activators that need to register a custom service that can dynamically produce class adapters.

To replace a library class with your own version, you can implement your bundle activator class as shown in Listing 9-7.

Listing 9-7. *Replacing a Class with Your Own Implementation Using TIMs*

```
package org.myfavoriteframework;

import org.osgi.framework.Bundle;
import org.osgi.framework.BundleContext;
import org.terracotta.modules.configuration.TerracottaConfiguratorModule;

public class MyConfiguratorModule extends TerracottaConfiguratorModule {
  protected void addInstrumentation(BundleContext context) {
    super.addInstrumentation(context);
    Bundle bundle = getExportedBundle(
                      context,
                      "org.myfavoriteframework.tim-myfavoriteframework");
    addClassReplacement(bundle, "org.myfavoriteframework.Impl",
                          "org.myfavoriteframework.ClusteredImpl");
  }
}
```

This example overrides the `addInstrumentation()` method in the bundle activator. First, it calls `super.addInstrumentation()` to add any standard instrumentation (at the moment, there is none). Next, you obtain your own bundle instance using the `getExportedBundle()` method, and finally, you replace the original `org.myfavoriteframework.Impl` with an alternate implementation.

There is more than one way to do class modification, but the easiest way to do so is add a custom class adapter for a particular class. For example, you could add the lines in Listing 9-8 to install a class adapter for a particular class in the `addInstrumentation()` method.

Listing 9-8. *Adding Your Own Class Adapter*

```
ClassAdapterFactory adapterFactory = new ImplAdapterFactory();
configHelper.addCustomAdapter("org.myfavoriteframework.Impl", adapterFactory);
```

The key here is, of course, how to create a `com.tc.object.bytecode.ClassAdapterFactory`. This class comes from ASM, the bytecode manipulation framework. ASM works by reading class files through a visitor, pumping them through your custom visitor(s), and writing them back out through another visitor. The ClassAdapterFactory has only one method that knows how to create a ClassAdapter, which is the visitor that will be used by ASM when the class is loaded in the JVM.

It is typical to create one class that implements the ClassAdapterFactory to return an instance of itself, which should also extend ClassAdapter. Writing class adapters is outside the scope of this book, and for further information, you should see either the ASM documentation located at http://asm.objectweb.org or examples of these classes in the TIM source code. Take a look at the Ehcache TIM or the Lucene TIM in the Terracotta Forge, as both use ASM and create custom visitors. The possibilities are effectively unlimited—class adapters can add, remove, and modify fields, methods, bytecode within methods, access modifiers, and so on.

Using Maven to Create TIMs with Code

The prior documentation on creating TIMs with contributed code focused on how to do so by modifying the manifest to specify a bundle activator and rebuilding the JAR with the compiled code.

You can also create a TIM with Maven using contributed code by making a few modifications to the Maven pom.xml in your TIM project.

Listing 9-9 outlines the major changes.

Listing 9-9. *Modifying Maven pom.xml for Creating TIMs*

```
<project xmlns="http://maven.apache.org/POM/4.0.0"
  xmlns:xsi="http://www.w3.org/2001/XMLSchema-instance"
  xsi:schemaLocation="http://maven.apache.org/POM/4.0.0
                              http://maven.apache.org/maven-v4_0_0.xsd">

  <dependencies>
    <dependency>
      <groupId>org.terracotta</groupId>
      <artifactId>terracotta-api</artifactId>
      <version>2.6.0</version>
    </dependency>
  </dependencies>

  <build>
    <plugins>
      <plugin>
        <groupId>org.terracotta.maven.plugins</groupId>
        <artifactId>tc-maven-plugin</artifactId>
        <version>1.0.0</version>
        <configuration>
          <bundleActivator>
            org.myfavoriteframework.MyConfiguratorModule
          </bundleActivator>
          <importPackage>
              org.terracotta.modules.configuration
```

```
        </importPackage>
      </configuration>
    </plugin>
  </plugins>
 </build>
</project>
```

First, it is important that the POM declare a dependency on the `terracotta-api` Maven module. Doing so will bring in all dependencies needed to compile the TIM. You may need to specify a `SNAPSHOT` version in this section if you are developing against an unreleased version of Terracotta.

Second, you must specify the bundle activator for the JAR manifest using the `BundleActivator` element under configuration. Also, you must import packages you are using in your code from the `terracotta-api` module. Similarly, the `<exportPackage>` element can be used to export portions of your module for use by other modules. For a full list of the properties that can be set in the `<configuration>` element for the Terracotta Maven plug-in, see Table 9-5.

Once these items are in place, you can then run Maven commands as normal, such as `compile`, `package`, and `install`. During the build life cycle defined by Maven, the manifest will be generated automatically and included in the JAR created in the target directory along with other artifacts of the Maven build.

Table 9-5. *Exportable Properties and Options for Maven-Based Builds*

Configuration Element	Description	Default
bundleActivator	OSGi Bundle-Activator manifest attribute	
bundleCategory	OSGi Bundle-Category manifest attribute	
bundleCopyright	OSGi Bundle-Copyright manifest attribute	
bundleDescription	OSGi Bundle-Description manifest attribute	${project.description}
bundleName	OSGi Bundle-Name manifest attribute	
bundleRequired ExecutionEnvironment	OSGi Bundle-RequiredExecutionEnvironment manifest attribute	
bundleSymbolicName	OSGi Bundle-SymbolicName manifest attribute with invalid character replacement	${project.groupId}. ${project.artifactId}
bundleVendor	OSGi Bundle-Vendor manifest attribute	${project.organization. name}
bundleVersion	OSGi Bundle-Version manifest attribute	${project.version} with invalid character replacement
exportPackage	OSGi Export-Package manifest attribute	
importPackage	OSGi Import-Package manifest attribute	
manifestFile	Location for the generated manifest file	${project.build. directory}/MANIFEST.MF
remoteRepositories	List of remote repositories	Remote repositories declared in the POM

Continued

Table 9-5. *Continued*

Configuration Element	Description	Default
requireBundle	OSGi Require-Bundle manifest attribute	Generated from the dependencies listed in the POM, excluding dependencies with test and runtime scopes

Summary

Terracotta Integration Modules (TIMs) provide a powerful mechanism for using Terracotta in an abstracted form. By "abstracted," we mean that users of libraries that you build and frameworks that you cluster do not need to manually integrate the required Terracotta directives into their application's tc-config.xml. Your users can, instead, use your library in a clustered environment with simpler <module> directives, just as you can with TIMs such as Hibernate and Ehcache, or for synchronized Java collections.

With Terracotta, it is possible to include XML configuration directives, much like the concept of #include in the C programming language. It is also possible to ship new code that can be added to or otherwise change classes and code in a package or library that is not well suited to clustering out of the box.

In fact, the very notion of integration modules was first created to make it easy to bundle Terracotta support in various open source projects. You too should use this bundling capability to make your own projects and products more stable and easier to understand.

In Chapter 10, you will learn how to build a master/worker, or grid, computing framework using Terracotta. All the classes and interfaces in the framework are available on Terracotta's Forge as a library for use in projects. The library consists only of POJO collections, multi-threaded execution logic, and appropriate locking to make everything thread-safe. You implement the notions of work and routing of work in the grid.

As you will learn in the next chapter, all of the configuration for the master/worker framework is abstracted through a TIM. Knowing how TIMs are constructed helps you understand frameworks like master/worker, and that knowledge also enables you to build your own frameworks and libraries that other developers can use without manual inclusion or integration. If you find yourself keeping recipes of configuration fragments and associated source code for inclusion across various projects, consider implementing those fragments and recipes in a module. Let's look at the master/worker framework now, keeping in mind that you can use that framework through TIMs.

■■■

CHAPTER 10

Thread Coordination

In a computer, just like the rest of the world, more work can get done if there are more workers working at the same time. In a computer, these workers take the form of multiple concurrently executing processes and, inside of a single process, multiple concurrent threads of execution. In the real world, if more than one worker is working on the same thing or if workers need to perform their work in a certain order relative to each other, they must have some form of communication and coordination between them. Just as in the physical world, if more than one thread is working on the same object or if those threads need to mutate objects in a certain order relative to each other, they must have some way to coordinate with each other.

With Terracotta, thread coordination constructs that exist in the Java language will transparently work across JVM process boundaries. One thread in one JVM can call wait() on an object and another thread in another JVM on another machine can call notify() to wake up the waiting thread. The challenge is that not all Java developers have experience with thread coordination and concurrency. Treat this chapter as a cookbook for concurrency with Terracotta. It works as a cookbook, because it is designed to steer you toward use cases and coordination models that will be easy to code and debug and will simultaneously scale very well in a Terracotta world. Let's dive in to the concurrency recipes now.

Terracotta and Thread Coordination

Thread coordination comes in two flavors:

- *Coordination of access to data*: For example, if thread A is sorting a list and thread B is iterating over the elements in list, thread A needs to finish sorting the list before thread B starts iterating.

- *Coordination of activities*: For example, assume thread A and thread B need to leave an apartment together, and thread A needs to turn out the lights, and thread B needs to close the door. In that case, threads A and B need to wait until thread A has turned off the light; likewise, thread B must wait until the light is off and both threads have walked over the threshold before closing the door.

The JVM has simple and elegant built-in mechanisms for coordinating threads: the bytecode instructions MONITORENTER and MONITOREXIT (also known as the synchronized method or synchronized block) and the various signatures of the `Object` methods `wait()`, `notify()`, and `join()`. As of Terracotta 2.6, `join()` is not supported as a clustered thread interaction. Since Java 1.5, higher level concurrency constructs have been added to the Java library to provide canonical implementations of commonly used coordination techniques. These higher-level thread coordination tools can be found in the `java.util.concurrent` package. Figure 10-1 depicts the way in which Terracotta instruments Java synchronized blocks.

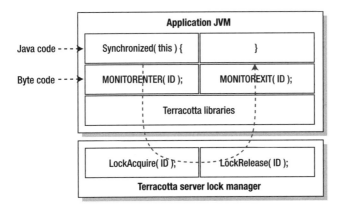

Figure 10-1. *Terracotta hooks into the MONITORENTER and MONITOREXIT bytecodes.*

Terracotta's virtual heap extends the utility of Java's built-in thread coordination to allow threads on multiple JVMs to coordinate with each other using exactly the same techniques as threads on the same JVM. This means that the number of workers that can be brought to bear to execute your program is no longer limited to the number of threads and processors available to a single JVM; Terracotta lets your program, which was written to run on a single JVM, run on many JVMs as if they were all one big JVM. The power of Terracotta's virtual heap lies in this ability to write software for a single JVM but run it on as many JVMs as you want—without the complexity and intrusiveness of a special inter-JVM signaling and data-sharing framework.

Clustering Threads

To see Terracotta inter-JVM thread coordination in action, let's look at a few thread clustering examples.

Thread Coordination Using Concurrency Primitives

The first example shows how to coordinate the actions of threads using just the concurrency primitives available in JDK 1.4.2 and above. The code for this example is available on this book's page at `http://www.apress.com`.

This example contains a configuration file and a single Java class with a `main()` method and some coordination code. The Java class is displayed in Listing 10-1.

Listing 10-1. *WaitNotify.java*

```
package org.terracotta.book.coordination.jdk14;
/**
 * This sample shows the use of wait and notify to coordinate 2 or more processes
 * as if they were threads.
 * It also demonstrates how one might share a clustered configuration
 * across processes in the same way that it is shared across threads.
 *
 * In this case the passed in number of nodes (2 by default) will startup
 * and wait for the number to join (like a cyclic barrier).
 *
 *
 */
public class WaitNotify {
  private static final int MINIMUM_EXPECTED_PARTICIPANTS = 2;
  private Configuration config;
  private int nodesJoined;

  public WaitNotify(Configuration aConfig) {
    this.config = aConfig;
    synchronized (this.config) {
      config.setMyNodeID(++nodesJoined);
      System.out.println("Nodes Joined:" + nodesJoined);
      this.config.notifyAll();
    }
  }

  public void run() throws Exception {
    synchronized (config) {

      while (nodesJoined < config.getTotalNodeCount()) {
        System.out.println("Node " + config.getMyNodeID()
            + " is waiting for more nodes to join.");
        config.wait();
      }
      System.out.println("All " + config.getTotalNodeCount()
          + " nodes joined! I'm node:" + config.getMyNodeID());
    }
  }

  public static void main(String[] args) throws Exception {
    int expectedParticipants = MINIMUM_EXPECTED_PARTICIPANTS;
    if (args.length == 0) {
      System.out.println("Node count NOT specified. Setting count to "
          + MINIMUM_EXPECTED_PARTICIPANTS);
    } else {
      try {
```

```
        expectedParticipants = Integer.parseInt(args[0]);
        if (expectedParticipants < 1) {
          throw new Exception("Invalid node count");
        }
      } catch (Exception e) {
        System.out.println("Invalid node count:" + args[0]);
        System.exit(1);
      }
    }

    Configuration c = new Configuration(expectedParticipants);
    new WaitNotify(c).run();
  }

  private static class Configuration {
    private int totalNodeCount;
    private transient int myNodeID;

    public Configuration(int totalNodeCount) {
      this.totalNodeCount = totalNodeCount;
    }

    public int getMyNodeID() {
      return myNodeID;
    }

    public void setMyNodeID(int myNodeID) {
      this.myNodeID = myNodeID;
    }

    public int getTotalNodeCount() {
      return totalNodeCount;
    }
  }
}
```

The main() method checks the command line arguments for the number of participating threads, which, in the normal execution case, will equal the number of participating JVMs. It then creates an instance of the WaitNotify class and calls its run() method. The constructor of WaitNotify synchronizes on a shared Configuration object, increments the shared integer nodesJoined, and notifies all threads in the cluster waiting on the shared Configuration object.

In the run() method, each participating thread synchronizes on the shared Configuration object and enters a while loop that will cause the thread in the run() method to continually wait on the shared Configuration object until the shared nodesJoined integer is incremented to the value of the expected number of participants.

The configuration file is displayed in Listing 10-2.

Listing 10-2. *tc-config.xml for Concurrency Primitives*

```xml
<?xml version="1.0" encoding="UTF-8"?>
<con:tc-config xmlns:con="http://www.terracotta.org/config">
  <servers>
    <server host="%i" name="localhost">
      <dso-port>9510</dso-port>
      <jmx-port>9520</jmx-port>
      <data>terracotta/server-data</data>
      <logs>terracotta/server-logs</logs>
    </server>
  </servers>
  <clients>
    <logs>terracotta/client-logs</logs>
  </clients>
  <application>
    <dso>
      <instrumented-classes>
        <include>
          <class-expression>
            org.terracotta.book.coordination.jdk14.WaitNotify$Configuration
          </class-expression>
        </include>
        <include>
          <class-expression>
            org.terracotta.book.coordination.jdk14.WaitNotify
          </class-expression>
        </include>
      </instrumented-classes>
      <roots>
        <root>
          <field-name>
            org.terracotta.book.coordination.jdk14.WaitNotify.config
          </field-name>
        </root>
        <root>
          <field-name>
            org.terracotta.book.coordination.jdk14.WaitNotify.nodesJoined
          </field-name>
        </root>
      </roots>
      <transient-fields>
        <field-name>
          org.terracotta.book.coordination.jdk14.WaitNotify$Configuration.myNodeID
        </field-name>
      </transient-fields>
      <locks>
        <autolock>
          <method-expression>
            void org.terracotta.book.coordination.jdk14.WaitNotify.run()
```

```
        </method-expression>
        <lock-level>write</lock-level>
      </autolock>
      <autolock>
        <method-expression>
          void org.terracotta.book.coordination.jdk14.WaitNotify.__INIT__ ➡
(org.terracotta.book.coordination.jdk14.WaitNotify$Configuration)
        </method-expression>
        <lock-level>write</lock-level>
      </autolock>
    </locks>
  </dso>
 </application>
</con:tc-config>
```

The Terracotta configuration has four important sections in this example: <instrumented-classes>, <roots>, <transient-fields>, and <locks>. Instrumented classes include the WaitNotify class as well as the inner class Configuration. Including them for instrumentation makes them sensitive to Terracotta augmented behavior. The <roots> section declares which object graphs ought to be part of the virtual heap and thus shared across JVMs.

This example has two roots, WaitNotify.config and WaitNotify.nodesJoined. The field Configuration.myNodeID is relevant only for the local JVM and is, therefore, declared transient, which means that its value is not part of the virtual heap. When the Configuration object is materialized on the local heap of another JVM, the myNodeID field is null and must be explicitly initialized with the local value.

The <locks> section of tc-config.xml describes which methods ought to be sensitive to Terracotta locking. In this case, two methods need to be configured: the run() method and the constructor (specified as __INIT__). Any lock operations (synchronized(), wait(), and notify()) on shared objects in these methods are augmented to include the equivalent lock operations in the Terracotta server for that object in addition to the lock operations that occur on the local heap for that object. Lock operations on objects that aren't stored in Terracotta are not sensitive to clusterwide Terracotta lock augmentation. This is likewise true of all lock operations in methods not specified in the <locks> section.

If you run this example in Terracotta, the first execution will increment the nodesJoined counter from zero to one, and enter the while loop in the run() method, because the value of nodesJoined is less than the default participants count of two. Upon entering the while loop, this first instance of the program will request and acquire the clustered lock on the shared Configuration object and wait on that object, pausing the execution of the main thread in the first execution instance.

When you run a second execution instance, its main thread, upon executing the constructor of WaitNotify, will increment the shared nodesJoined integer from one to two and then call notifyAll() on the shared Configuration object. This method call will cause the main thread in the first execution instance to attempt to acquire the lock on the shared Configuration object. When the first execution instance's main thread is granted that lock, that instance will resume execution and retest the while clause. At this point, since the second execution instance has already incremented the nodesJoined integer value to the expected value of two, the first execution instance will exit the while loop, print out the message that all participating nodes have joined, and exit.

Subsequently, the main thread of the second execution instance will then enter the run() method and, upon testing the condition of the while loop, find that the value of nodesJoined is already at the expected value. The second execution instance will therefore bypass the while loop and proceed to print out the message that all participating nodes have joined. Then, it too will exit.

As this example shows, using the built-in concurrency primitives synchronized(), wait(), and notify(), Terracotta lets you write simple Java code that can be used to coordinate the activities of threads both in the same and in different JVMs.

Thread Coordination Using the java.util.concurrent Package

The java.util.concurrent package was introduced in Java 1.5 to provide higher order abstractions for performing common concurrency operations. This example uses a member of that package, CyclicBarrier, to perform the same coordination task found in WaitNotify but does so without using explicit synchronization, wait(), or notify(). Those low-level thread operations are performed inside the CyclicBarrier class.

Like the previous example, this one contains a single Java class and a Terracotta configuration file. The code for this example is available on the Apress web site.

The Java class is displayed in Listing 10-3.

Listing 10-3. *CoordinatedStages.java*

```java
package org.terracotta.book.coordination.jdk15;

import java.util.concurrent.BrokenBarrierException;
import java.util.concurrent.CyclicBarrier;

public class CoordinatedStages {

  private CyclicBarrier enterBarrier;
  private CyclicBarrier exitBarrier;

  private static int MINIMUM_EXPECTED_PARTICIPANTS = 2;

  /**
   * Create an instance, setting the number of VMs expected to participate in
   * the demo.
   *
   * @param expectedParticipants
   *            Description of Parameter
   */
  public CoordinatedStages(int expectedParticipants) {
    assert (expectedParticipants > 1);
    System.out.println("Expected Participants: " + expectedParticipants);
    this.enterBarrier = new CyclicBarrier(expectedParticipants);
    this.exitBarrier = new CyclicBarrier(expectedParticipants);
  }
```

```java
public void run() {
  try {
    // wait for all participants before performing tasks
    System.out.println(
      "Stage 1: Arriving at enterBarrier.  I'll pause here until all " +
      enterBarrier.getParties() + " threads have arrived...");
    enterBarrier.await();
    System.out.println(
      "Stage 2: Passed through enterBarrier because all threads arrived.");
    System.out.println("Arriving at exitBarrier...");
    exitBarrier.await();
    System.out.println(
      "Stage 3: Passed through exitBarrier.  All done.  Goodbye.");

  } catch (BrokenBarrierException ie) {
    ie.printStackTrace();
  } catch (InterruptedException ie) {
    ie.printStackTrace();
  }
}

public static final void main(String[] args) throws Exception {
  int expectedParticipants = MINIMUM_EXPECTED_PARTICIPANTS;
  if (args.length == 0) {
    System.out.println("Node count NOT specified. Setting count to "
        + MINIMUM_EXPECTED_PARTICIPANTS);
  } else {
    try {
      expectedParticipants = Integer.parseInt(args[0]);
      if (expectedParticipants < 1) {
        throw new Exception("Invalid node count");
      }
    } catch (Exception e) {
      System.out.println("Invalid node count:" + args[0]);
      System.exit(1);
    }
  }
  (new CoordinatedStages(expectedParticipants)).run();
}

}
```

The second example uses CyclicBarrier objects to coordinate the arrival and departure of a particular number of threads. As you saw in Chapter 4, a barrier provides a point past which no thread may continue until all expected threads arrive. A CyclicBarrier cycles back to its initial state after all threads have arrived. Using Terracotta, a CyclicBarrier may be used across JVMs to coordinate the efforts of multiple computers.

This example has two `CyclicBarrier` instances, `enterBarrier` and `exitBarrier`, each of which, by default, is configured to block until two threads arrive at each barrier. The Terracotta configuration file is much simpler in this example, because `CyclicBarrier` is automatically supported by Terracotta and doesn't need to be declared in the configuration—no configuration is needed for any Terracotta-supported class in the `java.util.concurrent` package. The only thing that needs to happen in the configuration is that the shared barriers must be declared as DSO root objects, as you can see in the `<roots>` section of `tc-config.xml`, which is displayed in Listing 10-4.

Listing 10-4. *tc-config.xml for the java.util.concurrent Package*

```xml
<?xml version="1.0" encoding="UTF-8"?>
<con:tc-config xmlns:con="http://www.terracotta.org/config">
  <servers>
    <server host="%i" name="localhost">
      <dso-port>9510</dso-port>
      <jmx-port>9520</jmx-port>
      <data>terracotta/server-data</data>
      <logs>terracotta/server-logs</logs>
    </server>
  </servers>
  <clients>
    <logs>terracotta/client-logs</logs>
  </clients>
  <application>
    <dso>
      <instrumented-classes/>
      <roots>
        <root>
          <field-name>
            org.terracotta.book.coordination.jdk15.CoordinatedStages.enterBarrier
          </field-name>
        </root>
        <root>
          <field-name>
            org.terracotta.book.coordination.jdk15.CoordinatedStages.exitBarrier
          </field-name>
        </root>
      </roots>
    </dso>
  </application>
</con:tc-config>
```

When running this example, you'll see the first execution instance arrive at the `enterBarrier` and exclaim the following:

```
Node count NOT specified. Setting count to 2
Expected Participants: 2
Step 1: Arriving at enterBarrier.  I'll pause here until all 2 threads
have arrived...
```

When you run a second execution instance and it arrives at the enterBarrier, both threads will be allowed through. The same thing will happen at the exitBarrier. Since two threads—albeit in different JVMs—are participating, when they both arrive at the exitBarrier, they will be allowed through. You should see the following text printed out:

```
Step 2: Passed through enterBarrier because all threads arrived.  Arriving at
exitBarrier...
Step 3: Passed through exitBarrier.  All done.  Goodbye.
```

As you can see, there is very little functional difference between the two examples. The main difference is that the policy of blocking all threads until the expected number of threads has arrived at an execution point has been abstracted into a generic library class, CyclicBarrier. The power of Terracotta comes into play once again by automatically supporting the CyclicBarrier class so that you may take advantage of its policy behavior for threads across multiple JVMs.

Thread Coordination and JMX Cluster Events

The next example is the same as the previous one with the addition of Terracotta cluster events. Cluster events are JMX events that get fired in a client JVM when JVMs join or leave the cluster. In order to receive the Terracotta cluster events, the example class has to be augmented to implement four methods:

- nodeConnected(Object nodeID): Called when another JVM joins the cluster

- nodeDisconnected(Object nodeID): Called when another JVM leaves the cluster

- thisNodeConnected(Object nodeID): Called when this JVM joins the cluster

- thisNodeDisconnected(Object nodeID): Called when this JVM leaves the cluster

Cluster events in Terracotta will eventually grow to include all logical stages a cluster or JVM can experience. A more robust solution for event handling must include methods such as these:

- nodeInit(Object nodeID): Called when this node starts.

- nodeConnecting(Object nodeID): Called when this node invokes the socket connect() method to the Terracotta server.

- nodeConnected(Object nodeID): Called when a TCP handshake is complete and a node has joined the cluster.

- nodeReconnecting(Object nodeID): Called when the network hiccups and a node is reconnecting.

- nodeOrphaned(Object nodeID): Called when a cluster no longer waits for a node and the node will never reconnect without exiting first. Note that the orphaned node will never find out it has been orphaned; the server and other nodes can find out.

- nodeReconnected(Object nodeID): A node successfully rejoined a cluster (the same as the nodeConnected() event but documented here for clarity's sake).

- nodeDisconnecting(Object nodeID): A node exiting normally.

- nodeDisconnected(Object nodeID): A node exited normally.

As you can see from the previous list of ideal cluster events, Terracotta plans significant updates to this subsystem. The current functionality, while sufficient, will change, and thus we ask that you refer to the web site for more information. A full description of how the Terracotta cluster events work can be found in the Terracotta documentation: http://www.terracotta.org/confluence/display/docs1/JMX+Guide.

This example class extends the adapter class org.terracotta.util.jmx.SimpleListener (available on the Terracotta Forge) in order to be notified of the cluster events. The code for this example is available on the Apress web site.

The Java class is displayed in Listing 10-5.

Listing 10-5. *CoordinatedStagesWithClusterEvents.java*

```
package org.terracotta.book.coordination.jmx;

import java.util.concurrent.BrokenBarrierException;
import java.util.concurrent.CyclicBarrier;

import org.terracotta.util.jmx.ClusterEvents;
import org.terracotta.util.jmx.SimpleListener;

/**
 * This sample shows the use of Cyclic barrier to coordinate two or more JVM
 * processes as if they were threads running in the same JVM.
 * It also shows how you can integrate cluster events to tell your code
 * when nodes join and leave the cluster.
 *
 * If you pass in a number at startup, it will be used as the number
 * of participants to wait for. If no number is passed in then it defaults to three.
 *
 * By extending the abstract class org.terracotta.util.jmx.SimpleListener,
 * instances of this class receive notification when this JVM or other JVMs join
 * or leave the Terracotta cluster.
 */
public class CoordinatedStagesWithClusterEvents extends SimpleListener {

  private CyclicBarrier enterBarrier;
  private CyclicBarrier exitBarrier;

  private static int MINIMUM_EXPECTED_PARTICIPANTS = 3;
```

```java
/**
 * Create an instance, setting the number of VMs expected to participate in
 * the demo.
 *
 * @param expectedParticipants
 *            Description of Parameter
 */
public CoordinatedStagesWithClusterEvents(int expectedParticipants) {
  ClusterEvents.registerListener(this);
  assert (expectedParticipants > 1);
  System.out.println("Expected Participants: " + expectedParticipants);
  this.enterBarrier = new CyclicBarrier(expectedParticipants);
  this.exitBarrier = new CyclicBarrier(expectedParticipants);
}

public void run() {
  try {
    // wait for all participants before performing tasks
    System.out.println("Stage 1: Arriving at enterBarrier. I'll pause here until "
        + "all "   + enterBarrier.getParties() + " threads have arrived...");
    enterBarrier.await();
    System.out.println("Stage 2: Passed through enterBarrier because all threads "
        + " arrived.  Arriving at exitBarrier...");
    exitBarrier.await();
    System.out.println("Stage 3: Passed through exitBarrier.  All done. "
        + "Goodbye.");
  } catch (BrokenBarrierException ie) {
    ie.printStackTrace();
  } catch (InterruptedException ie) {
    ie.printStackTrace();
  }
}

/**
 * This method, defined in the org.terracotta.util.jmx.SimpleListener class,
 * is called when another JVM joins the cluster
 */
public void nodeConnected(Object nodeID) {
  System.out.println("Another JVM has just connected to the Terracotta cluster: "
      + "node id " + nodeID);
}

/**
 * This method, defined in the org.terracotta.util.jmx.SimpleListener class,
 * is called when another JVM leaves the cluster
 */
```

```
  public void nodeDisconnected(Object nodeID) {
    System.out.println("Another JVM has just disconnected from the cluster: "
      + "node id " + nodeID);
  }


  /**
   * This method, defined in the org.terracotta.util.jmx.SimpleListener class,
   * is called when this JVM joins the cluster
   */
  public void thisNodeConnected(Object nodeID) {
    System.out.println("I just connected to the Terracotta cluster: node id "
      + nodeID);
  }


  /**
   * This method, defined in the org.terracotta.util.jmx.SimpleListener class,
   * is called when this JVM leaves the cluster
   */
  public void thisNodeDisconnected(Object nodeID) {
    System.out.println("I just disconnected from the Terracotta cluster: node id "
      + nodeID);
  }


  public static final void main(String[] args) throws Exception {
    int expectedParticipants = MINIMUM_EXPECTED_PARTICIPANTS;
    if (args.length == 0) {
      System.out.println("Node count NOT specified. Setting count to "
        + MINIMUM_EXPECTED_PARTICIPANTS);
    } else {
      try {
        expectedParticipants = Integer.parseInt(args[0]);
        if (expectedParticipants < 1) {
          throw new Exception("Invalid node count");
        }
      } catch (Exception e) {
        System.out.println("Invalid node count:" + args[0]);
        System.exit(1);
      }
    }
    CoordinatedStagesWithClusterEvents demo =
      new CoordinatedStagesWithClusterEvents(expectedParticipants);
    demo.run();
  }
}
```

The example class, CoordinatedStagesWithClusterEvents, has the same two barriers as those in Listing 10-3, but the default expected participants has been set to three so you can see the cluster event messages as they occur.

The configuration file is displayed in Listing 10-6.

Listing 10-6. *tc-config.xml for JMX Cluster Events*

```
<?xml version="1.0" encoding="UTF-8"?>
<con:tc-config xmlns:con="http://www.terracotta.org/config">
  <servers>
    <server host="%i" name="localhost">
      <dso-port>9510</dso-port>
      <jmx-port>9520</jmx-port>
      <data>terracotta/server-data</data>
      <logs>terracotta/server-logs</logs>
    </server>
  </servers>
  <clients>
    <logs>terracotta/client-logs</logs>
  </clients>
  <application>
    <dso>
      <instrumented-classes/>
      <roots>
        <root>
          <field-name>
            org.terracotta.book.coordination.jmx.CoordinatedStagesWith ➥
ClusterEvents.enterBarrier
          </field-name>
        </root>
        <root>
          <field-name>
            org.terracotta.book.coordination.jmx.CoordinatedStagesWith ➥
ClusterEvents.exitBarrier
          </field-name>
        </root>
      </roots>
    </dso>
  </application>
</con:tc-config>
```

The configuration file is nearly identical to the one from the previous example, except the name of the example class is different.

To run this example, start the first execution instance. It will reach the enterBarrier, and the example's running thread will block, waiting for two other threads to arrive at that barrier. You should see output that looks like this:

```
Node count NOT specified. Setting count to 3
Expected Participants: 3
Stage 1: Arriving at enterBarrier.  I'll pause here until all 3 threads have
arrived...
```

When you start a second execution instance, it will arrive at the enterBarrier and its thread of execution will block also, waiting for the final of the three expected threads to arrive. Additionally, the nodeConnected() method gets called on the first execution instance when the second execution instance joins the cluster. The output of the first execution instance should then print a new line:

```
Another JVM has just connected to the Terracotta cluster: node id 1
```

When you start the third execution instance, all three instances will pass through both the enterBarrier and the exitBarrier. The output of the first execution instance will look like this:

```
Node count NOT specified. Setting count to 3
Expected Participants: 3
Stage 1: Arriving at enterBarrier.  I'll pause here until all 3 threads have
arrived...
Another JVM has just connected to the Terracotta cluster: node id 1
Another JVM has just connected to the Terracotta cluster: node id 2
Stage 2: Passed through enterBarrier because all threads arrived.  Arriving at
exitBarrier...
Stage 3: Passed through exitBarrier.  All done.  Goodbye.
```

If you experiment with starting and stopping different combinations of execution instances before they all fall through the barriers, you will see the other cluster events fired. You will also see the effects of having JVM participants join and leave during the execution of an application, especially with respect to the naïve expectation that every execution instance will always execute all of the code from start to finish. Keep in mind that thread execution may be interrupted. When using Terracotta, especially keep in mind that threads participating in the application in different JVMs will stop participating in the execution of the application if their JVM is removed from the cluster.

Thread Coordination with Queues

The next example illustrates the use of queues to send messages from one JVM to another. The shared data structure is a list of queues, each of which is associated with the color red, orange, yellow, green, blue, indigo, and violet. The first JVM to join the cluster will spawn one thread for each queue in the list. The threads will block on taking messages from the queue. When a thread is unblocked and takes a message off of a queue, this first JVM will simply print to console the message sent to it on that particular queue and repeat the process. Each subsequent JVM that joins the cluster is assigned one of the seven colors and proceeds to place messages into its designated color queue. Figure 10-2 presents a picture of the interaction between the different JVMs.

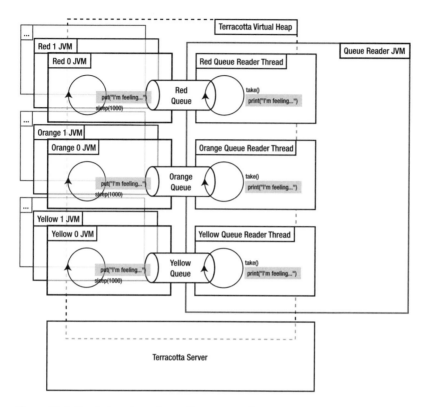

Figure 10-2. *Depicting thread coordination with queues graphically*

You can get the code on the Apress web site. The example class is presented in Listing 10-7.

Listing 10-7. *CoordinationWithQueues.java*

```java
package org.terracotta.book.coordination.queues;

import java.util.Date;
import java.util.HashMap;
import java.util.Iterator;
import java.util.LinkedList;
import java.util.List;
import java.util.Map;
import java.util.Random;
import java.util.concurrent.LinkedBlockingQueue;
import java.util.concurrent.atomic.AtomicInteger;

public class CoordinationWithQueues {

  private static final String[] MOODS = { "sleepy", "grouchy", "happy", "worried",
```

```
"sad", "like partying" };
  private static final String[] COLOR_NAMES = { "Red", "Orange", "Yellow", "Green",
"Blue", "Indigo", "Violet" };
  private static List<NamedQueue> QUEUES;
  private static final AtomicInteger sharedCounter = new AtomicInteger();

  private final String myColor;
  private final NamedQueue myQueue;
  private final Random random;

  public CoordinationWithQueues(final String color, final NamedQueue queue) {
    myColor = color;
    myQueue = queue;
    random = new Random();
  }

  private void run() {
    while (true) {
      try {
        String mood = MOODS[random.nextInt(MOODS.length)];
        myQueue.add(myColor + " says, \"I'm feeling " + mood + ".\"");
        Thread.sleep(1000);
      } catch (InterruptedException e) {
        // A real application would do something with this exception
        e.printStackTrace();
      }
    }
  }

  private static final class NamedQueue {
    private final String myName;
    private final LinkedBlockingQueue<Object> myQueue;

    public NamedQueue(final String name, final LinkedBlockingQueue<Object> queue) {
      this.myName = name;
      this.myQueue = queue;
    }

    public String getName() {
      return myName;
    }

    public void add(Object o) {
      myQueue.add(o);
    }

    public Object take() throws InterruptedException {
```

```
      return myQueue.take();
    }
  }

  private static final class QueueReader implements Runnable {
    private final NamedQueue myQueue;

    public QueueReader(NamedQueue queue) {
      this.myQueue = queue;
    }

    public void run() {
      while (true) {
        try {
          System.out.println(new Date() + ": message from the " + myQueue.getName()
            + " queue: " + myQueue.take());
        } catch (InterruptedException e) {
          // A real application would do something interesting with this
          // exception.
          e.printStackTrace();
        }
      }
    }
  }

  public static void main(final String[] args) {
    final int counterValue = sharedCounter.getAndIncrement();
    if (counterValue == 0) {
      // I'm the first JVM to join the cluster, so I'll initialized the queues
      // and start the queue reader threads...
      QUEUES = new LinkedList<NamedQueue>();
      synchronized (QUEUES) {
        if (QUEUES.size() == 0) {
          for (int i = 0; i < COLOR_NAMES.length; i++) {
            QUEUES.add(
              new NamedQueue(COLOR_NAMES[i], new LinkedBlockingQueue<Object>())
            );
          }
        }

        for (Iterator<NamedQueue> i = QUEUES.iterator(); i.hasNext();) {
          new Thread(new QueueReader(i.next())).start();
        }
      }
      final String color = COLOR_NAMES[counterValue % COLOR_NAMES.length] + " "
        + (counterValue / COLOR_NAMES.length);
      System.out.println("I'm the queue reader JVM.");
```

```
    }

    if (counterValue > 0) {
      // I'm not the queue reader JVM, so create and run the example...
      String color = (counterValue % COLOR_NAMES.length) + " "
        + (counterValue / COLOR_NAMES.length);
      System.out.println("I'm the " + color + " JVM.");
      NamedQueue queue;
      synchronized (QUEUES) {
        queue = QUEUES.get(counterValue % COLOR_NAMES.length);
      }
      (new CoordinationWithQueues(color, queue)).run();
    }
  }
}
```

The `main()` method uses a shared `AtomicInteger` as a counter of the number of JVMs that have joined. If the counter value is zero, this is the first JVM to join the cluster and is, therefore, assigned the queue reader/printer function. The first JVM performs the initialization task of instantiating the shared queues and adding them to the shared queue list. For each queue, it spawns a reader thread and creates an associated `QueueReader` object. The `QueueReader` is a `Runnable`, so when its thread is started, the `QueueReader.run()` method will get called. The `QueueReader.run()` method simply enters into a `while` loop, taking from the queue and printing the result to `System.out`.

Subsequent invocations of the example will be assigned one of the seven colors, again based on the value of the `AtomicInteger` counter. The `main()` method will choose the appropriate message queue for its color and invoke the `run()` method on an instance of the example class. This `run()` method simply enters a `while` loop, wherein it picks a mood at random from the available `MOODS` array, reports its mood by adding a message object to the queue, and sleeps for one second. Adding a message object to the shared queue will cause the thread in the first JVM, which is blocked trying to take from that queue, to remove the message object from the queue, print the message, and return to the queue to block on `take()` until another message arrives on that queue.

Listing 10-8. *tc-config.xml for CoordinationWithQueues*

```xml
<?xml version="1.0" encoding="UTF-8"?>
<con:tc-config xmlns:con="http://www.terracotta.org/config">
  <servers>
    <server host="%i" name="localhost">
      <dso-port>9510</dso-port>
      <jmx-port>9520</jmx-port>
      <data>terracotta/server-data</data>
      <logs>terracotta/server-logs</logs>
    </server>
  </servers>
  <clients>
    <logs>terracotta/client-logs</logs>
```

```
    </clients>
    <application>
      <dso>
        <instrumented-classes>
          <include>
            <class-expression>
              org.terracotta.book.coordination.queues.CoordinationWithQueues
            </class-expression>
          </include>
          <include>
            <class-expression>
              org.terracotta.book.coordination.queues.CoordinationWithQueues$ ➥
NamedQueue
            </class-expression>
          </include>
        </instrumented-classes>
        <roots>
          <root>
            <field-name>
              org.terracotta.book.coordination.queues.CoordinationWithQueues.QUEUES
            </field-name>
          </root>
          <root>
            <field-name>
              org.terracotta.book.coordination.queues.CoordinationWithQueues. ➥
sharedCounter
            </field-name>
          </root>
        </roots>
        <locks>
          <autolock>
            <method-expression>
              void org.terracotta.book.coordination.queues.CoordinationWith ➥
Queues.main(java.lang.String[])
            </method-expression>
            <lock-level>write</lock-level>
          </autolock>
        </locks>
      </dso>
    </application>
</con:tc-config>
```

The configuration for this example specifies that the CoordinationWithQueues example class must be instrumented and so must its inner class NamedQueue. Two roots are specified: the list of queues, QUEUES, and the shared counter, sharedCounter. The main() method is added to the <locks> section to make it sensitive to Terracotta locking, but, since LinkedBlockingQueue is implicitly configured by Terracotta, configuring locking for the queue's operations isn't necessary.

This fairly straightforward example illustrates the power Terracotta provides to simple Java programs by allowing them to send messages to each other using stock Java library classes, effectively providing an IPC/RPC mechanism that looks just like interthread communication.

Summary

The examples presented in this chapter illustrate how the simple concurrency utilities built into the JVM can be harnessed using Terracotta to provide an extremely powerful mechanism of inter-JVM coordination. Using simple Java constructs makes this approach easy to develop and, perhaps more importantly, testable at a unit level, because your application can be executed in a single JVM without Terracotta. Terracotta provides its power transparently, enabling it to stay out of the way of your code and allowing you to express your intent in the clearest possible manner.

The examples in this chapter are highly idealized for clarity, but with a little imagination, you can see how their principles may be applied to many different situations, including multi-step coordination, IPC/RPC, work partitioning or grid computing (see Chapter 11), policy enforcement, JVM or application configuration, application monitoring, workload load balancing, and more. And, because the state of the virtual heap is durable and highly available, should a particular member of the cluster go offline, another can be provisioned to seamlessly take its place. As such, you can easily add redundancy and failover systems to your implementation, so you can use these simple mechanisms in mission-critical environments.

■ ■ ■

CHAPTER 11

Grid Computing Using Terracotta

The Master/Worker pattern is one of the most well-known and common patterns for parallelizing work, and it is also one of the core patterns in grid computing to such an extent that most grid-enabling technologies can be seen more or less as industrial implementations of this pattern. In this chapter, we will explain the characteristics of the pattern, walk through some possible implementation strategies, and consider what's really behind all the buzz. We will briefly discuss what grids are really all about and how they use the Master/Worker pattern to solve very challenging real-world problems. We'll also show you, step by step, how you can implement a very scalable and high performing grid-style data processing and workload management framework with Terracotta. By the end of this chapter, you will have implemented your own grid running on Terracotta. The use case will walk you through building a distributed web crawler by hand. The resulting system will be able to run on as many JVMs as you want, crawl any web site as deeply as you want (following four levels of HREF links, for example), and store all the web pages on that site into your Terracotta grid.

What Are Grids?

A grid is a set of servers that together create a mainframe-class processing service where time-sensitive operations can be configured to adhere to business service-level agreements (SLAs) at an operating system level. In mainframes, tasks can be started, stopped, paused, and migrated across the hardware. In grids, data and operations can move seamlessly across the grid in order to optimize the performance and scalability of the computing tasks at hand. A grid scales through use of locality of reference and is highly available through effective use of data duplication. It combines data management with data processing.

Compute Grids vs. Data Grids

There are two main categories of grids: compute grids and data grids. The differences between these two are easier to understand in the context of a framework of load-balancing and partitioning. Grids are not like web applications, in that you don't need a load balancing switch and HTTP doesn't have to be the mode of communication. Grids are all about manually or programmatically partitioning work to a large number of low-cost servers. With partitioning in mind, now think of data grids as clusters of computers where the data has been spread out in memory across application nodes in order to avoid the roundtrips and latencies in retrieving the data from a database. Ten low-cost servers would each store and manage one-tenth of the data.

Compute grids split workload across application nodes; they only make sense for stateless workloads (e.g., only computational work tasks) or on top of data grids where the data has been partitioned. If a compute grid does not work in conjunction with the data grid, meaning that data and workload could be partitioned on different criteria, network bottlenecks could result when compute tasks running on server one of ten is accessing data on server seven.

From now on, our discussion will mainly relate to data grids, which provide both scalability and high availability. Data grids arguably provide the most interesting service for enterprise applications with their focus on fault tolerance and failover of stateful application-specific data as well as scalability in terms of access to this data.

How Grids Handle Scalability

One of the main reasons grids can scale so well is that grid engines can make intelligent choices between either moving data to its processing context or moving the processing context (the operations) to the data. Effectively moving the processing context to the data means that the processor can make use of locality of reference; therefore, data that is being processed on a specific node stays local to that node and will, in the ideal case, never have to leave that node. Instead, all operations working on this specific data set will always be routed to this specific node. The immediate benefits are that this approach minimizes the latency and can give close to unlimited and linear scalability. How well it scales is naturally use-case specific, and achieving scalability can take both effort and skill in partitioning the data and grouping the work items, as well as tuning potential routing algorithms.

The ultimate (and simplest) situation is when all work items are what we call embarrassingly parallel, which means that the work items have no shared state. All work items are self-contained and can execute their tasks in complete isolation, independently of all the other work items, which means that we do not need to worry about data partitioning or routing schemes. The most typical example of embarrassingly parallel work is an arithmetic calculation. Invoking some sort of add(), subtract(), multiply(), or divide() routine with two integer arguments requires no external context. All the data needed to execute work is available in the arguments to the worker. And the return results are well defined and need no further processing to be valuable: add(2, 2) should return 4. However, even though embarrassingly parallel work sets are fairly common, we are sometimes faced with more complicated situations that require both intelligent data partitioning and routing algorithms in order to scale well, something that we will take a look at later on in this chapter.

How Grids Handle Failover and High Availability

Grids are resilient to failure and down time by effectively copying all data across nodes two or three times. Grids can be seen as an organic system of nodes that is designed to handle failure of individual nodes outside the business logic. This is very different from traditional design of distributed systems in which each node is seen as an always-on unit, leaving the developer to deal with the possibility of node failure in source code. Failure in a grid system—meaning failure of a node, a work task, the network, and so on—is not a problem, since the infrastructure will address the problem accordingly. For example, pending work item(s) can be rescheduled to another node; the node can be restarted, and so forth.

Use Cases

Applications that could benefit from being run on a grid are usually applications that need to work on large data sets and/or have a need to parallelize processing of the data to achieve better throughput and performance. Examples of compute grids are financial risk analysis and other simulations, searching and aggregation on large datasets as well as sales order pipeline processing. Examples of data grids are giant distributed Internet indexes such as Google's or Yahoo's.

Introducing the Master/Worker Pattern

The Master/Worker pattern is the key enabler in grid computing and one of the most well-known and common patterns for parallelizing work. In this chapter, we will explain the characteristics of the pattern and walk through some possible implementation strategies.

The Master/Worker pattern consists of three logical entities: a master, a shared workspace, and one or more instances of a worker. The master initiates the computation by creating a set of work tasks, puts them in the shared workspace, and waits for the work tasks to be picked up and completed by the worker(s). The shared workspace is usually some sort of queue, but it can also be implemented as a tuple space (for example, in Linda programming environments, such as JavaSpaces, where the pattern is used extensively).

■Note Linda programming was invented at Yale University by a team led by David Gelernter. The system is made up of shared memory spaces for multiple processes to post and take objects. The shared memory is augmented with the concept of mutual exclusion, where a thread must take what it needs out of the shared space before operating on the object. By taking objects from shared memory while working on them, a thread can safely assume no other operations can occur, and thus no concurrency or transactions are required.

One of the advantages of using the Master/Worker pattern is that the algorithm automatically balances the load. This balancing is possible because the workspace is shared, and the workers continue to pull work tasks from the workspace as soon as those workers are able to do work until there are no more pending tasks. The algorithm usually exhibits good scalability as long as the number of tasks by far exceeds the number of workers and if the tasks take a fairly similar amount of time to complete. See Figure 11-1 for an overview of the algorithm.

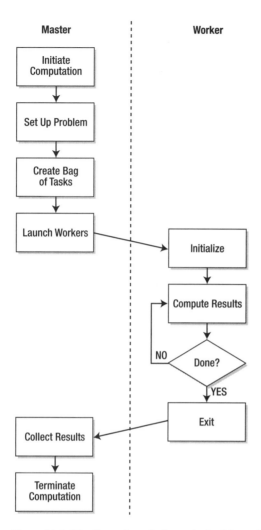

Figure 11-1. *The flow of work through the Master/Worker design pattern*

Master/Worker in Java

Let's now look at the different alternatives we have for implementing the Master/Worker pattern in Java. There might be more ways of doing it, but we will focus the discussion on three different alternatives, each one with a higher abstraction level.

Using the Java Language's Thread Coordination Primitives

The most hard-core approach is to use the concurrency and threading primitives that we have in the Java language itself as defined in the Java Language Specification (JLS), for example, the wait() and notify() methods and the synchronized and volatile keywords. The benefit of using this approach is that everything is really at your fingertips, meaning that you could customize the solution without limitations (well, you will still be constrained by the Java language abstractions and semantics). However, this is also its main problem, since implementing Master/Worker this way is both very hard and tedious to implement yourself and will most likely be even worse to maintain. These low-level abstractions are seldom something that you want to work with on a day-to-day basis. What we need to do is to raise the abstraction level above the core primitives in the JLS, and that is exactly what the data structure abstractions in the `java.util.concurrent` library, introduced by JDK 1.5, does for us.

Using the java.util.concurrent Abstractions

Given that using the low-level abstractions in the JLS is both tedious and difficult, the concurrency abstractions in JDK 1.5 are a very welcome and natural addition to the Java libraries. This very rich API provides everything from locks, semaphores, and barriers to implementations of the Java collections interfaces highly tuned for concurrent access.

It also provides an `ExecutorService`, which is mainly a thread pool that provides direct support for the Master/Worker pattern. This service is very powerful, since you're implementing the Master/Worker pattern using a single abstraction and framework, as shown in Figure 11-2.

Even though this approach would be sufficient in many situations and use cases, it has some problems. First, it does not separate the master from the worker, since they are both part of the same abstraction. In practice, this means that you cannot control and manage the master independently of the workers, which will prove to be a serious limitation when we cluster the implementation with Terracotta to scale it out onto not only multiple threads but multiple JVMs. The problem here is that clustering the `ExecutorService` as it is, even though possible and sometimes even sufficient, will not allow us to scale out the master independently of the workers but force us to run them all on every JVM.

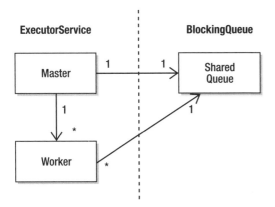

Figure 11-2. *The ExecutorService has limitions; it does not allow us to maintain a many-to-many relationship (instead of one-to-many) where masters and workers are more loosely coupled and we are able to communicate using shared queues (instead of thread pools and threading primitives).*

The second, and perhaps even more important, limitation is that `ExecutorService` is lacking a layer of reliability and control. Since the `ExecutorService` is implemented as a black box, we have no way of knowing if a specific work task has been started, completed, or rejected due to some error. Consequently, we have no way to detect if a work item has failed and retry the work item, on the same node or on another node. We need a way to deal with these things in a simple and, if possible, standardized way.

■**Note** The Oswego `util.concurrent` library provides most of the abstractions found in the Java 5 concurrency library but works with JDK 1.2 and above. The library can be downloaded at `http://g.oswego.edu/dl/classes/EDU/oswego/cs/dl/util/concurrent/intro.html`

Using the CommonJ Work Manager Specification

Spawning and coordinating threads inside an EJB container is something that has been prohibited by the EJB specification. However, enterprise applications very often have a need to coordinate tasks both in a synchronous and asynchronous manner. This is something that was partly solved in a fairly verbose way with Message-Driven Beans (MDB) and was the main motivation for IBM and BEA to create a joint specification that solves this problem by providing a standardized and well defined way of executing concurrent tasks in a JEE environment. The specification is called CommonJ and has support for the Master/Worker pattern in its Work Manager API. BEA provides a good article on getting started with the CommonJ interface at `http://dev2dev.bea.com/wlplatform/commonj/`.

Interestingly, the specification not only defines an API for submitting work and getting the result back but also provides functionality for tracking work status, in that it allows you to register listeners that will receive callback events whenever the state of the work has changed. This functionality for tracking work status makes it possible to not only detect work failure but also to acquire a handle to the work that failed, including the reason why it failed, which gives us enough information to deal with the failure in a sensible way.

Each of the three approaches we have looked at so far has been built on the previous one and has gradually raised the abstraction level, and even more importantly, minimized and simplified the code that we as users have to write and maintain.

The most natural choice is to base our implementation on the CommonJ Work Manager specification. It is a simple and minimalist specification and seems to provide most of the functionality that we need to build a reliable master/worker container.

Let's take a look at the interfaces in the specification. First, we have the `Work` interface; this is the only interface that will be implemented not by the framework but by the user of the master/worker implementation—this should be expected because the actual work to be executed is always use-case specific. The Interface extends the `java.lang.Runnable` interface with its `run()` method, the method that the user should use to implement the actual work task:

```
public interface Work extends Runnable { }
```

The second interface is the `WorkManager`, which provides the main API for our master. It defines two methods for scheduling work; both return an instance of `WorkItem` (which is discussed next), wrapping and giving us a handle to the `Work` instance. The difference between the two methods is that one allows us to pass in an optional `WorkListener` so we can listen to changes to the state of the `Work`. Two more methods give us different ways to wait for work to be completed. The `waitForAll()` method blocks and waits until all `Work` has been completed or the method has timed out, while the waitForAny() method returns immediately with a collection of all the completed Work so far:

```
public interface WorkManager {
  WorkItem schedule(Work work);
  WorkItem schedule(Work work, WorkListener listener);
  boolean waitForAll(Collection workItems, long timeout);
  Collection waitForAny(Collection workItems, long timeout);
}
```

The WorkItem interface, which acts as a wrapper around the pending Work instance adds a method returning status information about the Work being wrapped. This simple addition allows us to build a layer of reliability for our master/worker implementation.

```
public interface WorkItem {
  Work getResult();
  int getStatus();
}
```

The WorkListener is an optional abstraction that provides a set of callback methods that will be invoked whenever state for a Work item has changed:

```
public interface WorkListener {
  void workAccepted(WorkEvent we);
  void workRejected(WorkEvent we);
  void workStarted(WorkEvent we);
  void workCompleted(WorkEvent we);
}
```

Finally, the WorkEvent interface encapsulates the event that is sent to the WorkListener whenever the state for a Work has changed. In the case of a failure (e.g., the status flag is set to WORK_REJECTED), we will be able to use the WorkEvent interface to retrieve the WorkException, which holds additional information about the cause of the failure:

```
public interface WorkEvent {
  int WORK_ACCEPTED  = 1;
  int WORK_REJECTED  = 2;
  int WORK_STARTED   = 3;
  int WORK_COMPLETED = 4;
  public int getType();
  public WorkItem getWorkItem();
  public WorkException getException();
}
```

Our goal is to take all these interfaces and methods and create implementations of these things using only the JLS. When we implement this POJO implementation of CommonJ—one that does not depend on BEA or IBM application server internal libraries—we can use tc-config directives to cluster our CommonJ implementation in any context or container. Let's now implement CommonJ by hand, as this will serve as the basis for our master/worker engine.

Getting Started: Naïve Single Work Queue Implementation

We have looked at three different approaches to implement the Master/Worker pattern in Java, each one with a slightly higher abstraction level than its predecessor. Let's now make use of this knowledge by bringing it all together to create a master/worker implementation—let's call it container—that will implement CommonJ WorkManager interfaces. We'll build our container using java.util.concurrent abstractions, so we will get a standard API with rich enough abstractions to give us the level of reliability that we need, while utilizing the full performance, stability, and correctness of the standard Java concurrency libraries.

We will implement three different versions of the master/worker container. The first one will be trivial—actually not even trivial but naïve. We will then use it to bring together the concepts and set the stage for our journey toward a real-world implementation. After each implementation, we will take some time to look at how we can utilize Terracotta and its Network-Attached Memory to scale it out onto multiple nodes.

Sound like a good plan? Let's put it into action.

Implementing a Single-JVM Naïve Master/Worker Container

Our first, naïve implementation simply consists of a single work queue, one master, and an arbitrary number of workers (we will soon learn what makes this naïve).

The first thing that we need to do is build our single work queue, which will simply be a wrapper around an instance of the java.util.concurrent.LinkedBlockingQueue class. The semantics of this class are sufficient for our crossthread or cross-JVM communication needs. We will wrap it, however, simply to add a basic fault-handling strategy—if we catch an InterruptedException when trying to add a new work item to the queue, we set the status of the work item to WORK_REJECTED, passing along the offending exception before rethrowing the exception to the caller. Listing 11-1 shows our single work queue. Here, the DefaultWorkItem is our implementation of the WorkItem interface

Listing 11-1. *SimpleQueue CommonJ Implementation*

```
package org.terracotta.book.masterworker.naive;

import commonj.work.WorkException;

import java.util.concurrent.BlockingQueue;
import java.util.concurrent.LinkedBlockingQueue;

import org.terracotta.book.masterworker.DefaultWorkItem;

/**
 * Implements a single work queue which wraps a linked blocking queue.
 */
public class SimpleQueue {
```

```
// Terracotta Shared Root
private final BlockingQueue<DefaultWorkItem> m_workQueue =
  new LinkedBlockingQueue<DefaultWorkItem>();

public void put(final DefaultWorkItem workItem) throws InterruptedException {
  m_workQueue.put(workItem); // blocks if queue is full
}

public DefaultWorkItem peek() {
  return m_workQueue.peek(); // returns null if queue is empty
}

public DefaultWorkItem take() throws WorkException {
  try {
    return m_workQueue.take(); // blocks if queue is empty
  } catch (InterruptedException e) {
    Thread.currentThread().interrupt();
    throw new WorkException(e);
  }
}
}
```

The second artifact that we need to write is the Worker, which holds on to a reference to our SimpleQueue instance. It is shown in Listing 11-2. When the Worker starts up, it uses a thread pool to spawn a number of worker threads that continuously grab and execute work items from our SimpleQueue instance. Recall our issue with the ExecutorService and its inability to factor the master away from the workers by itself. Now, you can see that the queue is separating the master and his thread pool from the workers and their pools. The thread pool is an instance of the ExecutorService, exactly the same class from util.concurrent that we discussed in detail earlier in this chapter. During the execution of the work, work status is maintained by managing a flag in the wrapping WorkItem—the flag can have one of the following states: WORK_ACCEPTED, WORK_STARTED, WORK_COMPLETED, or WORK_REJECTED.

Listing 11-2. *Naïve CommonJ Worker Implementation*

```
package org.terracotta.book.masterworker.naive;

import commonj.work.Work;
import commonj.work.WorkEvent;
import commonj.work.WorkException;

import java.util.concurrent.ExecutorService;
import java.util.concurrent.Executors;

import org.terracotta.book.masterworker.DefaultWorkItem;
import org.terracotta.book.masterworker.worker.Worker;
```

```
/**
 * Worker bean, receives a work item from the same single work queue. It grabs the
 * next pending work and executes it.
 */
public class SimpleWorker implements Worker {

  protected final ExecutorService m_threadPool = Executors.newCachedThreadPool();

  protected final SimpleQueue m_queue;

  protected volatile boolean m_isRunning = true;

  public SimpleWorker(final SimpleQueue queue) {
    m_queue = queue;
  }

  public void start() throws WorkException {
    while (m_isRunning) {
      final DefaultWorkItem workItem = m_queue.take();
      final Work work = workItem.getResult();
      m_threadPool.execute(new Runnable() {
        public void run() {
          try {
            workItem.setStatus(WorkEvent.WORK_STARTED, null);
            work.run();
            workItem.setStatus(WorkEvent.WORK_COMPLETED, null);
          } catch (Throwable e) {
            workItem.setStatus(WorkEvent.WORK_REJECTED, new WorkException(e));
          }
        }
      });
    }
  }

  public void stop() {
    m_threadPool.shutdown();
    m_isRunning = false;
  }
}
```

Finally, we need to implement our Master, or in the context of CommonJ, our
WorkManager, as shown in Listing 11-3. Here, we had to implement the four different methods
in the WorkManager interface. The first two methods are for scheduling the work. They're both
called schedule(), and the difference between them is that one of them takes an optional
WorkListener instance in order to get callback notifications when work items change state.
Apart from that, both methods work the same; they take the work, wrap it in a WorkItem
instance, and add it to the queue. They also return the newly created WorkItem instance,
which gives the caller a reference to the pending Work for tracking or management.

The other two methods are waitForAll() and waitForAny(), whose contracts have been discussed in the previous section. At this stage, it is fine to go for the simplest thing that could possibly work: a busy wait loop. But, as you might guess, you can implement these methods more efficiently using wait() and notify(), which we will take a look at later on in this chapter. This is, after all, a simple and naïve implementation.

Listing 11-3. *Naïve CommonJ WorkManager Implementation*

```java
package org.terracotta.book.masterworker.naive;

import org.terracotta.book.masterworker.DefaultWorkItem;

import commonj.work.Work;
import commonj.work.WorkEvent;
import commonj.work.WorkException;
import commonj.work.WorkItem;
import commonj.work.WorkListener;
import commonj.work.WorkManager;

/**
 * Implementation of the WorkManager abstraction that is scheduling all work to
 * the same work single queue.
 */
public class SimpleWorkManager implements WorkManager {

  private final SimpleQueue m_queue;

  public SimpleWorkManager(final SimpleQueue queue) {
    m_queue = queue;
  }

  public WorkItem schedule(final Work work) {
    return schedule(work, null);
  }

  public WorkItem schedule(final Work work, final WorkListener listener) {
    DefaultWorkItem workItem = new DefaultWorkItem(work, null);
    try {
      m_queue.put(workItem);
    } catch (InterruptedException e) {
      workItem.setStatus(WorkEvent.WORK_REJECTED, new WorkException(e));
      Thread.currentThread().interrupt();
    }
    return workItem;
  }

  public boolean waitForAll(Collection workItems, long timeout)
      throws InterruptedException {
```

```
      long start = System.currentTimeMillis();
      do {
        synchronized (this) {
          boolean isAllCompleted = true;
          for (Iterator<WorkItem> it = workItems.iterator();
               it.hasNext() && isAllCompleted;) {
            int status = it.next().getStatus();
            isAllCompleted = status ==
                WorkEvent.WORK_COMPLETED || status == WorkEvent.WORK_REJECTED;
          }
          if (isAllCompleted) {
            return true;
          }
          if (timeout == IMMEDIATE) {
            return false;
          }
          if (timeout == INDEFINITE) {
            continue;
          }
        }
      } while ((System.currentTimeMillis() - start) < timeout);
      return false;
    }

    public Collection waitForAny(Collection workItems, long timeout)
        throws InterruptedException {
     long start = System.currentTimeMillis();
     do {
        synchronized (this) {
          Collection<WorkItem> completed = new ArrayList<WorkItem>();
          for (Iterator<WorkItem> it = workItems.iterator(); it.hasNext();) {
            WorkItem workItem = it.next();
            if (workItem.getStatus() == WorkEvent.WORK_COMPLETED ||
                workItem.getStatus() == WorkEvent.WORK_REJECTED) {
              completed.add(workItem);
            }
          }
          if (!completed.isEmpty()) {
            return completed;
          }
        }
        if (timeout == IMMEDIATE) {
          return Collections.EMPTY_LIST;
        }
        if (timeout == INDEFINITE) {
          continue;
        }
```

```
        } while ((System.currentTimeMillis() - start) < timeout);
        return Collections.EMPTY_LIST;
    }
}
```

What About My Work?

Now, we have the three main artifacts in place; the Master, the Worker, and the SimpleQueue. But what about the Work abstraction, and what role does the WorkItem play?

Let's start with the Work, which is an interface in the CommonJ Work Manager specification. We cannot implement this interface generically in our master/worker container. Instead, the user of the framework should implement it, since the implementation of the actual work that is supposed to be done is by its nature use case specific.

Let's look at the DefaultWorkItem, which as we've noted previously, is our implementation of the WorkItem interface; see Listing 11-4. Again, its purpose is simply to wrap a Work instance and provide additional information, such as status, and an optional WorkListener. If such a listener is available, it will instantiate a WorkEvent defining the work's state transition and pass it on to the listener.

Listing 11-4. *Default WorkItem Wrapper for Your Work*

```java
package org.terracotta.book.masterworker;

import commonj.work.Work;

import commonj.work.WorkEvent;
import commonj.work.WorkException;
import commonj.work.WorkItem;
import commonj.work.WorkListener;

/**
 * The work item holds the work to be executed, status of the progress and the
 * future result.
 */
public class DefaultWorkItem implements WorkItem {

    protected volatile int m_status;

    protected final Work m_work;

    protected final WorkListener m_workListener;

    public DefaultWorkItem(final Work work, final WorkListener workListener) {
        m_work = work;
        m_status = WorkEvent.WORK_ACCEPTED;
        m_workListener = workListener;
    }
```

```java
public Work getResult() {
  return m_work;
}

public synchronized void setStatus(
    final int status, final WorkException exception) {
  m_status = status;
  if (m_workListener != null) {
    switch (status) {
    case WorkEvent.WORK_ACCEPTED:
      m_workListener.workAccepted(
          new DefaultWorkEvent(WorkEvent.WORK_ACCEPTED, this, exception));
      break;
    case WorkEvent.WORK_REJECTED:
      m_workListener.workRejected(
          new DefaultWorkEvent(WorkEvent.WORK_REJECTED, this, exception));
      break;
    case WorkEvent.WORK_STARTED:
      m_workListener.workStarted(
          new DefaultWorkEvent(WorkEvent.WORK_STARTED, this, exception));
      break;
    case WorkEvent.WORK_COMPLETED:
      m_workListener.workCompleted(
          new DefaultWorkEvent(WorkEvent.WORK_COMPLETED, this, exception));
      break;
    }
  }
}

public synchronized int getStatus() {
  return m_status;
}

public WorkException newWorkException(final Throwable e) {
  e.printStackTrace();
  WorkException we = new WorkException(e.getMessage());
  setStatus(WorkEvent.WORK_REJECTED, we);
  Thread.currentThread().interrupt();
  return we;
}

public int compareTo(Object compareTo) {
  // check if Work is implementing Comparable
  Work work = ((WorkItem) compareTo).getResult();
  if (m_work instanceof Comparable) {
    Comparable<Comparable<?>> comparableWork1 =
```

```
            (Comparable<Comparable<?>>) m_work;
      if (work instanceof Comparable) {
        Comparable<?> comparableWork2 = (Comparable<?>) work;
        return comparableWork1.compareTo(comparableWork2);
      }
    }
    return 0; // ordering is not specified
  }

  public String toString() {
    String status;
    switch (m_status) {
    case WorkEvent.WORK_ACCEPTED:
      status = "WORK_ACCEPTED";
      break;
    case WorkEvent.WORK_COMPLETED:
      status = "WORK_COMPLETED";
      break;
    case WorkEvent.WORK_REJECTED:
      status = "WORK_REJECTED";
      break;
    case WorkEvent.WORK_STARTED:
      status = "WORK_STARTED";
      break;
    default:
      throw new IllegalStateException("illegal (unknown) status " + m_status);
    }
    return m_work.toString() + ":" + status;
  }
}
```

We now have a single-JVM, multithreaded, master/worker container based on the
CommonJ Work Manager specification and the `java.util.concurrent` abstractions. This application is potentially useful as it stands, but to fully scale it out, we need to be able not only to
schedule work onto multiple threads but also to divide the threads across machines in an easy
way. Let's bring in Terracotta.

Clustering Our Master/Worker with Terracotta

To cluster our current `WorkManager` implementation with Terracotta, all we have to do is create
a Terracotta configuration file in which we define three things: roots, includes, and locks.

Let's start with roots. First, we have to define the state that we want to share across the
cluster. In our case, we want to share the work queue, which means the instance of the
`LinkedBlockingQueue` in the `SimpleQueue` instance. Let's add this as a root now:

```
<roots>
  <root>
    <field-name>
```

```
        org.terracotta.book.masterworker.naive.SimpleQueue.m_workQueue
      </field-name>
    </root>
</roots>
```

We also need to define the set of classes that we want to include for instrumentation. This set should include all the classes that have instances that will join a shared object graph. In our case, those that can be referenced from our previously defined root collection must be instrumented:

```
<instrumented-classes>
  <include>
    <class-expression>
      org.terracotta.book.masterworker..*
    </class-expression>
  </include>
</instrumented-classes>
```

Finally, we have to define the potential lock/transaction boundaries. Here, we are using an auto-lock. We'll define a match-all pattern for the locking, since the impact of matching all synchronization is countered by the fact that we only instrumented classes in our own package. Normally, we wouldn't use such broadly scoped automatic locking configuration.

```
<locks>
  <autolock>
    <method-expression>* *..*.*(..)</method-expression>
    <lock-level>write</lock-level>
  </autolock>
</locks>
```

Now, we could try to run the application, but to make it a bit more interesting, we will wait until we have refactored our naïve implementation to prepare it a bit better to meet the real (evil and scary) world.

Handling Real-World Challenges

So far, we have built a distributed master/worker container ready for use, but we haven't run it, because it is a very naïve implementation. Even though it implements a clustered Master/Worker pattern, it will not scale very well. Sending too much work to our current implementation will essentially bottleneck on our work queue. Bottlenecks in a framework designed to deliver linear scale block us from achieving our goals. The current implementation also doesn't handle failure and resubmission of work.

Now, we will refactor and extend our implementation a bit to address some of these challenges that are likely to arise if we were to use SimpleQueue in the real world solving real-world problems.

We will look at the following challenges:

- Very high volumes of data

- Routing

- Work failure and failover

- Worker failure and failover

- Dynamic cluster management (workers can attach and detach from the grid at run time)

Refactoring for Large Workloads, Routing, and Work Failover

The first challenge to tackle is scaling workload throughput linearly. What makes the Simple-Queue naïve is that it uses one queue for all masters and works to communicate through. Using one queue is like putting every employee of every company in the city of San Francisco on a bus together, driving each one to work, one at a time, while all the others wait for their turn to be dropped off at the office. Instead, we will minimize contention through queue striping techniques.

Minimizing Contention and Maximizing Locality of Reference

One of the main problems with our current implementation is that one queue is shared by all the masters and workers. This might give acceptable performance and scalability when used under a small to moderate work load. However, if we need to deal with very high volumes of data, the single queue will be a bottleneck.

One solution is to stripe queues by creating one queue per worker and have the master do some more intelligent load balancing of work onto discrete work queues, one per worker. Partitioning data will enable the following:

- *Maximized use of locality of reference*: If all work operating on the same data set is routed to the same queue with the same worker working on it, no workers will share objects across JVMs, and thus no object updates will result in cluster traffic to other nodes. This is a good start toward linear scale where each node must avoid conversations with other nodes.

- *Minimized contention*: Since there will be only one reader and one writer per queue—the master on one end and the worker on the other—workers will not have to wait behind other workers to receive or respond to workload requests.

To reduce the contention even more, we can split up each work queue into two queues, one for pending work requests from the master and the other one for completed work responses from the worker. This refactoring calls for a new abstraction that wraps up both queues as a single unit—let's call this abstraction a pipe. We should go ahead and build some sort of pipe manager that holds on to and manages the different pipes. Each one of these pipes will be assigned a unique ID. Work will be routed to different queues according to predefined routing algorithms and failover schemes (something that we will talk more about later in this chapter).

First, let's introduce two new classes: RoutableWorkItem and Pipe. We'll start with RoutableWorkItem in Listing 11-5, which extends our DefaultWorkItem class by adding a routing ID. The purpose of this ID is to decide on which pipe the master should send work. The routing ID also gives the master the ability to change the ID to reroute the work onto another pipe if necessary, normally due to worker failure, which we will take a look at later in this chapter.

Listing 11-5. *A New RoutableWorkItem to Intelligently Balance Load Across Our Worker Grid*

```java
package org.terracotta.book.masterworker.routing;

import org.terracotta.book.masterworker.DefaultWorkEvent;
import org.terracotta.book.masterworker.MutableWorkItem;
import org.terracotta.book.masterworker.routing.Routable;
import org.terracotta.book.masterworker.routing.RoutableWorkItem;

import commonj.work.Work;
import commonj.work.WorkEvent;
import commonj.work.WorkException;
import commonj.work.WorkItem;
import commonj.work.WorkListener;

public class RoutableWorkItem<ID> implements Routable<ID>, MutableWorkItem {

  public static int CANCEL_WORK_STATUS_TRACKING = 1 << WorkEvent.WORK_STARTED;

  protected final int m_flags;

  protected final Work m_work;

  protected transient final WorkListener m_workListener;

  protected int m_status;

  protected boolean m_dirty;

  protected WorkException m_exception;

  protected ID m_routingID;

  public RoutableWorkItem(Work work, WorkListener workListener, ID routingID) {
    this(0, work, workListener, routingID);
  }

  public RoutableWorkItem(int flags, Work work, WorkListener workListener,
                          ID routingID) {
    m_flags = flags;
    m_work = work;
    m_status = -1;
    m_dirty = false;
    m_workListener = workListener;
```

```java
    m_routingID = routingID;
}

public Work getResult() {
  return m_work;
}

public int getFlags() {
  return m_flags;
}

public synchronized int getStatus() {
  return m_status;
}

public synchronized void setStatus(final int status,
  final WorkException exception) {
  m_status = status;
  m_exception = exception;
  m_dirty = true;
}

public synchronized ID getRoutingID() {
  return m_routingID;
}

public synchronized void setRoutingID(final ID routingID) {
  m_routingID = routingID;
}

public WorkListener getWorkListener() {
  return m_workListener;
}

public void fireListener() {
  if (m_workListener == null) {
    return;
  }

  int status;
  WorkException exception;
  synchronized (this) {
    if (!m_dirty) {
      return;
    }
    status = getStatus();
    exception = m_exception;
```

```java
      m_dirty = false;
    }

    switch (status) {
      case WorkEvent.WORK_ACCEPTED:
        m_workListener.workAccepted(
            new DefaultWorkEvent(WorkEvent.WORK_ACCEPTED, this, exception));
        break;
      case WorkEvent.WORK_REJECTED:
        m_workListener.workRejected(
            new DefaultWorkEvent(WorkEvent.WORK_REJECTED, this, exception));
        break;
      case WorkEvent.WORK_STARTED:
        m_workListener.workStarted(
            new DefaultWorkEvent(WorkEvent.WORK_STARTED, this, exception));
        break;
      case WorkEvent.WORK_COMPLETED:
        m_workListener.workCompleted(
            new DefaultWorkEvent(WorkEvent.WORK_COMPLETED, this, exception));
        break;
    }
  }
}

public WorkException newWorkException(final Throwable e) {
  e.printStackTrace();
  WorkException we = new WorkException(e.getMessage());
  setStatus(WorkEvent.WORK_REJECTED, we);
  Thread.currentThread().interrupt();
  return we;
}

public int compareTo(Object compareTo) {
  // check if Work is implementing Comparable
  Work work = ((WorkItem) compareTo).getResult();
  if (m_work instanceof Comparable) {
    Comparable<Comparable<?>> comparableWork1
        = (Comparable<Comparable<?>>) m_work;
    if (work instanceof Comparable) {
      Comparable<?> comparableWork2 = (Comparable<?>) work;
      return comparableWork1.compareTo(comparableWork2);
    }
  }
  return 0; // ordering is not specified
}

public static class Factory<ID> {
```

```
    private final int flags;

    public Factory() {
      this(0);
    }

    public Factory(final int flags) {
      this.flags = flags;
    }

    public RoutableWorkItem<ID> create(
        Work work, WorkListener listener, ID routingID) {
      return new RoutableWorkItem<ID>(flags, work, listener, routingID);
    }
  }
}
```

The Pipe class, shown in Listing 11-6, is fairly simple. It wraps two queues, one holding the pending work and the other the completed work.

Listing 11-6. *The Pipe Class*

```
package org.terracotta.book.masterworker.pipe;

import java.util.Set;

import org.terracotta.book.masterworker.queue.Queue;
import org.terracotta.book.masterworker.queue.QueueListener;

/**
 * A pipe is a two way queue for work management.
 * <p>
 * It is wrapping one queue for pending work and one for completed work as well as
 * two listeners that are receiving call backs whenever an item has been added to
 * one of its corresponding queues.
 *
 * @param <T>
 */
public interface Pipe<T, ID> {

  Queue<T> getPendingWorkQueue();

  Queue<T> getCompletedWorkQueue();

  QueueListener<T, ID> getQueueListener();

  void startQueueListener(Set<T> allCompletedWork);
```

```
  void clear();

  public static interface Factory<T, ID> {
    Pipe<T, ID> create(ID routingID);
  }
}
```

As you can see, the Pipe is using an abstraction called Queue, which is a simple generic interface for a queue abstraction. In this example's implementation in the SVN repository, you can
find three different implementations of this interface: ListBasedQueue (wrapping a
java.util.ArrayList), DmiBasedQueue (based on Terracotta's Distributed Method Invocation feature) and BlockingQueueBasedQueue (wrapping a java.util.concurrent.LinkedBlockingQueue).
Among these three, the third is the one that gives best throughput and scale (each of these Queue
implementations also has a Factory that creates the queue in question). The Queue class is
shown in Listing 11-7.

Listing 11-7. *The Queue Class*

```
package org.terracotta.book.masterworker.queue;

import java.util.Iterator;
import java.util.concurrent.TimeUnit;

/**
 * Represents a one-way communication channel. Abstract notion of putting
 * objects and receiving them (take or poll)
 *
 * @param <T>
 */
public interface Queue<T> {

  public static interface Factory<T> {
    public Queue<T> create();
  }

  T poll(long timeout, TimeUnit unit) throws InterruptedException;

  T put(T item) throws InterruptedException;

  T take() throws InterruptedException;

  int size();

  void clear();

  Iterator<T> iterator();
}
```

If we take a look at the current code, we discover that we need to refactor the SimpleQueue class—we need to rename it PipeManager and swap the single LinkedBlockingQueue to a ConcurrentHashMap with entries containing a routing ID mapped to our new Pipe abstraction.

In practice this means going from this

```
public class SimpleQueue {
  BlockingQueue<WorkItem> m_workQueue = new LinkedBlockingQueue<WorkItem>();
  ...
}
```

to this

```
public class PipeManager<ID> {
  private final Map<ID, Pipe<RoutableWorkItem<ID>, ID>> m_pipes =
      new ConcurrentHashMap<ID, Pipe<RoutableWorkItem<ID>, ID>>();
  ...
}
```

Finally, we need to change the Master implementation to start making use of the multiple pipes and their routing IDs by adding a Router abstraction that is responsible for putting the work on its dedicated pipe according to some predefined routing algorithm (more of which we'll see in the next section). In order to do that, we will have to slightly rewrite the schedule() methods to hand the work to a Router and not put it directly into the queue. This would mean changing the WorkManager from this

```
public class SimpleWorkManager implements WorkManager {
  ...
  public WorkItem schedule(Work work WorkListener listener) {
    WorkItem workItem = new DefaultWorkItem(work, listener);
    m_queue.put(workItem);
    return workItem;
  }
  ...
}
```

to this

```
public class StaticWorkManager<ID> implements WorkManager {

  private final Router<ID> m_router;
  ...

  public WorkItem schedule(final Work work, final WorkListener listener) {
    return m_router.route(work, listener);
  }
  ...
}
```

■Note The reason for naming the class StaticWorkManager is that this implementation reflects a static configuration with all the routing ids predefined and passed into the WorkManager at startup. This limitation is removed in the next refactoring session, in which we introduce a DynamicWorkManager that can handle workers joining and leaving the cluster on the fly.

While we are refactoring the WorkManager, we can take the time to get rid of the busy wait in our waitForAll() and waitForAny() methods (which we implemented in the previous section). Their functionality is implemented in terms of a new utility method also called waitForAny() (which is useful enough to actually expose in our public API even though it is not part of the CommonJ specification). You'll see the refactored original waitForAny() method at the end of the section.

This method waits until at least one WorkItem has been completed and returns only that WorkItem. Instead of relying on a busy wait, we use wait() and notify(). As you can see in the next code snippet, if we have a completed WorkItem in our set all completed work items would just return, but if the set is empty and the timeout is set to INDEFINITE, we will invoke wait() on the set, which will block until someone else calls notify() on the set (see the line in bold close to the end in the next code listing).

To get this method to work, we need to make sure that each time a WorkItem is added to the set with all the completed WorkItem objects, we call the notify method, which will then notify the thread blocked at the wait() in the waitForAny() method.

Using this utility method, refactoring the waitForAll() and waitForAny() becomes close to trivial. Here is the full source listing of the StaticWorkManager class:

```
/**
 * A routing aware WorkerManager that uses an implementation of the Router
 * interface to do the route work to different work queues.
 */
public class StaticWorkManager<ID> implements WorkManager {

  private final Router<ID> m_router;

  private final Set<RoutableWorkItem<ID>> m_completedWork;

  private int m_nrOfScheduledWork = 0;

  public StaticWorkManager(Router<ID> router) {
    m_router = router;
    m_completedWork = router.getAllCompletedWork();
  }

  public WorkItem schedule(final Work work, final WorkListener listener) {
    System.out.println("scheduled work #: " + m_nrOfScheduledWork++);
    return m_router.route(work, listener);
  }
}
```

```java
public Set<RoutableWorkItem<ID>> getCompletedWork() {
  return m_completedWork;
}

public WorkItem schedule(final Work work) {
  return schedule(work, null);
}

public boolean waitForAll(Collection workItems, long timeout)
    throws InterruptedException {
  final int nrOfPendingWorkItems = workItems.size();
  int nrOfCompletedWorkItems = 0;
  while (true) {
    WorkItem workItem = waitForAny(timeout);
    if (workItem == null) {
      return false;
    }
    nrOfCompletedWorkItems++;
    if (nrOfPendingWorkItems == nrOfCompletedWorkItems) {
      break;
    }
  }
  return true;
}

public Collection waitForAny(final Collection workItems, final long timeout)
    throws InterruptedException {
  final Collection<WorkItem> completedWorkItems = new ArrayList<WorkItem>();

  WorkItem workItem = waitForAny(timeout);
  if (workItem == null) {
    return Collections.EMPTY_LIST;
  }
  completedWorkItems.add(workItem);
  return completedWorkItems;
}

public WorkItem waitForAny(long timeout) throws InterruptedException {
  synchronized (m_completedWork) {
    while (true) {
      for (WorkItem workItem : m_completedWork) {
        if (workItem.getStatus() == WorkEvent.WORK_COMPLETED ||
            workItem.getStatus() == WorkEvent.WORK_REJECTED) {
          m_completedWork.remove(workItem);
          return workItem;
        }
      }
    }
```

```
        if (timeout == IMMEDIATE) {
          return null;
        }
        if (timeout == INDEFINITE) {
          int size = m_completedWork.size();
          while (m_completedWork.size() == size) {
            try {
              m_completedWork.wait();
            } catch (InterruptedException ie) {
              ie.printStackTrace();
              Thread.currentThread().interrupt();
              throw ie;
            }
          }
        }
      }
    }
  }
}
```

Routing Strategies

By splitting up the single work queue into multiple pipes, each with a unique routing ID, we are allowing for the possibility of providing different, pluggable routing schemes that can be customized to address specific use cases.

In the previous section, we introduced a new abstraction called Router. Here is the interface that we will use for it:

```
import commonj.work.Work;
import commonj.work.WorkItem;
import commonj.work.WorkListener;

public interface Router<ID> {
  RoutableWorkItem<ID> route(Work work);
  RoutableWorkItem<ID> route(Work work, WorkListener listener);
  RoutableWorkItem<ID> route(RoutableWorkItem<ID> WorkItem);
}
```

This interface can be used to implement various data partitioning and load-balancing algorithms, such as these:

- *Round-robin balancing*: The Router loops through all queues one by one. This is probably the least useful strategy; it's only useful if the work items have no state to share (i.e., they are embarrassingly parallel).

- *Workload-sensitive balancing*: The Router looks at queue depth and always sends the next pending work item to the shortest queue.

- *Data affinity*: Using sticky routing, meaning that the Router sends all pending work of a specific type to a specific queue, is useful for different data partitioning strategies, and is use case specific.

- *Roll your own*: To maximize locality of reference for your use-case-specific requirements, you can create your own balancing solution.

Here is an example of the load-balancing router implementation that takes an array of the routing IDs that are registered and always sends the next pending work to the shortest queue:

```
public class LoadBalancingRouter<ID> implements Router<ID> {

  private final PipeManager<ID> m_pipeManager;
  private final RoutableWorkItem.Factory<ID> m_workItemFactory =
      new RoutableWorkItem.Factory<ID>();

  public LoadBalancingRouter(PipeManager<ID> pipeManager, ID[] routingIDs) {
    m_pipeManager = pipeManager;

    // create all queues upfront
    for (int i = 0; i < routingIDs.length; i++) {
      m_pipeManager.getOrCreatePipeFor(routingIDs[i]);
    }
  }

  public RoutableWorkItem<ID> route(Work work) {
    return route(work, null);
  }

  public RoutableWorkItem<ID> route(final Work work, final WorkListener listener) {
    LoadBalancingRouter.PipeInfo<ID> shortestPipeInfo = getShortestPipe();
    RoutableWorkItem<ID> workItem = m_workItemFactory.create(
        work, listener, shortestPipeInfo.routingID);
    return scheduleWorkItem(shortestPipeInfo, workItem);
  }

  public RoutableWorkItem<ID> route(final RoutableWorkItem<ID> workItem) {
    LoadBalancingRouter.PipeInfo<ID> shortestPipeInfo = getShortestPipe();
    synchronized (workItem) {
      workItem.setRoutingID(shortestPipeInfo.routingID);
    }
    return scheduleWorkItem(shortestPipeInfo, workItem);
  }

  private RoutableWorkItem<ID> scheduleWorkItem(
      LoadBalancingRouter.PipeInfo<ID> shortestQueue,
      RoutableWorkItem<ID> workItem) {
    try {
      shortestQueue.pipe.getPendingWorkQueue().put(workItem);
```

```
      } catch (InterruptedException e) {
        workItem.setStatus(WorkEvent.WORK_REJECTED, new WorkException(e));
        Thread.currentThread().interrupt();
      }
      return workItem;
    }

    private LoadBalancingRouter.PipeInfo<ID> getShortestPipe() {
      ... // return the shortest pipe by looking at the number of items in each pipe's
          //pending queue
    }

    private static class PipeInfo<ID> {
      public ID routingID;
      public Pipe<RoutableWorkItem<ID>, ID> pipe;
      public int queueLength = Integer.MAX_VALUE;
    }
}
```

Dealing with Work Failure and Recovery

You might remember that we briefly mentioned that the CommonJ Work Manager specification provides APIs for event-based failure reporting and tracking of work status. Each Work instance is wrapped in a WorkItem instance, which contains status information about the work. It also gives us the possibility of defining an optional WorkListener, through which we can get callback events whenever the status of the work has been changed.

Let's recap what the WorkListener interface looks like (in case you have forgotten it):

```
public interface WorkListener {
  void workAccepted(WorkEvent we);
  void workRejected(WorkEvent we);
  void workStarted(WorkEvent we);
  void workCompleted(WorkEvent we);
}
```

As you can see, we can implement callback methods that subscribe to events triggered by work being accepted, rejected, started, and completed. In this particular case, we are mainly interested in doing something when receiving the rejected event. To do so, we need to create an implementation of the WorkListener interface and add some code in the workRejected() method:

```
import commonj.work.Work;
import commonj.work.WorkEvent;
import commonj.work.WorkItem;
import commonj.work.WorkListener;

public class RetryingWorkListener implements WorkListener {
```

```
  public void workRejected(WorkEvent we) {
    Exception cause = we.getException();
    WorkItem wi = we.getWorkItem();
    Work work = wi.getResult(); // the rejected work

    ... // reroute the work onto pipe with id X
  }

  public void workAccepted(WorkEvent event) {}
  public void workCompleted(WorkEvent event) {}
  public void workStarted(WorkEvent event) {}
}
```

Through the event passed to us in the callback method, we have access to the exception holding the cause of the failure and the work that was rejected. With this information, we can act accordingly, perhaps trying again (e.g., schedule the work on the same pipe), rerouting the work to another pipe, or if we can't recover, simply logging the error.

Refactoring the Worker

In the previous sections, we introduced the concept of a routing ID, which maps to a specific queue. Normally, we want each Worker to get its own queue to minimize contention and maximize data locality. In other words, we don't want the master or any other workers touching queues or pipes they do not need to access, as touching objects causes them to implicitly fault in to the heap. We can simply assign each worker an ID and use the worker's ID as the routing ID. To do so, we need to refactor our Worker a little bit to be able to define a routing ID and retrieve the work queue (called Pipe in our latest implementation). Let's do that now.

First, we add some member variables representing a pipe, pipe manager, and the routing ID:

```
protected Pipe<RoutableWorkItem<ID>, ID> m_pipe;
protected PipeManager<ID> m_pipeManager;
protected ID m_routingID;
```

Next, we refactor the constructor to be able to take a pipe manager and a routing ID as parameters, initialize them, and—most importantly—retrieve the pipe for the specific routing ID that is given:

```
public StaticWorker(PipeManager<ID> pipeManager, ID routingID) {
  m_routingID = routingID;
  m_pipe = pipeManager.getOrCreatePipeFor(m_routingID);
  m_pipeManager = pipeManager;
  System.out.println("Starting worker with routing ID: " + routingID);
}
```

We also need to change the run() method a little bit to have work with the queues for pending and completed work (wrapped up by the WorkerTask class, whose job is to put the completed WorkItem onto the queue with completed work and manage its status):

```
public void run() throws WorkException {
  while (m_isRunning) {
```

```
    final RoutableWorkItem<ID> workItem;
    try {
      workItem = m_pipe.getPendingWorkQueue().take();
    } catch (InterruptedException e) {
      Thread.currentThread().interrupt();
      throw new WorkException(e);
    }
    if (workItem != null) {
      m_threadPool.execute(new WorkerTask<RoutableWorkItem<ID>>(
        workItem, m_pipe.getCompletedWorkQueue()));
    }
  }
}
```

Finally, we need to add a statement to remove the pipe that the worker has used when it shuts down (this is not the best solution and will be addressed properly in the next refactoring session using Terracotta cluster events):

```
public void stop() {
  m_isRunning = false;
  m_threadPool.shutdown();
  m_pipeManager.removePipeFor(m_routingID);
}
```

Update the Terracotta Configuration

You might remember that, to make the first naïve implementation scalable, we had to change the SimpleQueue class with its single LinkedBlockingQueue to a PipeManager class with a java.util.concurrent.ConcurrentHashMap with multiple queues. When we did that, we changed both the name of the field holding our shared queue(s) and the name of the enclosing class. This is something that needs to be reflected in the Terracotta configuration file:

```
<roots>
  <root>
    <field-name>
      org.terracotta.book.masterworker.pipe.PipeManager.m_pipes
    </field-name>
  </root>
</roots>
```

Using the Master/Worker System

Let's define a completely useless work class that simply prints out a counter that counts the number of executed work instances:

```
public class MyWork implements Work {
  private int m_i = 0;
```

```
  public MyWork(int i) {
    m_i = i;
  }

  public void run() {
    System.out.println("work nr: " + m_i);
  }

  public boolean isDaemon() {
    return false;
  }

  public void release() {}
}
```

Next, let's take a look the worker. They both need to get a hold of the same PipeManager's factory; passing that factory to the master and worker using dependency injection (DI) might be more elegant, but for simplicity, we simply define it as a public final constant in the Master:

```
PipeManager<String> pipeManager = new PipeManager<String>(Master.PIPE_FACTORY);
Worker worker = new StaticWorker(pipeManager);
worker.run();
```

Finally, let's create a Master that creates the WorkManager, its Router, and an instance of PipeFactory. The master then schedules 100 instances of MyWork to be executed and waits until all of them have been completed:

```
Factory<RoutableWorkItem<String>, String> PIPE_FACTORY =
    new DefaultPipe.Factory<RoutableWorkItem<String>, String>(
        new BlockingQueueBasedQueue.Factory<RoutableWorkItem<String>>(1000));

PipeManager<String> pipeManager = new PipeManager<String>(PIPE_FACTORY);

// predefine the routing ids (e.g. pipes) to be used
String[] routingIDs = new String[] {…};

Router<String> m_router = new LoadBalancingRouter<String>(pipeManager, routingIDs);

WorkManager workManager = new StaticWorkManager(router);

List<WorkItem> workList = new ArrayList<WorkItem>();
for (int i = 0; i < 100; i++) {
  workList.add(workManager.schedule(new MyWork(i)));
}

try {
  workManager.waitForAll(workList, Long.MAX_VALUE);
} catch (Exception e) {
```

```
    // handle the exception
}

pipeManager.shutdown();
System.out.println("All work completed successfully");
```

Running the Master/Worker System

Now, let's run it. But before we spawn the master and the workers, we must first start the Terracotta server. Invoke the `start-tc-server` script in the `bin` directory in the Terracotta distribution.

When you have done that, you can start up the master and the workers (in any order you like). Since this implementation is static in terms of routing IDs, we have to feed the master all the routing IDs that will be used by the workers and start up each worker with its unique routing ID.

Refactoring Work Batching, Worker Failover, and Dynamic Worker Management

In the previous refactoring section, we tried to minimize the contention on the work queue by adding concepts, such as a pipe with incoming and outgoing queues, routing IDs for each worker to subscribe, and some helper classes to help us manage routing and pipes. However, the current implementation still has some problems.

First, the communication between the masters and the workers is too chatty: every pending work item or completed work item is immediately put on the corresponding queue. Since each put (or get) on the queue has to be locked, it can easily lead to high lock contention.

Second, the current worker management implementation is too static. All routing IDs have to be known in advance, and new workers are not allowed to join the cluster after the computation has begun. But perhaps most importantly, we do not have a failover mechanism for workers. This means that if a worker crashes, we have no way of detecting it and rerouting all the pending work that the worker has in its queue. This shortcoming can be worked around by, for example, letting two workers subscribe to each pipe in order to get failover behavior, but this is far from an ultimate solution.

In this section, we will address both of these issues. The first one will be addressed by using the oldest trick in the book, batching, while the solution for the other one is based on Terracotta cluster events.

Work Batching

Earlier in this chapter, we discussed two of the most important things to think about when you are developing with Terracotta: locality of reference and lock contention. Minimizing lock contention means trying to minimize the wait time for the different threads to further utilize the CPU (i.e., improving the throughput). However, another thing closely tied to lock contention is worth considering—the granularity of locking. In multithreaded programming, making the lock granularity (i.e., the scope of the critical section) as small as possible is generally best. But it is important to understand is that this is not always true with Terracotta. As we discussed in the first chapters, Terracotta treats critical sections of code (i.e., synchronized blocks and methods) as a single transaction and collects all changes made within this transaction into one atomic change set that is flushed to the server when the transaction commits (which happens just before the lock is released).

If you stop and think about this for a moment, collecting all the changes is fairly cheap, while flushing them to the server, which requires sending data over the network, is relatively expensive. Implicit network chatter underneath fine-grained locking means that aiming for the most fine-grained locking you can get is not always best. The optimal lock granularity is typically use case specific, but in some cases, you'll see improved throughput by using coarse-grained locks.

Making the locking (and thus the transactions) more coarse-grained in master/worker–based use cases can sometimes improve throughput immensely. The good news is that, in the master/worker container, the problem can be solved in a generic fashion using batching. The actual implementation is out of the scope of this book (see the accompanying code for details) but can be solved fairly straightforwardly. Instead of adding each WorkItem to its specific Pipe's pending work queue immediately after it has been created, collect them in a work set, and define a batching threshold; whenever the threshold is reached, put all the work items in the queue in one single Terracotta transaction. The workers can use the same strategy when adding completed work items to the work queue of completed work items.

Dynamic Worker Management

The master/worker container we have implemented so far has a rather static configuration. It requires knowledge about all pipes that will ever be needed and used for work scheduling, since their routing ids have to be fed to the master at startup time. This setup naturally poses very limiting and sometimes unacceptable constraints in the management and operation of the master/worker cluster, especially in regard to worker failure and failover, which is something we will discuss in the next section.

Terracotta provides a high-level event subscription system where nodes can subscribe to events triggered by other nodes as they either leave or join the cluster. These events are regular JMX events and can therefore be consumed and used by any JMX-compliant library or tool. In order to make things simpler for the developer, Terracotta has provided a utility library that makes it very easy and straightforward to start making use of these events. The library is called jmx-util and is replicated in the SVN repository for this chapter for simplicity. A walkthrough of this library is out of scope for this chapter (see Chapter 4 for more information), but we will show you how to make use of the library to simply and efficiently implement dynamic worker management and worker failover. We will now refactor the code from previous sessions to make use of Terracotta cluster events to enable transparent worker management, meaning being able to add and remove workers on the fly.

The first thing we need to do is to let our master (now renamed org.terracotta.book. masterworker.dynamic.DynamicWorkManager) implement the org.terracotta.util.jmx. ClusterEvents.Listener interface. This interface has a set of callback methods that we can use to bind application logic to certain node life cycle events. Let's take a look at this interface.

```
public static interface Listener {
  public void thisNodeId(Object nodeId);
  public void initialClusterMembers(Object[] nodeId);
```

```
public void nodeConnected(Object nodeId);
public void nodeDisconnected(Object nodeId);
public void thisNodeConnected(Object nodeId);
public void thisNodeDisconnected(Object nodeId);
}
```

First, we add a node ID to the DynamicWorkManager and a callback registering the DynamicWorkManager in the Terracotta cluster events subsystem.

```
private Object m_nodeId;

public DynamicWorkManager(final Router<String> router) {
  m_router = router;
  m_completedWork = router.getAllCompletedWork();
  ClusterEvents.registerListener(this);
}
```

Then, we can start implementing the Listener interface. We start with the thisNodeId(Object nodeId) method; this method, is called by Terracotta when the node is joining the cluster and is passing in the node ID for the specific node (in this case the DynamicWorkManager).

Next, we add the nodeConnected(Object nodeId) and nodeDisconnected(Object nodeId) methods. Here, this example starts getting interesting. These two methods are callbacks from Terracotta, signaling that another node (e.g., Worker) has joined or left the cluster. This means that we can use these callbacks to register and unregister the Worker from the Router.

Let's take a look at the code for these three callback methods:

```
public synchronized void thisNodeId(final Object nodeId) {
  System.out.println("work manager node id: " + nodeId);
  m_nodeId = nodeId;
  notify();
}

public void nodeConnected(Object nodeId) {
  if (isMasterNode(nodeId)) {
    return; // this is the master node
  }
  System.out.println("registering worker node with ID: " + nodeId);
  m_router.register(nodeId.toString());
}
private boolean isMasterNode(Object nodeId) {
  return nodeId.equals((String)m_nodeId);
}

public void nodeDisconnected(Object nodeId) {
  System.out.println("unregistering worker node with ID: " + nodeId );
  m_router.unregister(nodeId.toString());
}
```

```
// these two callbacks are not needed
public void thisNodeConnected(Object arg0) { }
public void thisNodeDisconnected(Object arg0) { }
```

Finally, we need to implement the initialClusterMembers(Object[] nodeIds) method. This method is passed the IDs for all the nodes that are currently connected to the cluster. It is always called by Terracotta on start-up and gives us a way to register all the workers that might have joined the cluster before the master (DynamicWorkManager):

```
public void initialClusterMembers(Object[] nodeIds) {
  // first time around for work manager - clean up potential previous state
  m_router.reset();

  for (Object nodeId : nodeIds) {
    if (isMasterNode(nodeId)) {
      return; // this is the master node - do nothing
    }
    System.out.println("registering worker node with ID: " + nodeId);
    m_router.register(nodeId.toString()); // register worker
  }
}
```

The only part of this code that might not be self-explanatory is the first statement, in which we reset the state for the Router. This is necessary once at master start-up in case the master crashes while pending or completed but uncollected work may still be in the pipes. On recovery, resetting the system and clearing all the pipes before continuing is important. The framework would otherwise drop work on the floor, so to speak.

This takes care of the master, but we also need to make the worker aware of cluster events. Now, we create a new worker called DynamicWorker that is implementing the org.terracotta. util.jmx.ClusterEvents.Listener interface. Like we did for the DynamicWorkManager class, we first need to add a field holding the node ID as well as a callback to register itself in the Terracotta cluster events subsystem. But we only need to implement a single callback method from the ClusterEvents.Listener interface: thisNodeId(Object nodeId). This method creates a Pipe for the specific node and its nodeId (the rest of the methods can have no-op implementations). As you might recall, this method is called when the node (in this case the worker) joins the Terracotta cluster and therefore provides a natural place to put initialization code like this.

```
public synchronized void thisNodeId(final Object nodeId) {
  System.out.println("worker node id: " + nodeId);
  m_routingID = nodeId.toString();
  m_pipe = m_pipeManager.getOrCreatePipeFor(m_routingID);
  notifyAll(); // worker is registered  - notify the worker
}
```

But before we can call it a day, we will have to take care of a couple of other things. For example, we need to modify the different routers slightly in order to take the new dynamicity into account. Now, the worker registration is initiated when the worker is started up but executed asynchronously using Terracotta cluster events. This means that we now need to use wait()/notify() to block the usage of the Router until the worker has been fully initialized.

Here is the new DynamicWorker implementation:

```java
package org.terracotta.book.masterworker.dynamic;

import java.util.concurrent.ExecutorService;
import java.util.concurrent.Executors;

import org.terracotta.util.jmx.ClusterEvents;
import org.terracotta.book.masterworker.pipe.Pipe;
import org.terracotta.book.masterworker.pipe.PipeManager;
import org.terracotta.book.masterworker.routing.RoutableWorkItem;
import org.terracotta.book.masterworker.worker.Worker;
import org.terracotta.book.masterworker.worker.WorkerTask;

import commonj.work.WorkException;

/**
 * Worker that is aware of routing. Each instance of the
 * RoutingAwareWorker class gets a routing ID from the Terracotta server and
 * gets a unique work queue mapped to this routing ID.
 */
public class DynamicWorker implements Worker, ClusterEvents.Listener {

  private Pipe<RoutableWorkItem<String>, String> m_pipe;
  private final ExecutorService m_threadPool = Executors.newCachedThreadPool();
  private PipeManager<String> m_pipeManager;
  private volatile boolean m_isRunning = true;
  private String m_routingID;

  public static final int WORKER_TIMEOUT_IN_SECONDS = 60;

  public DynamicWorker(final PipeManager<String> pipeManager) {
    m_pipeManager = pipeManager;
    ClusterEvents.registerListener(this);
  }

  public void start() throws WorkException {
    while (m_isRunning) {
      waitForRegistration();
      RoutableWorkItem<String> workItem;
      try {
        workItem = m_pipe.getPendingWorkQueue().take();
      } catch (InterruptedException e) {
        Thread.currentThread().interrupt();
        throw new WorkException(e);
      }
```

```
        if (workItem != null) {
          m_threadPool.execute(
              new WorkerTask<RoutableWorkItem<String>>(
                  workItem, m_pipe.getCompletedWorkQueue())));
        }
      }
    }

    public void stop() {
      m_isRunning = false;
      m_threadPool.shutdown();
      m_pipeManager.removePipeFor(m_routingID);
    }

    public synchronized void thisNodeId(final Object nodeId) {
      System.out.println("worker node id: " + nodeId);
      m_routingID = (String) nodeId;
      m_pipe = m_pipeManager.getOrCreatePipeFor(m_routingID);
      notifyAll(); // worker is registered  - notify the worker
    }

    private synchronized void waitForRegistration() {
      try {
        while (m_pipe == null) {
          System.out.println("waiting for registration");
          wait();
        }
      } catch (InterruptedException e) {
        Thread.currentThread().interrupt();
      }
    }

    public void initialClusterMembers(Object[] arg0) {}
    public void nodeConnected(Object arg0) {}
    public void nodeDisconnected(Object arg0) {}
    public void thisNodeConnected(Object arg0) {}
    public void thisNodeDisconnected(Object arg0) {}
}
```

Worker Failover

In a world clustered without Terracotta where you would use sockets or JMS to send messages among cluster nodes, you will find that detecting death of workers is quite difficult. With Terracotta, however, cluster membership events are all we need. The networking library in-side Terracotta sends periodic heartbeat messages to and from JVMs in the grid. There are several timeouts that can be set at a networking level to detect deadlocked, hung, or otherwise crashed workers (and masters). The only case you should address in code, then, is long-running work for which the JVM and the node and network remain healthy yet the work still takes too long to complete. If you want to eject a worker and send its work to another node, simply augment the master/worker framework using JDK 1.5 `util.concurrent` locking and `wait()`/`notify()` API options that include a timeout. Terracotta will honor those timeouts on attempts to wait for or lock objects (using `wait()` or `synchronized()`.

In all of the strategies, we need to take proper action when worker failure has been detected. In the context of master/worker, among other things, this need means we must reroute all pending, uncompleted work to another pipe to be consumed by its specific worker. Using cluster membership events is by far the simplest, most straightforward, and most stable way of integrating our code for handling failures.

What we have to do is to add a bit of logic to the `nodeDisconnected(Object nodeId)` method from the previous section. As you know, this method will be invoked whenever a node leaves the cluster, either unexpectedly due to a failure or by a clean shutdown.

So what kind of failover logic do we need to write? Well, if we base the implementation on the event notifications that we implemented previously for the dynamic worker management, the logic turns out to be quite simple. Since we are getting a callback event each time a `Worker` disconnects, we will know exactly when a `Worker` has died and can take proper action to failover all pending work to some other `Worker`.

If we map these ideas to code then we end up with a `nodeDisconnected(Object nodeId)` method looking like this:

```
public void nodeDisconnected(Object nodeId) {
  System.out.println("unregistering worker node with ID: " + nodeId);

  Pipe<RoutableWorkItem<String>, String> pipe =
    m_router.getPipeFor(nodeId.toString());

  // add all completed items to the completed work set
  Queue<RoutableWorkItem<String>> compWorkQueue = pipe.getCompletedWorkQueue();

  for (Iterator<RoutableWorkItem<String>> it = compWorkQueue.iterator();
       it.hasNext();) {
    m_completedWork.add(it.next());
  }

  // copy all pending work (needed since we will have to remove the pipe
  // before the rerouting)
  List<RoutableWorkItem<String>> pending =
    new ArrayList<RoutableWorkItem<String>>();

  Queue<RoutableWorkItem<String>> pendWorkQueue = pipe.getPendingWorkQueue();
```

```
for (Iterator<RoutableWorkItem<String>> it = pendWorkQueue.iterator();
    it.hasNext();) {
  pending.add(it.next());
}

// unregister the worker which also clears and removes the pipe
// remove pipe for disconnected worker before fail-over
m_router.unregister(nodeId.toString());

// reroute the pending work
for (RoutableWorkItem<String> workItem : pending) {
  m_router.route(workItem);
}
}
```

How to Use and Run the Fault-Tolerant Master/Worker System

There is very little difference in how we run this master/worker container and the one from the previous section. The only difference is that we have renamed some classes and do not need to pass in an array with all the routing IDs to the master, since that is taken care of by the Terracotta cluster events. In the next section, we will show you how you can use this implementation to build a real-world application.

Building a Distributed Web Spider

In the previous section, we discussed how we can implement a framework based on Terracotta, the Master/Worker pattern, and the CommonJ Work Manager specification, which is suitable for managing very large workloads in a scalable and efficient manner. What we didn't cover in much detail is how to use our framework (and similar techniques) to solve real-world problems. Therefore, we will now show you how you can make use of Terracotta and our master/worker container by implementing distributed Web search (á la Google). We will do that by developing a distributed web spider that can crawl the Internet and index the pages it finds using the Lucene search framework. Here is the basic algorithm defining the workflow:

1. Fetch the page from a starting URL.

2. Parse the page, and collect all outgoing URLs.

3. Index the page.

4. For each outgoing URL, go to step 1.

This is a classic recursive algorithm working on a tree structure. No work task shares state with any other task, which means that they are all embarrassingly parallel (i.e., the data is by nature perfectly partitioned). This algorithm is very well suited for a divide-and-conquer strategy such as the Master/Worker pattern. The three main artifacts that we have to implement are:

- SpiderMaster: Implements the core algorithm and manages the WorkManager

- SpiderWork: Implements the page parsing, indexing, and link aggregation

- Worker: Spawns the threads that are doing the actual computation (We'll reuse the one from the previous section.)

Let's start with the SpiderWork class. It has four variables: the URL for the page to fetch and parse, the maximum depth that the spider should crawl, a flag that decides if the spider should follow external links outside its initial domain, and finally a list with all the outgoing links (represented as a list of PageLink instances, which simply wraps the current depth in the search tree and the URL). Here's the class:

```java
package org.terracotta.book.masterworker.spider;

import java.io.IOException;
import java.net.URL;
import java.util.ArrayList;
import java.util.List;

import commonj.work.Work;

import au.id.jericho.lib.html.Source;
import au.id.jericho.lib.html.StartTag;

/**
 * The implementation of the work to do on each worker node.
 * <p>
 * Each <code>SpiderPageWork</code> processes an input page and returns a list
 * of {@link PageLink} objects that contain the depth of the page (relative to
 * the visited graph, i.e. one more than the current page) and a url, one
 * <code>PageLink</code> per page reference.
 */
public class SpiderWork implements Work {

  private final String m_url;
  private final int m_depth;
  private final boolean m_followExternalLinks;
  private final List<PageLink> m_links  = new ArrayList<PageLink>();

  public SpiderWork(String url, int depth, boolean followExternalLinks) {
    m_url = url;
    m_depth = depth;
    m_followExternalLinks = followExternalLinks;
  }
```

```java
public List<PageLink> getLinks() {
  return m_links;
}

public void run() {
  try {
    URL resource = new URL(m_url);
    Source source = retrievePage(resource);

    List<StartTag> tags = source.findAllStartTags();
    System.out.println(m_url + " has " + tags.size() + " tags to process.");

    for (StartTag tag : tags) {
      if (tag.getName().equals("a")) {
        addLink(m_links, resource, tag.getAttributeValue("href"));
        continue;
      }
      if (tag.getName().equals("frame")) {
        addLink(m_links, resource, tag.getAttributeValue("src"));
        continue;
      }
    }
  } catch (IOException e) {
    throw new PageNotFoundException(
        "Skipping page; couldn't parse URL: " + m_url);
  }
  System.out.println("Returning " + m_links.size() + " links.");
}

private static Source retrievePage(URL resource) throws IOException {
  Source source = null; // cache.getPage(resource.toString());
  if (source != null) {
    System.out.println("Processing " + resource);
  } else {
    System.out.println("Retrieving " + resource);
    // get the url into the parse structure
    source = new Source(resource);
    source.fullSequentialParse();

    source = SpiderMaster.cachePage(resource.toString(), source);
  }
  return source;
}

private synchronized void addLink(
    List<PageLink> links, URL url, String relativeLink) {
```

```java
    // don't follow anchor links
    if (relativeLink == null ||
        relativeLink.length() == 0 ||
        relativeLink.contains("#")) {
      return;
    }
    // relative links will not have a ':' in them, otherwise, they are external
    if (relativeLink.indexOf(":") < 0) {
      try {
        relativeLink = new URL(url, relativeLink).toString();
      } catch (Exception e) {
        // one url failure should not stop the parsing process
        e.printStackTrace();
        return;
      }
    } else {
      // leave if we don't support external links
      if (!m_followExternalLinks) {
        return;
      }
    }
    links.add(new PageLink(m_depth + 1, relativeLink));
  }
  …
}
```

The retrievePage() method is not really interesting for our current discussion; in our implementation, we are using a third-party JAR (au.id.jericho.lib.html) to grab a page, and its implementation is, however simple, out of scope for the current discussion. More interesting is the addLink() method which parses HTML tags, looks for <a> and <frame> tags to extract their outgoing URLs (found in the href and src attributes), and for each one of these, it filters out all local anchor links before it creates a PageLink for the URL at the current search depth.

The second thing that we need to implement is the SpiderMaster class, which is responsible for creating a PipeFactory, PipeManager, Router, WorkManager, and WorkListener and holding a cache of the URLs to all the pages that have been visited. The arguments needed to initialize the master are a starting URL, maximum search depth, and a flag deciding if we should follow outgoing links (links that are external and leads outside our initial domain). Here's the SpiderMaster class:

```java
package org.terracotta.book.masterworker.spider;

import java.util.Collection;
import java.util.HashSet;
import java.util.List;
import java.util.Set;

import org.terracotta.book.masterworker.pipe.DefaultPipe;
import org.terracotta.book.masterworker.pipe.PipeManager;
import org.terracotta.book.masterworker.pipe.DefaultPipe.Factory;
```

```java
import org.terracotta.book.masterworker.queue.BlockingQueueBasedQueue;
import org.terracotta.book.masterworker.routing.RoutableWorkItem;
import org.terracotta.book.masterworker.routing.Router;
import org.terracotta.book.masterworker.statik.LoadBalancingRouter;
import org.terracotta.book.masterworker.statik.SingleQueueRouter;
import org.terracotta.book.masterworker.statik.StaticWorkManager;

import au.id.jericho.lib.html.Source;

import commonj.work.Work;
import commonj.work.WorkEvent;
import commonj.work.WorkException;
import commonj.work.WorkItem;
import commonj.work.WorkListener;
import commonj.work.WorkManager;

public class SpiderMaster implements Runnable {

  public final static int QUEUE_SIZE = 100;
  public final static int BATCH_SIZE = 100;

  // public static so I can reuse the same factory in the RetryWorkListener
  public static final Factory<RoutableWorkItem<String>, String> PIPE_FACTORY =
    new DefaultPipe.Factory<RoutableWorkItem<String>, String>(
      new BlockingQueueBasedQueue.Factory<RoutableWorkItem<String>>(QUEUE_SIZE));

  private final static PageCache s_pageCache = new SimplePageCache();

  // the work queue manager
  private final PipeManager<String> m_pipeManager;

  // the router
  private final Router<String> m_router;

  // the work manager
  private final StaticWorkManager<String> m_workManager;

  // the work listener
  private final WorkListener m_workListener;

  private final Set<String> m_visitedPages = new HashSet<String>();
  private final String m_startURL;
  private final int m_maxDepth;
  private final boolean m_followExternalLinks;
  private int m_nrOfCompletedWork = 0;

  public SpiderMaster(String startURL,
```

```
                                    int maxDepth,
                                    boolean followExternalLinks,
                                    String[] routingIDs,
                                    String routingIdForFailOverNode) {

    m_startURL = startURL;
    m_maxDepth = maxDepth;
    m_followExternalLinks = followExternalLinks;

    m_pipeManager = new PipeManager<String>(
        PIPE_FACTORY, PipeManager.Initiator.MASTER);

    m_router = new LoadBalancingRouter<String>(m_pipeManager, routingIDs);
    m_workListener = RetryWorkListener(routingIdForFailOverNode);
    m_workManager = new StaticWorkManager<String>(m_router);
  }

  public static Source cachePage(String link, Source page) {
    return s_pageCache.setPage(link, page);
  }

  public void run() {
    WorkItem firstWorkItem;
    try {
      // schedule first work
      // IN: start URL
      // OUT: first pending work item
      firstWorkItem = scheduleWork(m_startURL);
    } catch (WorkException e) {
      System.err.println("WorkException: " + e.getMessage());
      return;
    }

    // keep track of all pending work
    final Set<WorkItem> pendingWork = new HashSet<WorkItem>();
    pendingWork.add(firstWorkItem);

    // loop while there still is pending work to wait for
    while (!pendingWork.isEmpty()) {

      // wait for any work that is completed
      Collection completedWork;
      try {
        completedWork = m_workManager.waitForAny(
            pendingWork, WorkManager.INDEFINITE);
      } catch (InterruptedException e) {
        throw new RuntimeException(e); // bail out
```

```java
    }

    // loop over all completed work
    for (Object o : completedWork) {
      WorkItem workItem = (WorkItem) o;

      // check work status (completed or rejected)
      switch (workItem.getStatus()) {
      case WorkEvent.WORK_COMPLETED:
        List<PageLink> linksToProcess = null;
        // if completed - grab the result
        SpiderWork work = ((SpiderWork) workItem.getResult());

        // grab the new links
        linksToProcess = work.getLinks();
        m_nrOfCompletedWork++;

        // remove work from the pending list
        pendingWork.remove(workItem);

        // process all the new links
        processLinks(linksToProcess, pendingWork);
        break;

      case WorkEvent.WORK_REJECTED:
        // work rejected - just remove the work
        pendingWork.remove(workItem);
        break;

      default:
        // status is either WORK_ACCEPTED or WORK_STARTED - should never
        // happen
        throw new IllegalStateException(
            "WorkItem is in unexpected state: " + workItem);
      }
    }
  }
  System.out.println("Completed successfully - processed " +
      m_nrOfCompletedWork  + " pages.");
}

private void processLinks(
    List<PageLink> linksToProcess, Set<WorkItem> pendingWork) {
  System.out.println("Processing " + linksToProcess.size() + " link results.");
  for (PageLink link : linksToProcess) {

    // loop over all new links
```

```java
      if (followLink(link)) {
        try {
          // schedule work for each link that is found
          WorkItem newWorkItem = scheduleWork(link.getUrl(), link.getDepth());

          // add the new work item to pending work list
          pendingWork.add(newWorkItem);
        } catch (WorkException e) {
          System.err.println("WorkException: " + e.getMessage());
          continue;
        }
      }
    }
  }
}

private boolean followLink(PageLink link) {
  if (m_visitedPages.contains(link.getUrl())) {
    return false;
  } else if (link.getDepth() >= m_maxDepth) {
    return false;
  } else if (link.getUrl().endsWith(".pdf") || link.getUrl().endsWith(".gz") ||
             link.getUrl().endsWith(".tgz") || link.getUrl().endsWith(".zip") ||
             link.getUrl().endsWith(".doc") || link.getUrl().endsWith(".ppt")) {
    // don't follow binary content links
    return false;
  } else if (!link.getUrl().startsWith("http")  &&
               !link.getUrl().startsWith("file")) {
    // we're only going to support http and file for now
    return false;
  } else {
    return true;
  }
}

private WorkItem scheduleWork(String url, int depth)
    throws WorkException {
  System.out.println("Submitting URL: " + url);
  m_visitedPages.add(url);

  // create new work for the link
  Work work = new SpiderWork(url, depth, m_followExternalLinks);

  // schedule the work in the work manager
  return m_workManager.schedule(work, m_workListener);
}

private WorkItem scheduleWork(String url) throws WorkException {
```

```
    return scheduleWork(url, 1);
  }
}
```

The most interesting part of the master is the run() method, which implements the algorithm that we recently discussed. For those who have forgotten it, here is a refresher.

1. Fetch the page from a starting URL.

2. Parse the page, and collect all outgoing URLs.

3. Index the page.

4. For each outgoing URL, go to step 1.

As you can see in our web crawler examples, in this recursive algorithm, which we implement as a regular loop, we start by trying to fetch the page for our initial URL by passing it into the scheduleWork() method. In return, we get our first pending WorkItem, which serves as a handle to the ongoing work. We keep track of this and all future WorkItem objects by adding them to a Set of all pending work. Now that we have at least one WorkItem in our Set, we can start a loop that will continuously iterate over all items in this Set (until the set is empty). The first thing we do in this loop is to check if there are any completed WorkItem objects by consulting the waitForAny() method in our WorkManager. This method will return a Collection with least one completed WorkItem; we can iterate over the collection, check the status for each completed WorkItem, and filter out all successfully completed ones. Filtering is necessary, since the WorkItem can be "completed" due to failure and will then have its status flags set to WORK_REJECTED instead of the successful WORK_COMPLETED. Now, we will pass each successfully completed WorkItem into the processLinks() method, which will, for each of its outgoing links, create a new SpiderWork object that it passes into the scheduleWork() method. This SpiderWork item will give us a handle to a new pending WorkItem, and we can continue with another round in the loop.

Finally, we have to implement two wrapper classes who can start up the master and the worker, StartWorker and StartMaster:

```
public class StartMaster {
  public static void main(String[] args) throws Exception {
    ... // parse command line options

    new SpiderMaster(startURL, maxDepth, followExternalLinks).run();
  }
}

public class StartWorker {
  public static void main(String[] args) throws Exception {
    PipeManager<String> pipeManager = new PipeManager<String>(
        SpiderMaster.PIPE_FACTORY,  PipeManager.Initiator.WORKER);
    new DynamicWorker (pipeManager).run();
  }
}
```

That's it. Now, let's try to run it as a distributed spider that can scale out by distributing out the page processing and data aggregation onto multiple nodes. We can reuse the tc-config.xml from the previous sections, but we have to add a couple of include statements to add a couple of include statements to tell Terracotta to include our spider classes for instrumentation as well as a third-party JAR (for Jericho) that we have used to parse the pages. When we ran the spider, we also realized that we have to add the commonj.work.WorkException for instrumentation to allow the spider's state to be managed by Terracotta (in case of a Work failure); for example, its state can be sent over the wire, from the worker to the master.

```
<instrumented-classes>
  <include>
    <class-expression>
      org.terracotta.book.masterworker..*
    </class-expression>
    <honor-transient>true</honor-transient>
  </include>
  <include>
    <class-expression>au.id.jericho..*</class-expression>
  </include>
  <include>
    <class-expression>commonj.work.WorkException</class-expression>
  </include>
</instrumented-classes>
```

When we run the master and the worker, we have to feed this XML configuration to Terracotta with a call to dso-java. You would normally start up many workers and have each one of them up and running for a long period of time serving multiple master initiated sessions. For example purposes, here is how to start a single worker and a single master instance:

```
dso-java -Dtc.config=tc-config.xml  -cp ... \
  org.terracotta.book.masterworker.spider.StartWorker

dso-java -Dtc.config=tc-config.xml  -cp ... \
  org.terracotta.book.masterworker.spider.StartMaster
```

When Not to Use the Master/Worker Pattern

In working with large-scale use cases in financial services and telecommunications industries, we have developed best practices around where Terracotta is most effective and, additionally, where the Terracotta Master/Worker approach should not be used. The two biggest cautions for developers are around rogue clients and WAN load balancing. Because Terracotta is an extension of your application memory, the Master/Worker pattern is focused on somewhat uniform large grids of servers in reasonably close proximity to each other.

Rogue clients were first a demonstrable problem when a Terracotta developer built a distributed cache where some nodes in the cluster were servers in a data center while others were end users' laptops. When the laptops were shut down for the day, the cluster would stop running. We commonly refer to these laptops as rogue clients. A similar problem arises in slow consumption off the queue. If some servers in your grid are eight core and have16 gigabytes of RAM while others are two core and have 2 gigabytes of RAM, the two classes of machine will work at different speeds. The slower consumer will throttle Terracotta's entire grid to its speed unless perfectly partitioned in its work.

The Master/Worker pattern seems like a perfect way to sandbox or otherwise fence off these rogue clients and slow consumers, and it does work in many cases. But be cautioned that as soon as rogue and slow consuming clients, acting as workers, begin to share data with any node other than a master, these slower nodes will slow down their peers in the grid.

As for WAN, the Master/Worker pattern is simply insufficient. In fact, WAN-based replication should be done with messaging services. Interestingly, if you take the Master/Worker pattern and customize it as we have shown, you can create what we call a "worker on the edge." Imagine building a cluster with POJO/Terracotta-based workers who communicate using a linked blocking queue and simultaneously act as a bridge on the WAN. These bridge workers would take messages off of the local grid and relay them to another grid across the WAN. Thus the nomenclature: these special bridging-workers are on the edge of your local datacenter's grid.

Summary

In this chapter, you learned how to extend your skills from Chapters 5 through 10 to use Terracotta for scaling out POJO-based applications and a host of popular frameworks. Now, you should also be able to use Terracotta for multithreaded, multi-JVM, scaled out custom processing.

Data grids and compute grids built on Terracotta are highly flexible, because every aspect of the framework is open and in your control. You decide what the unit of work is. You decide the batching levels. You decide on the routing capabilities, and you edit the interfaces as you see fit.

You learned how to scale your grid using only one Terracotta server by simply tuning the locality and granularity of your grid operations. While Terracotta requires more custom code when used in grid use cases than when with other enterprise use cases, the resulting applications and frameworks remain flexible and easy to understand and maintain.

In Chapter 12, you will learn the one remaining technique you will need for tuning and scaling applications: visualization techniques and tools are important to understanding what a cluster is doing and why it is going fast or slow. Visualization is especially valuable for grids where the application is never contained on any one node but is, in fact, a loosely coupled grid of nodes working together as one big server. Visualization is the only way to understand what a grid is doing. Let's take a look at visualization and general tuning techniques now.

■■■

CHAPTER 12

Visualizing Applications

Tuning applications that run in a cluster is hard. What makes tuning difficult is that the application is a logical entity running across processes and machines, while the available tools work almost exclusively at the process or machine level.

For example, you know from Chapter 5 that Terracotta helps distribute application cache data. We also know an application that accesses the cache in a random way will not scale, because the objects have to move around the cluster through the Terracotta server. But none of the tools that exist for performance tuning (including CPU and memory monitoring tools, JVM heap monitoring tools, and Java application profilers) would show that a distributed cache is slow, because random JVMs in a cluster keep updating the cache contents in a manner requiring notification to all other JVMs in the cluster.

This lack of tools for tuning and optimizing clustered applications led to the creation of clusterwide visualization tools at Terracotta. The idea is to stack all the relevant metrics and measurements a developer should be observing for every JVM in a single dashboard view along with the activities of the Terracotta server. Through visualization, we can study an application quite literally as it runs, without building custom tools to do so.

In this chapter, we will work with a derivative of the inventory application from Chapter 8. This demonstration will be altered so that it can generate lots of changes to objects and so that those changes can be either random or highly focused on specific objects. You will learn how to use Terracotta's tools to help visualize and point out what is causing slowness in various scenarios. By the end of the chapter, you should be comfortable with the concept of cluster visualization and, further, be able to apply the tools to solving real problems.

Observing an Application

In the practice of medicine, the concept underlying observing the electrical patterns transmitted by the body is that doctors can attach to key points on the body and visualize key information that helps determine what the heart and brain are doing. With applications, we can do the same. Specifically, it is possible to connect to key data points in the application stack and, by taking repeated measurements over time, learn what the application is doing. Making this data-driven approach successful depends on providing a centralized view of all this information as well as on showing the appropriate information.

The information that must be observed can be thought of as a stack of data streams. This stack is depicted in Figure 12-1 and is composed of the operating system information at the bottom to information about application objects at the top.

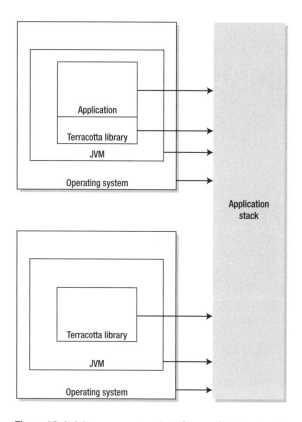

Figure 12-1. *Measurement points for application tuning*

In a cluster, one node could be slowing down the others. In that cluster, observing an individual node will show us only that it is slow, and not why. Terracotta concluded that the stack of information is less helpful when viewed on a JVM-by-JVM basis. The visualization tool and administration console are designed to help us correlate performance across processes. The visualization tool shows us all the JVMs in the cluster at once, allowing us to drill into any metric across JVMs or any JVM across metrics as the need arises.

Visualization Tools and Architecture

Terracotta provides the tools and internal architecture for gathering and managing perform-ance data emanating from application JVMs as well as from the Terracotta server. The system is designed to gather the clusterwide data depicted in Figure 12-1 in a single database. This strategy is useful when performance tuning applications before deploying into a production environment. The system provides not just visualization tools but also tools for taking snap-shots of the cluster's performance for offline analysis of production performance issues. Figure 12-2 depicts the architecture of the system.

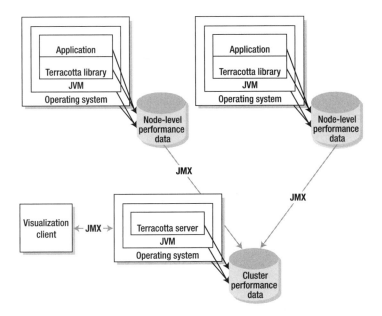

Figure 12-2. *Terracotta cluster visualization database architecture*

When using the system, you have the choice to view real-time data in the visualization client or to ask the system to only gather data into the cluster database inside the Terracotta server. In either mode, the system records all the data in its central database and can export the records in a comma-delimited format for transfer to other developers or even to Terracotta engineers during offline analysis.

The data that the Terracotta server gathers is also streamed via JMX to any tool of your choice. Just as Terracotta's server and visualization client can manage and display performance data, so too can your existing monitoring and management tools.

■**Tip** In fact, in order to gather statistics at the operating system level, Terracotta uses a plug-in from Hyperic (http://www.hyperic.com/). Hyperic offers an excellent example of a monitoring framework through which Terracotta can be managed.

Now that you understand the system architecture, let's build an application that exhibits performance problems and discover its problems together, using the visualization tools in the kit.

The Sample Inventory Application

The application we will use to learn about visualization is included in the Terracotta kit. The inventory application is located in the following directory on Unix:

```
$TC_HOME/samples/pojo/inventory
```

or this one on Windows

```
<drive>:\$TC_HOME\samples\pojo\inventory
```

The application was initially designed to illustrate anemic domain modeling in a clustered environment. Anemic domain models are those where the tools and frameworks restrict freedom of expression of the Java language. The restriction usually is embedded in the marshalling of POJOs to and from clustering, messaging, or database infrastructure. Terracotta users do not suffer the pitfalls of anemic domain modeling, because the service is transparent.

The inventory application illustrates freedom in modeling by representing the data inside a store in a manner that is well suited to supporting two different use cases. The first use of the inventory application's data is in selling products to consumers. An inventory system must track the quantity on hand for every item the store sells. The second usage of the data is in merchandizing products that are related in one way or another. The domain model is captured in Figure 12-3.

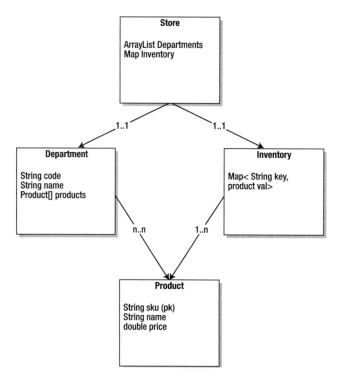

Figure 12-3. *Inventory application schema*

The domain model enables the application to efficiently update items by ID, named Stock Keeping Unit (SKU) numbers in retail terminology. When the retailer buys more basketballs, for example, the warehouse must receive the goods against the SKU. In this domain model, the warehouse worker needs to enter the SKU of the basketballs, and then the system can look up the SKU as a key in the inventory Map. The worker can then ask the system to update the quantity available for sale to reflect the new stock received into the warehouse. Storing the inventory in a map makes sense, because there are many uses where the product will be accessed by its SKU.

Simultaneously, the e-commerce web site that fronts this example needs to convince web users to buy products. This task, referred to as merchandizing, might have the business deciding to sell basketballs as toys and sporting goods simultaneously. Thus, the basketballs need to be represented in a navigational tree or hierarchy of some sort. Ideally, the basketball items could be stored in the map and simultaneously in the tree so that, when the price changes, the application uses the SKU to update the price on the web site automatically.

The inventory application is focused on illustrating the freedom of domain modeling inherent to the Terracotta approach to scale out. As a result, the application can do only two things. We can change the price of products in the map, and we can also ask the system to display the merchandizing hierarchy under which this fictitious store is selling its products. The application runs at the command line, which is ideal for the purpose of tuning and visualization. We can make a few changes to the application and end up with a system for changing different objects across JVMs or changing the same objects. We can make these decisions at run time and, thus, will have the flexibility to test the various scenarios under which Terracotta performs well or not so well.

Modifying to Generate Load

What makes this application interesting is that we can easily extend it to generate interesting workload for the Terracotta server. The best way to do this is provide a way to have many JVMs mutating the same object at the same time, versus different objects at the same time. Our hope is to end up with a system where changing different objects delivers linear scale, while changing the same object causes bottlenecks. If the tools work, we will be able to visualize good or poor parallelism, depending how we run the system.

Before we change the application, let's first review the structure of the application on disk. As with all Terracotta samples, the `samples/pojo/inventory` directory comes with the tools to run the sample as well as recompile it when we want to make changes.

You can use `ant` and the file named `build.xml` in this directory to compile the application once we make changes. The script named `run.sh` (or `run.bat` on Windows) is used to start and stop the application. The file named `tc-config.xml` contains the root and lock definitions needed to run the inventory application inside Terracotta. The directory named `classes` contains the compiled application, and the directory named `src` contains the Java files we will now modify.

The package name is `demo.inventory`, so there are two directories nested inside `src`. Table 12-1 explains each of the Java files inside `demo.inventory`.

Table 12-1. *The Source Files in the demo.inventory Directory*

File	Purpose
`Product.java`	Contains the definition of a product object
`Department.java`	Contains the tree where products get stored for web display
`Store.java`	Wrapper class to products, inventory, and departments that contains our map and tree
`Main.java`	The command line interface driver that instantiates an instance of `Store` and preloads a database into the map and tree

The changes we will make are documented in Table 12-2.

Table 12-2. *Changes to the Source Files*

Step	Description	Goal
Copy	Copy the entire demonstration to a new location.	Leave the original sample in place for future reference.
Pounder	The core load-generating logic.	Insert methods that change product prices in a loop. Products are clustered in Terracotta.
Lock tuning	Ensure that the demonstration locks properly.	Make the lock more coarse gained for visualization.
Separate roots	Add a second root to the `Store` object.	Allow us to test with two JVMs pounding one root or separate roots in order to measure scalability.
Update the CLI	Change the command line interface so that we can call the pounder we insert.	Provide a way to make the whole test work.
Update Terracotta configuration	Update `tc-config.xml` to support our changes.	Make sure the locks and objects are properly clustered.

Copying the Sample

Change directories to the inventory sample in the Terracotta distribution. Note that we will refer to the directory where you unpacked Terracotta as $TC_HOME. If, for example, you decompress Terracotta into /Users/ari/terracotta-2.6 (something like c:\Documents and Settings\ari\terracotta-2.6 under Windows), you want to issue the following command.

```
> cd /Users/ari/terracotta-2.6/samples/pojo (c:\Documents and Settings\ari\
terracotta-2.6)
```

Next, copy the inventory sample. On Unix, the command would look something like this:

```
> cp -R inventory inventory.pounder (xcopy inventory inventory.pounder)
```

■**Note** You can avoid making all the manual changes to the inventory application by downloading the `inventory.pounder` application from `http://www.apress.com`.

Pounder Methods

A pounder is a test that continually calls some routine, effectively pounding or exercising an aspect of a system to create load or attempt to fatigue or break the system at a key stress point. We will now introduce a pounder that takes one SKU from inventory and changes its price to random values a certain number of times. First, change directories as follows:

```
> cd inventory.pounder/src/demo/inventory
% cd inventory.pounder\src\demo\inventory (in Windows)
```

Now, edit Main.java with your favorite editor, and add the following method:

```java
private void poundRandomProducts() {
  ArrayList productArray = new ArrayList( 4 );

  productArray.add( store.getInventory().get( "1GFR" ) );
  productArray.add( store.getInventory().get( "TRPD" ) );
  productArray.add( store.getInventory().get( "WRPC" ) );
  productArray.add( store.getInventory().get( "USBM" ) );

  for( int i = 0; i < max; i++ ) {
    synchronized( productArray.get( i % 4 )) {
      ( ( Product ) productArray.get( i % 4 ) ).setPrice(i);
    }
  }
}
```

The first part of this new method initializes an array of Product objects to four discrete values. The second section takes the productArray and loops through, changing one of the four products to some monotonically increasing price, i. We will use this method to run a clustered pounding routine that updates any of the objects in the array so that all JVMs in the cluster are making changes that the others will hear about. The call to synchronized(productArray.get(i%4)) may or may not cause a problem that we will visualize later.

Let's now add another pounder that does something different:

```java
private void poundOneProduct( ) {
  Product p = null;
  // if we run separate_roots, this returns one of 2 Inventory copies
  Map inventory = store.getInventory();
  assert( inventory != null );
  printInventory();

  boolean failedToLoad = true;
  do {
    out.println("\nEnter SKU of product to update:");
    out.print("> ");
    out.flush();
    String s = getInput().toUpperCase();
    p = (Product) inventory.get(s);
    if (p != null) failedToLoad = false;
    else out.print("[ERR] No such product with SKU '" + s + "'\n");
  } while( failedToLoad == true );

  double newPrice;
  assert( p != null );
  newPrice = p.getPrice( );
```

```
  for( int i = 0; i < max; i++) {
    synchronized( p ){
      p.setPrice( newPrice );
    }
    newPrice = 1234.34;
  }
}
```

Whereas the poundRandomProducts() method changes any and all products in the array, poundOneProduct() can be made to change just one. This new pounder is naïve in nature, because it allows the user to specify one product to incessantly change. If the user were to set up two instances of the modified inventory application to pound on one product, those two JVMs would have to yield to each other all the time, just like HelloClusteredWorld from Chapter 3. But, if each inventory instance pounds on a different product, perhaps two JVMs needn't yield to each other at all and can run in parallel. Hopefully, visualization will help us validate the performance differences among all three options: pounding the same product in each of two JVMs, pounding separate products in each JVM, and pounding random products in all JVMs.

Before we finish with Main.java, we have to wire up the ability to accept a command line argument regarding the use of separate roots. We will explain separate roots soon. For now, you should change the main() method to check for a command line argument named separate_roots. If that argument is present, pass a Boolean to the Store constructor; we will edit the Store constructor shortly. First, let's add a couple of fields to the Main class:

```
public class Main {
    /**
     *  Description of the Field
     */
    public Store store;
    private PrintWriter out = new PrintWriter(System.out, true);
    Map serverCount = new HashMap();
    private static Boolean separateRoots = false;
    private static int max = 50000;
```

Making the Boolean a member field of the class allows the main() method to configure the test and for the pounder methods to react when invoked later. The integer max field will be used to enable the pounder methods to execute dynamic loop iterations. You will learn later in this chapter why separate roots are faster or slower than shared roots across JVMs (one of the two types of roots is so much faster than the other that we need to increase the number of iterations to compensate for testing in that particular mode; otherwise, the test duration will be too short for you to run the visualization tools). Next, let's change the main() method to set these two new fields:

```
public static void main(String[] args) {
        if( ( args.length > 0 ) && args[ 0 ].equals( "separate_roots" ) ) {
          System.out.println( "[INFO] Running With 2 roots." );
          separateRoots = true;
          max = 200000;
```

```
    }

    try {
        new Main().run( );
    }
    catch (Exception e) {
        e.printStackTrace();
        System.out.flush();
    }
}
```

Also, we should change the run method to pass the Boolean for separate roots to the Store constructor:

```
private void run( ) {
    store = new Store( separateRoots );
    menu_main();
}
```

Tuning the Locks

The two pounder methods we just added include synchronization. Inside the synchronized blocks of code, both methods call Product.setPrice(), which is also synchronized. Given the way synchronization works with regard to the Java Memory Model (recall JSR 133 discussed in Chapter 1), Terracotta must push data whenever a lock is released. Figure 12-3 demonstrates a scenario when one thread can hold a lock on object B, then acquire a lock on object A and mutate A, while, at some later point in time, a second thread can acquire a lock on A before B has been unlocked.

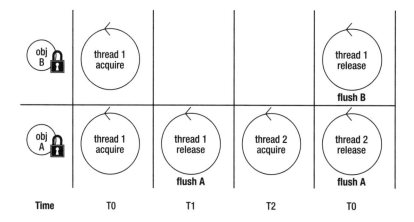

Figure 12-4. *Lock batching*

Thread two must see the changes to A made by thread one. If we look at the Product class in the file named Product.java, we will find that the setPrice(double p) method synchronizes internally.

```
public void setPrice(double p) {
    synchronized (this) {
        price = p;
    }
}
```

By leaving this synchronization in place, we will end up with an application that is bottle-necked somewhere we don't really want, because the pounder methods change the price of Product objects as rapidly as possible. Given the requirement to flush the changes at each lock release, every time setPrice() is called, network I/O will occur. If both the pounder method and setPrice() lock the object, we will flush changes twice each time through the loop. So we have to either comment out the synchronization in the setPrice() method or change tc-config.xml to avoid automatically locking this method. Without synchronization on setPrice(), the synchronization in the two pounder methods will take effect.

■**Note** With synchronization on setPrice(), the synchronization in the two pounder methods will have no data to flush, since setPrice() will cause the flush on its own. You should try to observe this locking behavior yourself using the visualization tools we are about to launch. Leave the synchronization in place in the setPrice() method first, then remove it, and compare the performance.

We will not bother to show you how to comment out the synchronization, but if you are interested in changing the configuration file, the following example illustrates what to change in the tc-config.xml file located in the inventory demonstration's root directory. Change the <locks> stanza:

```
<locks>
  <autolock>
    <method-expression>* *..*.*(..)</method-expression>
  </autolock>
</locks>
```

to the following

```
<locks>
  <autolock>
    <method-expression>* Demo.inventory.Department.*(..)</method-expression>
  </autolock>
  <autolock>
    <method-expression>* Demo.inventory.Store.*(..)</method-expression>
  </autolock>
  <autolock>
    <method-expression>* Demo.inventory.Main.*(..)</method-expression>
  </autolock>
</locks>
```

Now the application is almost ready to run. The last change to the domain model is to introduce separate roots

Using Separate Roots

Separate roots are going to prove helpful when we start looking for bottlenecks. "Separate roots" means that one instance of the inventory application will be able to connect to its own copy of the shared object data, and no other JVM will see or share objects with this JVM. With separate roots, you baseline the application's performance with Terracotta integrated as well as with more than one instance of the application running at once, which will help isolate any bottlenecks in our own application logic, versus bottlenecks that may exist in the Terracotta server.

Do not assume that Terracotta is slow or that Terracotta causes high overhead to your application based solely on initial observations after getting Terracotta up and running. Instead, use a methodical approach such the one as we are about to undertake together. The approach as outlined thus far includes pounding on random products in an array as well as pounding on a single product. In fact, the tests will be run several times, both to get valid sample data and to run various scenarios. poundOneProduct will be run where two JVMs each pound on the same product as well as on different products. poundRandomProducts will be run only once.

With the addition of separate roots, all tests will be run again. The second set of tests will be with JVMs started such that, instead of sharing a root, each JVM gets its own root, yet all roots will be stored in the same Terracotta server. poundRandomProducts() running on two JVMs will therefore be pounding on two separate arrays. And poundOneProduct() can pound the same product ID on each JVM yet be mutating different objects in Terracotta. This separate roots mode may seem like extra work, but it allows us to confirm for ourselves that no objects in one JVM are required by the other JVM in the test. Let's make the appropriate changes now.

Open the file named Store.java. Change the member fields at the top of the class named Store as follows:

```
import java.util.concurrent.atomic.AtomicInteger;

public class Store {
public List departments = new ArrayList();
public Map inventory, inventory2;        // add inventory2

// This reference will point to inventory or inventory2
// The reference will be determined at constructor time
private Map _inventoryReference;

// Add an AtomicInteger which will be used to keep track
// of how many JVMs are in the cluster
// every odd JVM we start (1, 3, 5, ...) will reference inventory2
// every even JVM we start (2, 4, 6, ...) will reference inventory
private AtomicInteger sequence = new AtomicInteger();
```

Much of the rest of the class changes to accommodate the introduction of the new capability of dynamically mapping to one of two root objects.

```
public Store(boolean sep) {
    boolean separateRoots = sep;

    Product warandpeace = new Product("War and Peace", 7.99, "WRPC");
    Product tripod = new Product("Camera Tripod", 78.99, "TRPD");
    Product usbmouse = new Product("USB Mouse", 19.99, "USBM");
    Product flashram = new Product("1GB FlashRAM card", 47.99, "1GFR");

    Department housewares =
        new Department("B", "Books", new Product[]{warandpeace});
    Department photography =
        new Department("P", "Photography", new Product[]{tripod, flashram});
    Department computers =
        new Department("C", "Computers", new Product[]{usbmouse, flashram,});

    synchronized(departments) {
        departments.add(housewares);
        departments.add(photography);
        departments.add(computers);
    }

    if(separateRoots == false) {
        inventory = new HashMap();
        _inventoryReference = inventory;
    }
    else {
        if(sequence.getAndIncrement() % 2 == 0) {
            inventory2 = new HashMap();
            _inventoryReference = inventory2;
        }
        else {
            inventory = new HashMap();
            _inventoryReference = inventory;
        }
    }

    synchronized(_inventoryReference) {
        _inventoryReference.put(warandpeace.getSKU( ), warandpeace);
        _inventoryReference.put(tripod.getSKU( ), tripod);
        _inventoryReference.put(usbmouse.getSKU( ), usbmouse);
        _inventoryReference.put(flashram.getSKU( ), flashram);
    }

}
```

```
Map getInventory( ) {
    return(_inventoryReference);
}
}
```

Now that you have changed Store, make sure to change Main.java so that it passes a Boolean to the Store constructor.

Figure 12-5 illustrates the change to the object model. Notice that each JVM connects to either inventory or inventory2 by examining the AtomicInteger sequence value.

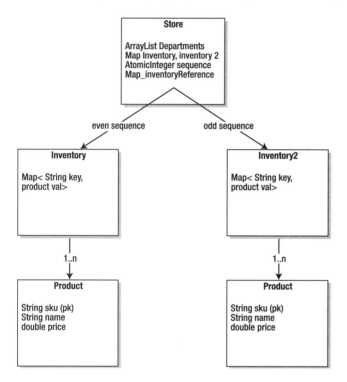

Figure 12-5. *Using separate roots means there are two copies of inventory for isolating JVMs.*

Updating the CLI

We need to add a command line mechanism for invoking the newly inserted pounder methods. Find the method named menu_main() in Main.java. Edit the switch() block by appending two more cases:

```
case 'O':
  poundOneProduct();
  continue;
case 'R':
  poundRandomProducts();
  continue;
```

Updating the Terracotta Configuration

You should have already updated the `<locks>` section of `tc-config.xml` or commented out the synchronization logic in the `setPrice()` method at your discretion. It is not necessary, however, to add the `productArray` from the pounder methods to the `<roots>` section of the configuration file. Just to remind you of the power of object identity and the flexibility of domain modeling in a Terracotta world, the objects stored in the array are already stored in other collections that are defined as roots. As a result of the objects having been shared through another object, there is no need to cluster the new data structures created in these new methods.

Make sure to add the second `inventory2` object as a new root. While Terracotta is powerful, it is not magical, and this new root will not be found without a configuration directive:

```
<root>
  <field-name>demo.inventory.Store.inventory2</field-name >
</root>
```

One last change is needed since the pounder will run twice or more times on the same physical computer. As depicted in Figure 12-2, each JVM has its own database of statistical data. The default file name for this database is based on the host IP address of the client where Java is running. Let's change this now to store data in a file named based on the time when the client was started. This way, each client we start will write to its own database, assuming the clients are not started at the same millisecond.

Change the `<clients>` block in the `tc-config.xml` file by adding a subdirective specifying where to write stats data:

```
<statistics>%(user.home)/terracotta/client-logs/pojo/inventory/statistics-%D ➥
</statistics>
```

In the preceding example, `%(user.home)` expands to your home directory, and `%D` expands at run time to the start time of the Java process. More information on runtime variable expansion in `tc-config.xml` is available at `http://www.terracotta.org`. If you do not get this correct, the client will disable gathering of statistics and warn you:

```
The statistics buffer couldn't be opened at
'/Users/ari/Desktop/terracotta/samples/pojo/inventory.pounder/
statistics-192.168.1.94'.
The CVT system will not be active for this node.

A common reason for this is that you're launching several Terracotta L1
clients on the same machine. The default directory for the statistics buffer
uses the IP address of the machine that it runs on as the identifier.
When several clients are being executed on the same machine, a typical solution
to properly separate these directories is by using a JVM property at startup
that is unique for each client.

For example:
  dso-java.sh -Dtc.node-name=node1 your.main.Class
```

You can then adapt the tc-config.xml file so that this JVM property is picked up when the statistics directory is configured by using %(tc.node-name) in the statistics path.

Compile and Run the Application

First, edit build.xml and run.sh by globally replacing inventory with inventory.pounder Compile the application by issuing the following commands (on Unix).

```
> cd $TC_HOME/samples/pojo/inventory.pounder
> ant clean; ant
```

You should see something similar to the following output.

```
Buildfile: build.xml

init:
    [mkdir] Created dir: /Users/ari/terracotta-2.6.0/samples/pojo/inventory.pounder/
classes

build:
    [javac] Compiling 4 source files to /Users/ari/terracotta-2.6.0/samples/pojo/
inventory.pounder/classes

BUILD SUCCESSFUL
Total time: 2 seconds
```

We are now ready to visualize the application. Start a new Terracotta server. To be safe, you should stop any running Terracotta server by issuing the command $TC_HOME/bin/stop-tc-server.sh. Then, run $TC_HOME/bin/start-tc-server.sh. Next, run the newly compiled demonstration by executing ./run.sh in two separate windows.

■Tip Watch closely to make sure both clients start without errors.

Confirm you are running in a clustered environment by starting the administration console. With the console running, display products and change prices using the command line interface. If you have trouble confirming that your application is running inside Terracotta, refer to Chapters 3 and 4 for more details on how to properly start applications in a Terracotta environment.

Taking Performance Snapshots

Now, let's start the snapshot tools. Figure 12-6 shows the location of this feature using Terracotta 2.6.

Figure 12-6. *Snapshot feature inside the administration console*

Click "Statistics recorder" in the tree control illustrated in Figure 12-6 to reveal the snapshot tool. Figure 12-7 shows the snapshot tool. You can start recording data by clicking the button labeled "Start recording", highlighted in the figure, and stop recording by clicking "Stop recording". You can also manage multiple recording sessions in the section of the tool highlighted at the bottom of Figure 12-7.

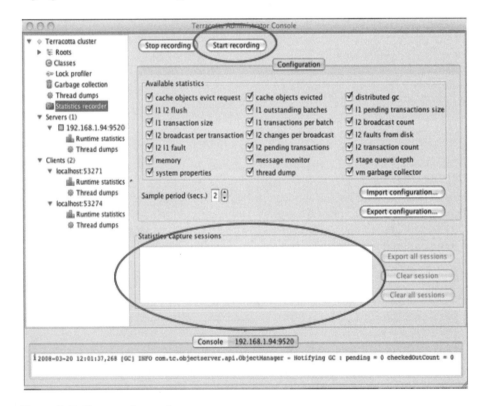

Figure 12-7. *The snapshot tool*

Now, it is time to start the snapshot tool and run the pounders. First, make sure both inventory clients are running. Then click "Start recording" in the snapshot tool. Now, return to the command line window where an inventory application is running, and follow these steps at the prompt:

1. Type **I** to get inventory faulted in to both JVMs.

2. Type **r\<enter\>** in each JVM.

Let the process run until completion. Once both JVMs finish, run the other pounder method twice. The first time, hit the same object in both JVMs:

1. Type **o\<enter\>** in each JVM.

2. Type **1GFR\<enter\>** in each JVM.

Now, run the pounder hitting different objects.

1. Type **o\<enter\>** in each JVM.

2. Type **1GFR\<enter\>** in the first JVM.

3. Type **USBM\<enter\>** in the second JVM.

Once this completes, stop both `inventory.pounder` instances by pressing either Q or Ctrl+C (on Unix). Rerun the entire set of tests, this time with separate roots. To run the application in this fashion, issue the command that follows:

`./run.sh separate_roots`

Once you have invoked `poundRandomProducts()` and `poundOneProduct()` with separate roots, return to the administration console, and select "Stop recording" in the snapshot tool. There is now data to analyze.

Download the visualization tool from Terracotta's web site simply by starting the administration console and clicking "view" on the Statistics Recorder pane. Clicking the view button will invoke your default web browser and take you to the correct URL. You will need your Terracotta.org username and password to download the visualization tool.

Now click Retrieve in the user interface. Note that Import is used for exported test data sent to you from another user or system (the import and export features will be explained at the end of this chapter). Retrieve the test data from the Terracotta server by providing its address in the dialog box as shown in Figure 12-8.

Figure 12-8. *Retrieving performance data for graphical analysis*

The retrieval tool will download all sessions available on this Terracotta server, regardless of which session you pick. By picking a specific recording session, however, you are guiding the tool to do analysis of only a specific subset of the data in this Terracotta server. Pick the snapshot session that corresponds to the run you just made. There should be only one if you are following along for the first time. But every time you start a snapshot session, you will automatically create another session.

■**Tip** The Terracotta administration console provides tools for managing performance recording sessions and snapshots. You can delete any and all sessions using that tool.

Now, generate the graphs for every application JVM as well as for the Terracotta server. To do so, you must click the "Generate graphs" button in the user interface (see Figure 12-9). Any time you change the snapshot session or the JVMs for which you want data, you must click "Generate graphs" again.

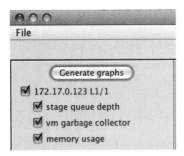

Figure 12-9. *Generating graphs for all performance data*

So far we have built a set of pounder methods to exercise the Terracotta infrastructure. We have also run those methods while recording performance snapshot data on every JVM as well as on the Terracotta server. And we have generated graphs to view. Before we view these graphs and make sense of them, you should understand what to look for.

Potential Bottlenecks

Before jumping in to analysis of the output of the test runs, you should understand what the various graphs display. Any of these graphs can represent a bottleneck in a specific application. Understanding the statistic underlying any graph tells us what the bottleneck in a specific application is.

Recalling the Motherboard

Recall from Chapter 2 that we view Terracotta as enabling applications to scale out as if the application were running on one large computer. We refer to Terracotta's libraries as L1 clients and the Terracotta server as an L2 instance—as in the motherboard and CPU cache analogy. Figure 12-10 demonstrates the concept.

Virtual memory
Core 1
Cache
Page fault/ context switch
Core 2
Cache
Operating system
Application threads
Operating system abstracts multiple cores.
Terracotta abstracts multiple JVMs
Terracotta memory
JVM 1
Cache
Object fault/ context switch
JVM 2
Cache
Application cluster
Application threads
Application threads

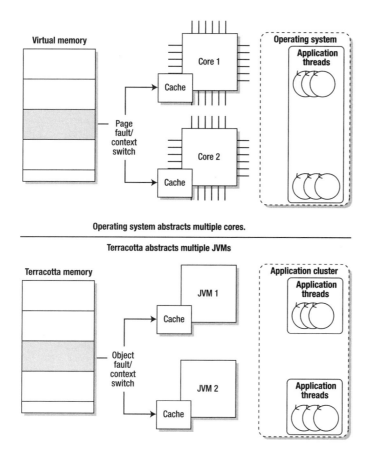

Figure 12-10. *Terracotta is analagous to the SMP motherboard.*

Each graph in the visualization tool corresponds to a check box option in the administration console, as Figure 12-11 shows. The visualization tool allows graphing of specific stats for specific Java machines in the cluster. Each statistical graph can be enabled or disabled. Nodes can also be entirely ignored.

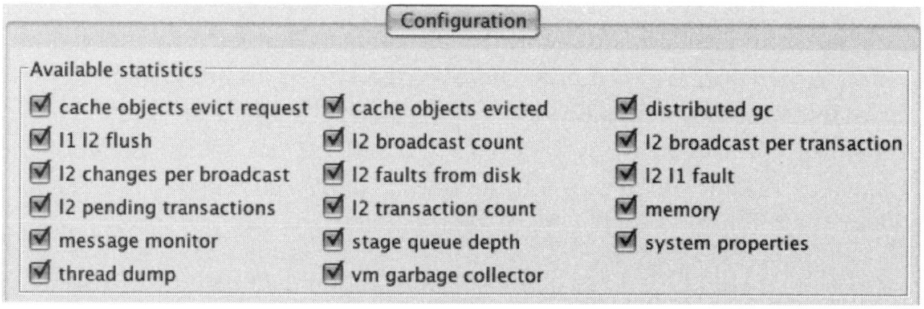

Configuration
Available statistics
cache objects evict request
cache objects evicted
distributed gc
l1 l2 flush
l2 broadcast count
l2 broadcast per transaction
l2 changes per broadcast
l2 faults from disk
l2 l1 fault
l2 pending transactions
l2 transaction count
memory
message monitor
stage queue depth
system properties
thread dump
vm garbage collector

Figure 12-11. *Administration console snapshot options*

We'll define every metric that the snapshot tool offers, as these are key Terracotta components that can cause trouble:

- *Cache objects evict request*: This statistic tracks the number of times objects need to get evicted from the Terracotta server to disk.

- *L1 L2 flush*: The L1 is a nickname in Terracotta for one of your application JVMs. The L2 is a nickname for the Terracotta server. "Flush," just as in the motherboard analogy, refers to point in time when the L1 runs out of memory or garbage collects objects and flushes some objects to the L2 to free heap space.

- *L2 changes per broadcast*: The L2 updates each field of each changing object discretely on disk. If a broadcast occurs, one or many changes in the L2 can occur as a result. This statistic tracks the ratio of L2 changes that result from each broadcast.

- *L2 pending transactions*: The L2 holds on to transactions for a while before applying the deltas to its disks. Those pending transactions take memory while in flight. Furthermore, any object that is part of a pending transaction cannot be updated again until the transaction is completed. The system holds transactions in the pending state so that redundant changes to objects can be folded together, or compressed out of updates when possible. Transactions remain pending while being compressed and folded into the fewest number of disk updates possible. So this statistic represents the situation where lots of updates occur redundantly to objects, and those objects are, therefore, temporarily locked by the system while being updated.

- *Message monitor*: This statistic tracks the network message count flowing over TCP from clients to server.

- *Thread dump*: This data is a marker that decorates all the performance graphs with a milestone mark that notes when the thread dump happened. In the visualization tools, these marks are clickable and will display the thread dump as recorded when requested during performance testing and recorded into the snapshot. While we never clicked the "Take thread dump" button in the administration console, feel free to experiment with this feature.

- *Cache objects evicted*: This statistic is directly related to evict requests. While evict requests tracks the number of times eviction should happen, this statistic tracks how many objects actually are evicted from memory.

- *L2 broadcast count*: The L2 will broadcast any deltas to objects that are resident in more than one L1 JVM. "Broadcast" is a misnomer, because the L2 determines which L1 needs certain updates and never actually sends updates to JVMs that won't end up needing the changes. The system keeps track of each broadcast that occurs, meaning this statistic provides visibility into every time an object changes in one JVM and that object is resident in another JVM and needs to be updated.

- *L2 faults from disk*: When the L2 has too little memory to maintain all objects in RAM on the Java heap, it spills objects to disk. This statistic represents how many times the L2 has to load objects from disk to serve L1 object demand.

- *L2 transaction count*: In Terracotta, a transaction is defined as a group of changes to objects marked by synchronization boundaries. When an object is unlocked in the JVM, all the changes made in a particular thread will be flushed. A Terracotta transaction is neither a single object field change nor a single object change. A transaction is an application-specific number of field changes bundled together using a Java lock. As an example, one application might change one object field inside a setter method within a lock. Another might change one thousand objects in a `for` loop before releasing an object lock. A single transaction for application one equals one field change. A single transaction in the other application equals 1,000 field changes. Whatever the application's definition of a transaction, this metric counts them.

- *Stage queue depth*: The L2 is asynchronous in nature meaning, like a modern operating system, it uses a fixed set of resources and splits its time among all pending work doing a little bit of each task at a time. As an example, when one JVM needs objects from Terracotta, the task of retrieving those objects is broken into stages, and each stage can have many JVM requests waiting for work at that point. Stage queue depth tracking allows visibility into all the L2 stages and shows how much work of each type is pending in the server. Use this metric to determine if your application is causing a specific type of bottleneck inside Terracotta. This lets you know what is slow or bottlenecked in detail, all in hopes that you can change your application to avoid potential slowdowns.

- *JVM garbage collector*: This statistic tracks the garbage collector's behavior on any and all JVMs.

- *Distributed gc*: This Terracotta-specific concept is better thought of as a collector of distributed garbage rather than a distributed garbage collector. This tool never crawls memory across all JVMs in order to locate clustered garbage. It instead runs only inside the L2. At critical points during distributed garbage collection, however, the L2 pauses all other types of work, making sure that no object being actively referenced gets flagged as garbage. Just like Java garbage collection, this L2 collection can cause bottlenecks while pausing the system.

- *L2 broadcast per transaction*: This statistic represents the ratio of broadcasts to transactions. If your application updates objects 1,000 times per second, and each update causes a broadcast, the ratio would be one-to-one. A ratio of one-to-one means all transactions are causing broadcasts, which implies poor locality of reference and most likely limited scalability. A broadcast ratio of zero implies that no objects are simultaneously resident in more than one JVM at a time. Such a configuration should be linearly scalable.

- *L2 L1 fault*: This statistic tracks the opposite of a flush. A fault occurs when a JVM needs an object it doesn't have in the local heap. The L1 must wait for the L2 to send the object and thus is blocked by the L2 from making forward progress. Good locality combined with the appropriate number of JVMs implies that a JVM should always have enough memory to keep all the objects it uses in the local heap. Less faulting implies better scalability.

- *Memory*: This statistic tracks the heap usage over time. This data is available standalone through JConsole for JDK 1.5 or newer, but Terracotta puts the data in the same place as all other statistics for easy correlation.

- *System properties*: This is not a statistic at all but a snapshot of all the Java properties passed in and set at startup time for each JVM. This helps determine if one JVM is configured differently from others. It also helps determine what the settings for a particular snapshot of data were.

Inside the Terracotta Server

Now would be a good time to explain why the L2 is not automatically a bottleneck. The notions of broadcasting, flushing/faulting, and lock bottlenecks are a direct result of the internal implementation details of the L2. Understanding these concepts fully requires understanding the internals of the Terracotta server.

SEDA

Since its first release, Terracotta has been designed on an asynchronous workflow under the principles of staged event driven architecture (SEDA). SEDA is a concept where any task gets broken into its component parts and then gets managed through its execution life cycle via an external workflow execution engine. In Chapter 11, you learned about master/worker relationships, which can be used to spread work across a cluster of JVMs. The concept behind SEDA is just like master/worker, but SEDA is used to spread work across threads in a single JVM, in a manner where each work stage is unaware of those that come before or after.

SEDA is made up of building blocks. Specifically, queues, drains, and faucets make up the interface. A queue represents a bucket of work. A drain represents an outgoing connection from one bucket to another, and a faucet represents an input to a bucket. Picture water flowing through a series of buckets and hoses. Now, imagine taking a servlet container and breaking up its various internal stages of processing an HTTP request using this paradigm.

The SEDA-based servlet container can provide all the capabilities of a multithreaded servlet container. The main difference is that the SEDA-based containers do not take a system resource per user request, whereas the Tomcat 5.*x* container, for example, does. On the other hand, Tomcat's core developers can easily provide for security and context management while processing an HTTP request using thread local variables. A SEDA-based container would have an object scoping problem if it used only thread local objects, since one thread would do only part of the work and must, therefore, bundle up the objects it created for other threads to be able to reach.

While SEDA may or may not be for you because of the burden of decoupled, asynchronous programming it places, it is definitely good for the Terracotta server. The server does not cause unnecessary thread contention in the JVM. It also doesn't increase in size and resource utilization as the number of transactions flowing through the system increases. SEDA makes the latency and throughput of a Terracotta server very efficient and predictable.

The advantage of breaking up a seemingly singular task into parts and then spreading those parts across threads does not have the same value as the master/worker model. SEDA is meant to help an architect break up a task in a logical manner so that the stages of work that can be serialized are separated from those that can go parallel while at all times, work moves through parallel and serial stages in a consistent manner. While in master/worker scenarios we get parallelism, SEDA can provide for both parallelism and serial execution at various stages in a system. Understanding the SEDA workflow inside the Terracotta server will help you understand why some operations that a clustered application executes will run faster than others.

Terracotta's SEDA Pipeline

The SEDA pipeline that runs inside the Terracotta server is made available to Terracotta users through the visualization tools. It is, therefore, important to understand the pipeline and what the tools might be indicating. Figure 12-12 represents the internal structures inside the Terracotta server. These structures have to communicate among themselves in order to complete any work.

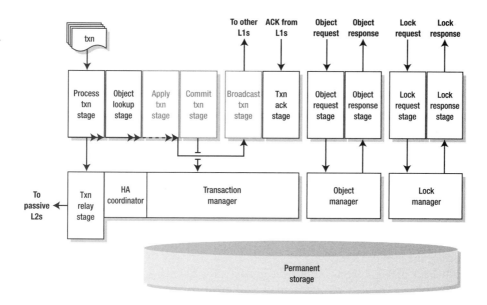

Figure 12-12. *The SEDA stages inside the Terracotta server*

The stages inside the L2 can be grouped into four segments. The first is transaction processing and is depicted in the figure as the cluster on the far left. The second is broadcast management represented by the broadcast transaction and transaction acknowledgement stages ("broadcast txn stage" and "txn ack stage" in Figure 12-12). The last two sections are the ones you would expect, namely object request/response and lock request/response. Since these segments are separate SEDA stages, locks can be acquired, objects faulted and flushed, and transactions committed in parallel. In fact, an L1 is allowed to continue as soon as it flushes a transaction to the server. The server must ensure that all other L1s acknowledge this transaction when necessary. So while most of the time, the system is asynchronous, broadcasts put the server into synchronous mode, having to manage all the acknowledgements and guarantee delivery.

Using the visualization tools, we can tell how much work the server is doing in each of the four groups. And using the tools, we can tell if the server is keeping up with the workload the application is generating. Before confirming in the tools what we expect, let's review our expectations.

Looking for Locality Issues

The Terracotta server will become a bottleneck when more and more of its internal SEDA stages must be involved in an object update. For example, if an update to an object requires a broadcast to several JVMs and a flush to disk and that update is to the same objects that were updated in a recent transaction, the server must order all the operations and make pending several stages of processing while waiting for others to complete. The less object updates overlap across JVMs, the faster the system will go. The concept of keeping objects out of JVMs that don't need them and keeping objects resident in memory as close to the processor as possible is referred to as locality of reference.

One of the secrets to successfully tuning an application is to try to maintain locality of reference. "Reference" refers to object references and "locality" to keeping object references as close to L1 and L2 as possible. L1 will not be able to maintain locality if the data Terracotta is managing takes more space than available memory, and it will then spill to the L2 anything it doesn't need or cannot retain. L2 will not be able to maintain locality if the data Terracotta is managing must spill to disk.

Any and all I/O—be it disk, network, or even memory—can result in application bottlenecks. The data gathered by the snapshot and visualization tools provides a targeted view of each of the points at which the system can execute I/O and end up waiting for that I/O.

Use the tool to confirm for yourself that your application exhibits good locality, meaning that object faults from L2 to L1 and from disk to L2 are not required much of the time. Recall that we executed `inventory.pounder` application in different ways. The pounder worked on random elements in the `productArray`, meaning both JVMs were making changes to the same objects all the time. `poundOneProduct()` instead updated the same product, namely the 1 gigabyte flash card in a loop, explicitly breaking locality of reference and forcing the object changes to be pushed and acknowledged between both JVMs. The last model worked on two different objects, one in each JVM.

Think of locality of reference as akin to linear scalability. As long as our application runs without sharing objects across JVMs, no communication other than to L2 needs occur. This is the fastest way to run, because the L2 will not block transaction flow from any one L1, waiting for other L1s to acknowledge updates. Let's confirm for ourselves that the `inventory.pounder` application running in a highly localized mode runs much faster than when updating random objects in all JVMs.

Specific Bottlenecks in inventory.pounder

The pounder we created at the beginning of this chapter was run in essentially two different modes. The modes were carefully designed to illustrate the key bottlenecks that a real-world application will experience when running in a Terracotta environment. Given your new understanding of the Terracotta server's internals, let's review the three tests.

Broadcasting Changes

One issue that occurs whenever the same object is touched by more than one JVM is that all changes in one context must be sent to all JVMs where the object lies resident. The specific broadcast rate (broadcasts per transaction as measured by the tools) in each of our pounder tests is different. This will directly lead to different performance characteristics. We will vali-date this assertion by examining the transaction throughput for two JVMs pounding on the same product versus on different products in the same map and on different maps (inventory versus inventory2 when running with separate roots).

Lock Acquisition

Now let's consider the cost of acquiring a lock. Acquiring a lock over the network can be expensive for two reasons. The first problem is that JVMs can lock and unlock much faster if they do not have to traverse the network to L2 to request the lock in the first place. The second problem is that Java locking is exclusive, meaning only one thread at a time is allowed inside a lock.

Throughout this book, we have mentioned the greedy lock optimization. We can confirm this optimization is present simply by viewing the locking statistics recorded during the vari-ous pounder test runs. Consider running the pounder again on just one JVM. In such a modified test, the JVM would keep all locks local to itself and will not make any lock requests to L2. So such a modification should produce a significant increase in transactions per second or a corresponding decrease in elapsed time to complete the scenario.

In the tests you ran, poundRandomProducts() randomly updated objects and exhibits less greediness than a test where the same product, 1GFR, is updated in a loop. In the second sce-nario, the Terracotta server will grant the lock greedily, and L1 will keep the lock for several iterations before yielding to its peer. In the first scenario, the system cannot tell that such an optimization where L1 is granted the locks for an extended period of time would be beneficial, because L1 grabs a different lock every time through the loop.

Since the objects that L1 works with change over time, the greedy lock optimization works less efficiently when working with random objects, and thus lock acquisition is an interesting bottleneck. We will study lock greediness in the test results.

Visualizing the Bottlenecks

Now that you have a deep understanding of the various layers in the stack, visualizing the sub-tle interplay across layers will be illuminating. First, start the Terracotta visualization tool again.

```
> cd $TC_HOME/lib; java -cp tc.jar com.tc.admin.cvt.ClusterVisualizerFrame
```

Use the retrieval feature to grab the data from the three pounder runs. Leave all check boxes selected, and click Generate Graphs. Figure 12-9 demonstrates how to do this.

Scroll through the various graphs in the right pane. Note the different transaction rates for each client and the Terracotta server. Remember that transactions can be committed in batches, and locks can be awarded greedily. So the L1s instances and the L2 CPU should have a different perspective on the number of times these events occur inside the system.

Let's focus in on two graphs: the transaction rate according to L2, represented in Figure 12-13, and the SEDA stages inside the L2, represented in Figure 12-14, for the same time period.

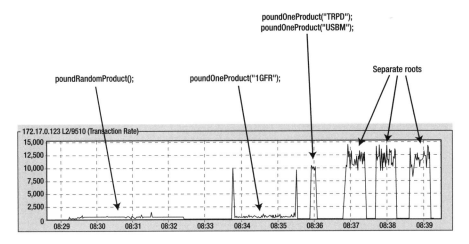

Figure 12-13. *Visualizing the differences in throughput between test runs*

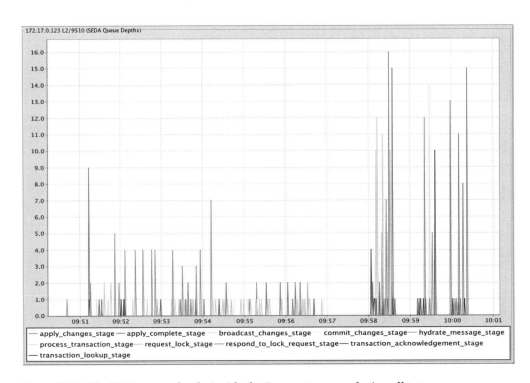

Figure 12-14. *The SEDA queue depths inside the Terracotta server during all tests*

Figure 12-13 shows transaction rates for each scenario. First, we observe that the highest transaction rates occur with separate roots. This makes sense, because the two JVMs share no information with each other and thus never have to wait for Terracotta to grant them locks or apply updates to memory. Terracotta detects that no objects in JVM one and two are shared and, therefore, never makes either JVM wait while L2 commits changes. All object updates become asynchronous. In other words, with perfect locality, a JVM always trusts its own heap and is never made to wait while writing data to heap. The JVMs in such a scenario will move at local CPU speeds.

The next fastest scenario is when roots are not separate yet the object that the test pounds is different in each JVM. When one JVM pounds on the price of the camera tripod, while the other pounds on the USB mouse, the cluster delivers about 10,000 updates per second as opposed to about 12,000 in the previous scenario. So we can conclude that locality was automatically in play under this scenario just as in the first, simply by keeping the JVMs from touching the same objects. This conclusion is also important. It is not necessary to separate JVMs at a root level. Just make sure the JVMs do not lock on and update the same objects, and as this exercise proves, the system will automatically make parallel updates and localize the objects as appropriate.

The remaining two scenarios (which we ran first) are slowest by far. Pounding on the same product produces about 800 transactions per second, and pounding on random products produces about 500 transactions per second. As we have stated, when we pound on one product in both JVMs, Terracotta invokes special greedy algorithms that allow each JVM to keep the lock for a long time. When accessing all objects randomly, no optimization is in play, and thus, all updates are broadcast between the two JVMs.

Now, go back to your test environment, and restart the inventory.pounder application with shared roots:

```
> ./run.sh
```

In the administration console, select "Lock profiler" (see Figure 12-15), and run the two pounders.

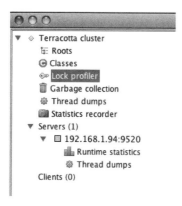

Figure 12-15. *Select the Lock profiler*

Run poundRandomProducts() and poundOneProduct(). Use a single product when running poundOneProduct(), such as 1GFR. In the lock profiler screen, while the tests are running, keep clicking the Refresh button and switching between the Clients and Server views. The Clients view shows how many times the JVMs lock and unlock your objects with or without talking to Terracotta. The Server view shows how many times the server was involved in a lock request. As in Figure 12-16, the administration console shows us that locking inside poundRandomProducts() leads to almost as many hops as lock requests. For a lock to hop, it has to be reclaimed from one JVM to hop over to another. This means the network and the Terracotta server are slowing down the application, because each JVM blocks on operations in the other.

Lock	Times Requested	Times Hopped	Average Contenders	Average Acquire Time	Average Held Time	Average Nested Lock Depth
▼ @61002 (demo.inventory.Product)	3,702	3,601	0	14,798	17,518	0
demo.inventory.Main.poundRandomP	3,702	3,601	0	14,798	17,518	0
@61005 (demo.inventory.Product)	3,702	3,601	0	14,672	17,522	0
demo.inventory.Main.poundRandomP	3,702	3,601	0	14,672	17,522	0
▼ @61006 (demo.inventory.Product)	3,702	3,602	0	14,598	17,516	0
demo.inventory.Main.poundRandomP	3,702	3,602	0	14,598	17,516	0
▼ @61009 (demo.inventory.Product)	3,702	3,602	0	14,642	17,521	0
demo.inventory.Main.poundRandomP	3,702	3,602	0	14,642	17,521	0

Figure 12-16. *Illustrating the lock hopping problem for poundRandomProducts()*

When running poundOneProduct(), we can see that the lock hops far fewer times than it was requested. In Figure 12-17, the system is granting locks approximately four times before reclaiming the lock to hand to the other JVM.

Lock	Times Requested	Times Hopped	Average Contenders	Average Acquire Time	Average Held Time	Average Nested Lock Depth
▼ @61006 (demo.inventory.Product)	4,691	1,424	0	7,905	3,084	0
demo.inventory.Main.poundOneProdu	4,691	1,424	0	7,905	3,084	0

Figure 12-17. *Illustrating greedy locks underneath poundOneProduct() for 1GFR*

You have just seen everything needed to understand what makes each inventory.pounder scenario fast or slow. The visualization tool can be used not just to see transactions per second and SEDA queue depths but broadcast rates, disk I/O, and more. The power of seeing all the data in a single place comes from the fact that a slowdown in one metric might be correlated to a high count of updates in another metric. For example, you should be able to use these tools to prove to yourself that bad garbage collection tuning leads to clusterwide slowdowns when one JVM pauses inside garbage collection when it was supposed to be acknowledging object broadcasts.

Managing Production Environments

The visualization tools and administration console are all designed with production application monitoring in mind. No tuning has been done, however, to make this safe. Terracotta has, instead, made every monitoring point an option. You can decide to monitor locking or not. You can decide to monitor transaction rates, garbage collection, or what have you. You can decide on the sample rate as well.

The safest way to set up the system for a production environment is to turn off all monitoring, run load at your application, and observe the transaction rate as reported by the Terracotta server in the administration console. Next, start turning on snapshot details and lock profiling details, and observe how much throughput is lost. Tune the sample rates and the data that is gathered until you strike an acceptable balance of loss in throughput versus increased visibility.

Note that all metrics gathering can be started and stopped through JMX events. This means that you can choose to gather no data at all and monitor only the default data such as the transaction rate. When the transaction rate dips or increases beyond expected thresholds, you can use a monitoring framework (like Hyperic) to issue a JMX event to Terracotta to instantaneously start recording more data.

You should do lots of testing with metrics on, off, and at increased and decreased rates, all under load. Observing a running system can, in fact, exacerbate performance problems, so the more you automate, the more you should validate that automation is safe.

All these graphical tools can be run on the developer's desktop. Run statistics snapshots. Then export them to zip files on the Terracotta server, and secure copy (SCP) or otherwise transfer the files to your desktop computer. After that, import the data into the visualization tools instead of retrieving the data from the running, production L2 as we did in this chapter thus far. As for the administration console, it is a Swing tool and can be run from your desktop, connecting over TCP to the Terracotta server. For most people, this option works fine, but when you have a slow network from your desktop to a production environment where the Terracotta server is running, consider running a virtual network computing (VNC) or remote desktop tool of some sort near your production Terracotta server. The administration console then runs over the local network, and only the graphical display data traverses the slow network back to your desktop.

Summary

Visualization is a powerful concept that has been leveraged for years inside profiling tools. When brought to bear against the problem of tuning and managing a clustered application that is spread across processes and machines, visualization might be the only way forward.

Terracotta provides transparent clustering, which means that much of your performance tuning work can be delivered at a unit level using traditional profilers. At some point, however, seeing and understanding what Terracotta is doing behind the scenes becomes important. To that end, we developed the `inventory.pounder` application in this chapter. However, the `inventory.pounder` application you built, ran, and analyzed in this chapter was not meant to dictate a rigid way for seeing what Terracotta is doing. Rather, it was meant merely to illustrate the concept of pounding your application in a test environment with Terracotta's monitoring tools turned on and gathering data.

Not only did you learn how to pound on an application and observe and measure the Terracotta inner workings, you learned about some of the internal details and how bottlenecks can occur. If we were to establish any rules of thumb in this chapter, those rules would include the need to profile locks. Never assume greedy locks are or are not working. Confirm, using the administration console, that lock acquisition does not require the network. Study transaction rates and broadcast rates. Also study system-level resources such as disk I/O, CPU utilization, heap utilization, and garbage collection activity.

Try to observe all these metrics in a single dashboard view, since sometimes, bottlenecks in one JVM can slow down throughput in another. The goal of this chapter was to explain the power of visualization, as opposed to simply providing one or two tricks. Hopefully, you can use the tools explained in this chapter to tune your application on your own using these powerful concepts and tools.

Index